HUGH T. LEFLER
WILLIAM S. POWELL

COLONIAL NORTH CAROLINA

A HISTORY

CHARLES SCRIBNER'S SONS, NEW YORK

ACKNOWLEDGMENTS

All maps and illustrations not otherwise credited have been provided by courtesy of The North Carolina Collection, University of North Carolina, Chapel Hill.

Printed in the United States of America
Library of Congress Catalog Card Number 73-5188
SBN 684-13536-1

In appreciation for the pioneer work of

SAMUEL A. ASHE
1840–1938

and

R. D. W. CONNOR
1878–1950

Historians of Colonial North Carolina

CONTENTS

ILLUSTRATIONS

EDITORS'
INTRODUCTION

The American colonies have not lacked their Boswells. Almost from the time of their founding, the English settlements in the New World became the subjects of historical narratives by promoters, politicians, and clergymen. Some, like John Smith's *General History of Virgina*, sought to stir interest in New World colonization. Others, such as Cotton Mather's *Magnalia Christi Americana*, used New England's past as an object lesson to guide its next generation. And others still, like William Smith's *History of the Province of New-York*, aimed at enhancing the colony's reputation in England by explaining its failures and emphasizing its accomplishments. All of these early chroniclers had their shortcomings but no more so than every generation of historians which essayed the same task thereafter. For it is both the strength and the challenge of the historical guild that in each age its practitioners should readdress themselves to the same subjects of inquiry as their predecessors. If the past is prologue, it must be constantly reenacted. The human drama is unchanging, but the audience is always new: its expectations of the past are different, its mood uniquely its own.

The tercentenary of John Smith's history is almost coterminous with the bicentenary of the end of the American colonial era. It is more than appropriate that the two occasions should be observed by a fresh retelling of the story of the colonization of

English America not, as in the case of the earliest histories, in self-justification, national exaltation, or moral purgation but as a plain effort to reexamine the past through the lenses of the present.

Apart from the national observance of the bicentennial of American independence, there is ample justification in the era of the 1970s for a modern history of each of the original thirteen colonies. For many of them, there exists no single-volume narrative published in the present century and, for some, none written since those undertaken by contemporaries in the eighteenth century. The standard multivolume histories of the colonial period—those of Herbert L. Osgood, Charles M. Andrews, and Lawrence H. Gipson—are too comprehensive to provide adequate treatment of individual colonies, too political and institutional in emphasis to deal adequately with social, economic, and cultural developments, and too intercolonial and Anglo-American in focus to permit intensive examination of a single colony's distinctive evolution. The most recent of these comprehensive accounts, that of Gipson, was begun as far back as 1936; since then a considerable body of new scholarship has been produced.

The present series, *A History of the American Colonies*, of which *Colonial North Carolina* is part, seeks to synthesize the new research, to treat social, economic, and cultural as well as political developments, and to delineate the broad outlines of each colony's history during the years before independence. No uniformity of organization has been imposed on the authors, although each volume attempts to give some attention to every aspect of the colony's historical development. Each author is a specialist in his own field and has shaped his material to the configuration of the colony about which he writes. While the Revolutionary Era is the terminal point of each volume, the authors have not read the history of the colony backward, as mere preludes to the inevitable movement toward independence and statehood.

Despite their local orientation, the individual volumes, taken

together, will provide a collective account that should help us
understand the broad foundation on which the future history of
the colonies in the new nation was to rest and, at the same time,
help clarify that still not completely explained melodrama of
1776 which saw, in John Adams's words, thirteen clocks somewhat amazingly strike as one. In larger perspective, *A History of
the American Colonies* seeks to remind today's generation of
Americans of its earliest heritage as a contribution to an understanding of its contemporary purpose. The link between past and
present is as certain as it is at times indiscernible, for as Michael
Kammen has so aptly observed: "The historian is the memory
of civilization. A civilization without memory ceases to be
civilized. A civilization without history ceases to have identity.
Without identity there is no purpose; without purpose civilization will wither." *

Although North Carolina was by 1776 the fourth most
populous of England's mainland colonies, no specialized study
of its colonial history has hitherto been published. Surely one
reason for this unwarranted neglect is the enigmatic character
of the colony's history which renders it the proverbial exception
to most generalizations about the origins of the American
Revolution. Founded in the seventeenth century as part of the
larger settlement called "the Carolinas," North Carolina was
from the beginning strikingly different from its southern sister:
it had few slaves, no plantation aristocracy, no centers of
commerce and culture, and despite the production of naval
stores that were highly prized in Britain was not closely bound
to the mother country. Its colonial history was also in sharp
contrast to that of its neighbors to the north: preoccupation with
local problems—conflicts between settlers and Indians, between
east and west, between assemblies and governors—combined
with geographic and cultural isolation to give North Carolina

* Michael Kammen, *People of Paradox* (New York, 1972), p. 13.

a uniquely parochial character at a time when events were causing other colonies to develop a more American outlook. Nevertheless, North Carolina joined the revolutionary movement, though largely for local reasons, and was the first state formally to enjoin its delegates in the Continental Congress to vote for independence. How does one explain this paradox? The authors of the present history offer the plausible and fruitful explanation that in 1776 North Carolina was seeking independence not merely from the mother country but from Britain's other mainland colonies, a status the new government did in fact secure a decade or so later by refusing for a year to join the other states in adopting the Federal Constitution.

Professors Lefler and Powell, drawing on their unique command of primary sources and their exemplary knowledge of recent monographic research, provide the first comprehensive account of the colonial history of North Carolina. Their full and balanced treatment helps to explain how complex an event the American Revolution was, drawing into the stream of rebellion as it did not only zealous colonies like Massachusetts but also those like North Carolina which demonstrated a curious mixture of indifference and ardor. North Carolina's colonial history, viewed in conjunction with the histories of the other twelve colonies, clarifies the meaning of a revolution whose inception, however fortuitous, produced consequences so momentous that they live with us still.

MILTON M. KLEIN
JACOB E. COOKE

PREFACE

In spite of the fact that North Carolina was the site of England's first American colony and that almost two centuries elapsed between the initial interest and the first step toward "the great dismemberment of the British Empire" which occurred in 1775, colonial North Carolina has not been the subject of a book-length study. Now, as the bicentennial of that momentous event is about to be noted, it seems appropriate that a careful look should be taken at the first half of the state's history. Reports of explorers, the kind of people who had the courage to settle here, and the effects of geography on both people and events were important factors in the development of North Carolina as an English colony and later as a state. From the first Tudor interest during the reign of Queen Elizabeth I, through Stuart settlement, and well into the reign of the House of Hanover, this region was a part of the empire. Tobacco and naval stores produced here made the name Carolina a familiar one from London to Liverpool, and especially in the tobacco factories of Scotland.

Lacking historians of national renown before the nineteenth century, North Carolina's early period was scarcely known outside the area. In the classic national histories, events in North Carolina often went unreported. It has been one of our purposes in this book to begin to change that fact. In addition to providing a continuous narrative, we have thought it proper to mention events which, had they occurred elsewhere and been carefully described, would now be a familiar part of the American story.

Our work has been made easier by the state historians who have preceded us, notably Samuel A'Court Ashe and Robert D. W. Connor, pioneer investigators of our colonial past to whose memory this book is dedicated. In recent years the careful research of diligent graduate students has brought to light many fascinating aspects of this period, some of which have published their findings in regional and national journals. We are especially indebted to two promising young scholars at the University of North Carolina at Chapel Hill, Jerry Cashion and Michael G. Martin, who frequently consulted with us and made many valuable suggestions. With her keen editorial eye, Mrs. Barbara Wrubel contributed much to our manuscript by way of stylistic emendation. Our wives, Virginia Waldrop Powell and Ida Pinner Lefler, joined with enthusiasm in many phases of our work and gladly labored to provide ideal conditions for research and writing.

Chapel Hill   WILLIAM S. POWELL
April 9, 1973   HUGH T. LEFLER

COLONIAL
NORTH CAROLINA

A HISTORY

1

THE FIRST EXPLORATIONS OF
NORTH CAROLINA

North Carolina was the site of England's only colony in America during the great Elizabethan Age when the foundations of the British Empire were laid. Both France and Spain had preceded her to the New World, but it was England, with her dauntless persistence, who was destined to win the country. The discovery of America by Columbus in 1492 had given Spain a virtual monopoly on the Western Hemisphere. However, neither England nor France was content to sit back and idly watch Spain reap all the rewards, and within a few years adventurous English sailors were trespassing on Spanish preserves in search of either more lucrative fishing sites or a shorter route to the Indies. The discovery of the North American continent by John Cabot in 1497 provided the basis for England's claim. From her abortive attempts to colonize an island off the coast of North Carolina in the 1580s, Britain at last gained the experience necessary to succeed in this sort of venture early in the next century on another island about a hundred miles away. To be sure, the founding of North Carolina was not an isolated event; it was simply one more step in the discovery, exploration, and settlement of the New World by various European nations. The first discovery on record of what was to become North Carolina was made by the French, and the first attempt at settlement was made by the Spanish.

Following Magellan's circumnavigations of the globe in 1519–1522 for Spain, Francis I of France became curious to know more of the fabled New World. When a group of expatriate Florentine and Portuguese merchants of Lyons sought his approval for an expedition to seek a new route to the Orient and to discover new lands, he eagerly assented. Giovanni da Verrazzano, who commanded their expedition, sighted land near Cape Fear on March 21, 1524. Verrazzano's report, the earliest description that we have of North Carolina, noted in glowing terms the valuable trees, abundant wildlife, and easy availability of fresh water. After his first treacherous anchorage at Cape Fear, he moved up the coast some sixty miles where he encountered the Indians for the first time. As the ship approached land, a sailor who had been tossing some sheets of paper, mirrors, bells, and other trifles to the natives, lost his footing and was swept ashore. Apparently the Indians treated him kindly, drying his clothes by a fire and making him comfortable. The natives were found to be "very courteous and gentle," and when the sailor signified his desire to return to his companions in the boat, "they with great love clapping him fast about with many embracings" accompanied him to the seaside. With the sailor safely on board ship, the expedition continued sailing up the North Carolina coast. Verrazzano saw Pamlico and Albemarle sounds behind the long chain of narrow islands that mark the coast, but he did not see the mainland beyond and consequently mistook these waters for the Pacific Ocean. A map of the New World that was drawn by his brother Girolamo da Verrazzano in 1529 shows an isthmus here joining the region known as Florida with the remainder of the continent. Map-makers and explorers for a century and a half afterward thought the Pacific Ocean or South Sea to lie not very far west of North Carolina.

Soon after his exploration of the North Carolina coast, Verrazzano returned home eager to find support for another expedition. France, however, was becoming so deeply embroiled in a series of wars that she was unwilling to back his new adventures. Determined to continue his explorations, Verrazzano turned to England for encouragement and help. He presented Henry VIII with a parchment map of his discoveries, and he may even have made one voyage under England's auspices, but actually he found very little enthusiasm or real support. Henry was too busy establishing England's independence, creating a new society, and perfecting the Reformation to take much interest in the New World. But he did, nevertheless, set a foundation for exploration upon which his daughter, Elizabeth, would begin to build.

Verrazzano's expedition in 1524 had stirred Spain to action. In July 1525 a civil official in Hispaniola, Lucas Vásquez de Ayllón, set sail to locate the region visited by Verrazzano. He found a land, which the natives called Chicora, between the Cape Fear and Santee rivers. In mid-July of the following year a colony of five hundred men and women from the Spanish West Indies arrived to establish a colony. Among the group were some Negroes, and they were probably the first slaves within the limits of what was to become the United States. Landing in the mouth of the Cape Fear River, one of their ships with all its provisions was lost. Undismayed by their misfortune, the colonists immediately began to build not only a replacement for the lost ship but also a smaller open boat that could be used for exploring the inland waters. Before long, however, the Spanish discovered that they had selected an unfortunate site for their colony; the land was swampy and unhealthy. To compound their woes, the loss of supplies proved a great deal more serious than was originally supposed. Severely reduced in number by disease, the colonists decided to move down the coast in search of a more habitable site. Failing to find anything better by early winter, the remaining 150 returned to Santo Domingo. They concluded that the value of a coastal colony was not equal to the enormous cost in human life.

Spain made several other attempts to explore the region to determine whether gold or other valuable resources might be found there. From 1539 to 1540 Hernando De Soto marched northward from Florida with more than five hundred men, two hundred horses, three hundred pigs, and some mules and bloodhounds. By the spring of 1540 they had reached the mountains of what is now North Carolina and there they were treated well by the Cherokee Indians who offered baskets filled with corn and entertained them for a whole month while they rested and searched for gold. Although nothing of value to Spain was actually found, it was reported that this country looked exceedingly promising for minerals. Marching west, the expedition soon crossed the Little Tennessee River, which was the first river they had found flowing west, and a year later they learned its ultimate destination when they discovered the Mississippi River. Information based on De Soto's reports began to appear on maps a few years later, but because he had so exaggerated the extent of the mountains, later explorers and settlers were discouraged from trying to approach or pass through this great mountain barrier.

During the succeeding years several expeditions flying the Spanish flag made accidental visits to North Carolina. Ships wrecked by the rough waters of the Atlantic off Cape Hatteras were washed ashore, and Indians later reported tales of their survivors. It would seem that the valuable iron spikes which the Indians removed from the timbers of the ships kept the events fresh in their memories. Early in 1566 a small group of Spanish explorers who were attempting to reach the Chesapeake Bay area accidentally landed on North Carolina's Currituck peninsula because of faulty navigation and heavy seas. They reported that there was nothing of value in the area, but before departing they erected a cross and claimed the unknown country in the name of Spain. Later that year, because France had attempted unsuccessfully to plant a colony in what is now South Carolina, Spain decided to make one final reconnaissance into North Carolina. From a base on the coast, an expedition set out to the west and occupied a log fort during the winter at the foot of the mountains. The group explored the same region that De Soto had seen, and they concluded that there was no hope of gold in the area. Having found neither the wealth she anticipated nor an inviting country for settlement, Spain withdrew, leaving to the natives what she considered to be a worthless wilderness.

When Elizabeth ascended the English throne in 1558, only a little over a quarter of a century had passed since Peter Martyr, the geographer, had published a book pointing out that America was a new world and that Columbus had not actually discovered a route to China. Elizabeth's subjects soon grew envious of the wealth that Spain was drawing from her colonies across the Atlantic. In many ways the two countries were rivals, and Spain's source of immense wealth gave her an advantage that was indeed threatening. England's commercial independence and even the nation's Protestant religion were challenged. Many Englishmen were aware of this and therefore supported Hawkins, Drake, Grenville, and Cavendish, the great "sea dogs" who were sent out to capture Spanish treasure ships and to burn and spoil the enemy's American outposts. The gold, silver, jewels, spices, lumber, and other goods that were brought home by these men excited everyone from Queen Elizabeth down to the lowest London servant.

No Englishman knew better than Walter Raleigh what was required if the country was to share in the new wealth. In order to destroy Spain's power, England had to build up her own, and the first step in this direction was the settling of English colonies in the New World. These would enlarge the extent of the empire and they could serve as bases of operation from which attacks could be launched against the enemy. To the accomplishment of these aims, Raleigh devoted his life and a great part of his fortune. Apparently he owed at least some of his ideas to his older half-brother, Sir Humphrey Gilbert. In November 1577 an anonymous person (but most likely Gilbert) presented to the queen a document marked "A discourse how Her Majesty may annoy the Kinge of Spaine by fitting out a fleet of shippes of war under pretence . . . to discover and inhabit strange places." Pondering this proposal through the winter and into the spring, Queen Elizabeth finally reached a decision and in June 1578 she signed a charter authorizing Gilbert "to discover, search, find out, and view such remote heathen and barbarous lands . . . not actually possessed of any Christian Prince or people, as to him . . . shall seem good." Gilbert was given the prerogative to govern any colonies that he established so long as the laws that were set up conformed to those of England. Citizens of the new land were to "have and enjoy all the privileges of free . . . persons native of England in such like ample manner and form as if they were born and personally resident within our said Realm of England." So that citizens in the New World might "live together in Christian Peace and Civil quietness" provisions were made for the maintenance of good order. The royal will was that nothing be done "against the true Christian faith or religion, now professed in the Church of England" or "to withdraw any of the subjects or people of those lands . . . from the allegiance of us, our heirs or successors, as their immediate sovereigns under God."

Without precise plans, Gilbert sailed to the West Indies in the fall of 1578, but he failed to accomplish anything worthwhile for England. He then proceeded to engage the Spanish off their home coast, but at the insistence of several prominent leaders at home he sailed in 1583 with a colony to be planted at Newfoundland. After spending a month ashore he decided to move on to Cape Breton. During the journey one of the vessels was wrecked and Gilbert became very discouraged. Finally he decided to sail for home with his colonists. In a storm in the North Atlantic, the small ship bearing Sir Humphrey Gilbert sank and he was lost.

When the remaining vessels in the expedition reached England late in September, Raleigh became interested in continuing the plans for exploration. On March 25, 1584 Queen Elizabeth renewed the Gilbert charter in Raleigh's name, and he lost no time in preparing a small exploratory expedition. He selected young Philip Amadas of Plymouth to command the reconnaissance voyage. Arthur Barlowe was captain of the second small ship and his pilot was Simon Fernandez (it is likely that he is the same Fernandez who accompanied the ill-fated Spanish expedition that was driven ashore at Currituck peninsula in 1566). John White, an artist, also accompanied the small group that finally departed England on April 27, 1584. On the 4th of July land was sighted, and the expedition spent the next nine days coasting slowly up the Atlantic until they found the entrance they were seeking, about midway between Cape Hatteras and Cape Lookout. After a brief service of "thankes given to God for our safe arrivall" some of the men went ashore to take possession of the land "in the right of the Queenes most excellent Majestie, as rightful Queene, and Princesse of the same."

For two days the little band of explorers examined the land around Roanoke Island where they established a base for themselves. They marvelled at the tall red cedars, the abundance of wild grapes, and the "goodly woods" full of deer, rabbits, and birds. On the third day they met some of the natives for the first time. The encounter was marked by signs of friendship on both sides; Amadas and Barlowe gave one of them a shirt and hat, some wine and food, and then they took him on a tour to inspect their ship. When the Indian left for his own boat he immediately "fell to fishing, and in lesse then halfe an howre, he had laden his boate as deepe as it could swimme." He took these fresh fish and divided them between the two English ships anchored in the sound. Afterward many Indians came, and the English exchanged various signs of joy and welcome with them.

In a report to Raleigh, Barlowe commented on the deer and buffalo skins that they received in trade from the Indians; on the meat, fish, corn, pease, pumpkins, melons, and grapes that the natives ate; on the Indian methods of farming and the near-miracle of growing three crops of corn in one season; on the kind of shelter the natives constructed and the weapons they used; on how the Indians made boats; on the religion and entertainments of the natives; on the awe and respect that was shown by the Indians for their leaders; and on the relations between the different tribes that he identified. Barlowe also mentioned having seen some metal, but whether it was copper or gold he was unable to determine. He noted that pearls were plentiful, and the

Romantic engraving said to depict the landing of the English on Roanoke Island.

explorers took Raleigh a little bracelet made from them. John White's watercolor drawings of the wonders of the region supplemented Barlowe's written report. After a stay of six weeks on and around Roanoke Island, the expedition made a fast voyage home, arriving in England in the middle of September. They took with them samples of the produce of the country and two of the natives, Manteo and Wanchese.

Raleigh was already at work on plans for a second expedition, and the safe return of the men and Barlowe's glowing reports served to spur him on and to interest a great many new people in his ideas. On Twelfth Day, the final day of medieval Christmas celebrations, Queen Elizabeth named the new country Virginia for herself, the Virgin Queen. Virginia was a name not too different from Wingina, chief of the Roanoke Indians, and that fact may not have escaped her notice. It was also later pointed out that the whole country "still seemed to retain the virgin purity and plenty of the first creation, and the people their innocency of life and manners." On the same day, January 6, 1585, Raleigh was knighted as a reward for his role in this new venture for England. But the queen had even better Christmas presents for her favorite courtier: she permitted Raleigh to obtain valuable stores of gunpowder from the Tower; she placed one of her own ships, the *Tiger*, at his disposal; and she had Ralph Lane relieved of his post in the government of Munster, Ireland—but his allowance and pay continued—so that he could serve Raleigh.

Raleigh's first colony was to be organized along military lines, and Sir Richard Grenville was selected to command it. The expedition sailed in seven ships early in April 1585 with a complement that may have numbered as many as six hundred men, including three hundred soldiers and specialists. It was intended that these men should establish an American base from which Spanish shipping could be attacked and from which the whole continent might be more carefully explored. Simon Fernandez returned as pilot; Thomas Cavendish, who was to circumnavigate the globe the following year, was high marshal;

and Ralph Lane was third in command. Captain Philip Amadas
was slated to become admiral of Virginia upon arrival. John
White, the artist who was along on the first expedition, Thomas
Hariot, one of England's most outstanding scientists, John
Harvey, the cape-merchant, and the natives Manteo and
Wanchese, were also present. The fleet made good time to the
West Indies where several stops were made for water, salt, and
additional supplies. During the last week in June the fleet
reached Wococon (now Portsmouth Island), but some of the
ships had difficulty in sailing through the narrow and shallow
inlet of the sound behind the Outer Banks, the long chain of
islands along the coast. The *Tiger* was damaged on the shallow
bar and was temporarily beached with the serious damage and
loss of many supplies. While stranded here, Grenville, Amadas,
White, and others took advantage of the opportunity to visit the
nearby mainland. White painted pictures of several Indian
towns, and his journal reports that the natives received his party
cordially. One Indian, however, stole a silver cup and in
retaliation Amadas burned a deserted village with its surrounding cornfields.

Once the *Tiger* was repaired the fleet was able to sail slowly
northward, reaching Roanoke Island before the end of July.
Here Manteo and Wanchese were returned to their homes and a
base was established. Amadas and a small party set out early in
August to explore the sounds north of the island and around
Currituck peninsula where the Spanish had been. At about this
same time Captain John Arundell sailed for England in one of
the smaller vessels to expedite the sending of additional supplies,
and before the middle of August other ships were preparing to
follow him. Grenville had failed to find a good harbor as a base
from which his vessels could raid the Indies, so Lane was left in
command of 107 men and the fort that they built on Roanoke
Island. He had adequate equipment but only modest supplies for
his force. Among the men under Lane's command there were
many who had specialized skills; particularly well represented
were miners and metalworkers. In addition, Thomas Hariot who

had learned much of the language of the Indians from long sessions with Manteo and Wanchese while they were all still in England, collaborated with White to record a great deal of information about the flora and fauna of the new country.

Many expeditions, most often to the west and north, were made from the base. One of these left in the fall for the Chesapeake Bay area where a camp was established. Members of the party spent considerable time exploring the waterways, which they hoped might provide a more suitable harbor for forays against the Spanish. The mainland was found "to bee the goodliest soile under the cope of heaven," but Lane found the Indians to be not altogether friendly and somewhat less generous than he had hoped in sharing their food with the hungry explorers. On one occasion, in fact, the Indians attempted to combine their forces for the purpose of slaughtering or at least driving away the invaders. Fortunately for the members of the expedition, word of the planned attack was slipped to Lane by a sympathetic native. Because of the necessarily meager supplies of food that could be transported on long expeditions and because of increasingly hostile Indians, Lane was forced to divide his men into three groups. One remained on Roanoke Island, a second went to Port Ferdinando near what is now Oregon Inlet, and the third set up camp at Croatoan, present-day Cape Hatteras. Winter was fast approaching, but the men were comforted by the expectation that relief would be arriving from home at any time. Near-miracle though it was, every member of the expedition survived the winter without the anticipated supplies from England. In the spring of 1586 corn was planted and they were confident that in June the harvest would replenish their store of food.

Sir Francis Drake was in the West Indies in 1585 and 1586 and he had plans to land at several places that were held by the Spanish. He hoped to drive them out and leave an English force in their stead. Although Drake attacked and successfully looted several places, he abandoned many parts of his scheme. He did, however, take a considerable number of prisoners from among

The manner of their fishing.

John White watercolor drawing illustrating the Indians and "the manner of their fishing." *Courtesy of University of North Carolina Press.*

John White drawing of the Indian village of Pomeiock near Lake Landing in
Dare County. In the interior of the houses can be seen the platforms on which
the Indians slept. *Courtesy of University of North Carolina Press.*

the Spanish, including Moorish galley slaves and soldiers, some Negro slaves (to whom he promised freedom), and about three hundred South American Indians. With these mixed passengers aboard, Drake sailed north to look in on the English colony left by Grenville on Roanoke Island. On June 8 he was sighted by Captain Edward Stafford's men at Croatoan.

Drake called on Lane at Roanoke Island and offered what he could to meet the needs of the outpost. He gave a limited amount of food, several ships and boats with masters and crew, weapons, tools, and clothing. Lane, disappointed that the fleet was not the long-expected relief from home, reluctantly accepted Drake's offering. The transfer of goods ashore was nearly completed when a severe hurricane blew up on June 13, dispersing and seriously damaging the fleet. Three days later most of it reassembled, but the best ship, which was to have been left with Lane for further exploration to the north, was lost. A bigger one was offered by Drake but it was entirely too large. Lane was by now deeply distressed and so he called some of his men together for advice. It was agreed to abandon the fort on Roanoke Island and to return to England. In loading the colony's goods in bad weather, some of the sailors impatiently pitched overboard books, maps, and papers as well as specimens of various kinds that had been gathered over the past year. The fleet sailed on June 19, taking Manteo and another Indian, Towaye, but leaving behind three of their own number who were off on an expedition. These three were never heard from again. Drake apparently also abandoned the South American Indians and the Negroes somewhere in the vicinity of Roanoke Island. They were not mentioned again, although the Moorish captives were sent back to Turkey as a gesture of goodwill from Queen Elizabeth.

Raleigh was delayed in sending the supply ship Grenville had requested because of the damage suffered by the *Tiger*. Lane had expected relief to arrive at Roanoke Island by Easter, but the ship that Raleigh finally sent did not set sail until then. Richard Hakluyt, historian and chronicler of England's expeditions, says that the ship carrying food and supplies reached the island "immediately" after Lane departed with Drake on June 19. Actually, she probably arrived between the 20th and the 25th and lingered perhaps until the first week in July. By this very short span of one to five days, the Ralph Lane colony on Roanoke Island may have failed to become England's first permanent American colony. Apparently the relief ship met with some unreported difficulty during its brief visit. On about July 15, or perhaps a little earlier, Grenville himself arrived with a larger expedition, which was intended to relieve and reinforce the Lane colony, and he and his men found the hanged bodies of an Englishman and an Indian. Grenville searched for the colonists and led several expeditions into regions that he had not explored during his earlier visit in 1585. He also captured three Indians, and one of them told him that Lane had left with Drake. Grenville had about four hundred men with him and ample supplies so that he might have left a holding party at Roanoke Island. Or he might have taken the option of completely abandoning the idea of an English colony being established here. Instead, he made the half-hearted decision to leave behind only a handful of men. Reports differ as to whether he left fifteen or eighteen men (perhaps the larger figure includes the three who were left by Lane) at the fort. With four pieces of ordnance and supplies for several years, the small contingent was put under the command of a Master Coffin (or Cofar) and another man named Chapman. Grenville sailed before the end of August, undoubtedly with the hope of repeating his previous good fortune of capturing valuable cargoes from Spanish ships.

In 1587 when Raleigh's final colony arrived, it was learned from a friendly native witness that about a dozen of the men left by Grenville had been invited by Indians for a "friendly" meeting when they were suddenly attacked. One was killed, but some of those who got away managed to reach the shore where they found a boat in which to escape. They picked up four of their comrades along the shore and then made their way to a small island near Port Ferdinando. From here, it was reported, the Englishmen left and were never seen again. The 1587 colonists found a skeleton near the fort on Roanoke Island as evidence of the fate of at least one of Grenville's small party.

Three extremely valuable products of Lane's expedition, which arrived home on July 28, 1586, were the written reports of Thomas Hariot, the watercolor drawings of John White, and several very good maps. A small book by Hariot, *A brief and true report of the new found land of Virginia*, was printed in London in 1588. One of the author's purposes was to discount rumors that were being spread by malcontents among the returned colonists who, "after gold and silver was not so soone found, as it was by them looked for, had little or no care of any other thing but to pamper their bellies; or of that many which had little understanding, lesse discretion, and more tongue then was needfull or requisite." To encourage future settlers, the book included reassuring accounts of the "Marchantable commodities" that existed or that might be produced. Hariot specified such things as flax and hemp; pitch, tar, rosin, and turpentine; sassafras, cedar, oak, and walnut; alum, iron, and copper; numerous furs and skins including otter, deer, and skunk; and various kinds of dyes and gums. Food, he confidently assured the reader, would be no problem, as several kinds of beans and peas, wheat, maize, pumpkins, melons, herbs, grapes, strawberries, and other edible plants grew easily in the fertile soil. Fish, fowl, and animal meat of various kinds were plentiful. Some prospective settlers would be pleased to know that from the Indian maize "wee made . . . some mault, whereof was brewed as good Ale as was to bee desired." Finally, Hariot provided the reader with a good account of the Indians in a section of the book headed "the nature and manners of the people."

John White's watercolors of plants, birds, Indians, and the various other things that he so carefully observed, complemented Hariot's text and also supplied additional new information. White and Hariot worked closely in mapping the region they visited, and their work has been called "the most thorough topographical survey of an extensive tract of North America made during the sixteenth century." In 1590 Theodor de Bry

Theodor de Bry engraving based on a John White watercolor showing the Indians' method of making canoes.

published Hariot's text and engraved many of White's paintings to illustrate it. It was printed in Frankfort in Latin, German, English, and French, thus making it possible for nearly every literate person in Europe to read about the wonders of the New World.

Raleigh's next plans called for a colony to be established on Chesapeake Bay, where a good deep water port would serve English ships. Ralph Lane's beachhead on Roanoke Island had been set up as a military base, but the new colony that Raleigh had in mind would be different. Composed of women and children as well as men, it would have a civil government, and the colonists would have grants of land and be investors in the scheme. John White, whose enthusiasm for the prospects of Virginia must have pleased Raleigh, was appointed governor of the new colony. On January 7, 1587, a corporate body was formed as the Governor and Assistants of the City of Raleigh in Virginia and a coat of arms secured.

The enterprise was initiated in London in late March or early April 1587, when two ships sailed for Portsmouth where additional supplies and passengers were picked up. On April 26 the little fleet called at the Isle of Wight for eight days, again to take on people and supplies. Before finally clearing on May 8, Governor White made one more stop, calling at Plymouth. The established route through the West Indies was followed and the colony arrived at Port Ferdinando on July 22 after seventy-six days at sea. Before going on to Chesapeake Bay, White was to leave the Indians Manteo and Towaye with Grenville's men on Roanoke Island. However, when preparations were being made to continue the journey from here, the pilot for the expedition, Simon Fernandez, seized control and refused to take the colony to its destination. He was anxious to get out into the shipping lanes, now that the season was so far advanced, in order to try his luck against the Spanish. He told the colonists that they had to remain on Roanoke Island, and White gave in to Fernandez with no apparent objection. Perhaps, after all, he preferred this familiar area to one about which he knew little or nothing from personal experience.

An advance party visited the fort site on July 23 and found the earthworks destroyed and some damage from fire. White reported that all of the houses from Lane's time were still in good condition, except for the downstairs rooms of some of them. Orders were promptly issued that all the men should immediately set about repairing the houses and building new cottages. The expedition had brought along a supply of roofing slate, which was probably intended for use on a chapel or the governor's house. Rather quickly, work was underway to establish homes and to make the seventeen women and nine children comfortable. Then, on July 28, a frightening event occurred. George Howe, one of the assistants, strayed two miles away from the fort site while catching crabs and some Indians who were hiding in the marsh grass shot him sixteen times with their arrows and then beat his head in with wooden swords. Although this brutal attack was certainly a horrifying and inflammatory incident, the colonists did not as a result totally break off attempts at securing peaceful and perhaps friendly relations with the natives. Governor White's brief journal records that on "the 13. of August, our Savage Manteo, by the commandement of Sir Walter Raleigh, was christened in Roanoak, and called Lord therof . . . in reward of his faithfull service." This is the earliest known Protestant baptismal service in America and the first granting of a title of nobility to an Indian. As lord of Roanoke, Manteo was recognized by Raleigh as a trusted friend of the English and as the person through whom negotiations with other Indians should be conducted.

Another important entry was made in the journal under the date of August 18. "Elenor, daughter of the Governor, and wife to Ananias Dare, one of the Assistants, was delivered of a daughter in Roanoak, and the same was christened there the Sunday following, and because this childe was the first Christian borne in Virginia, she was named Virginia." She was, in fact, the first English child to be born in America.

By the end of August the ships had just about finished unloading supplies and equipment and they were beginning to

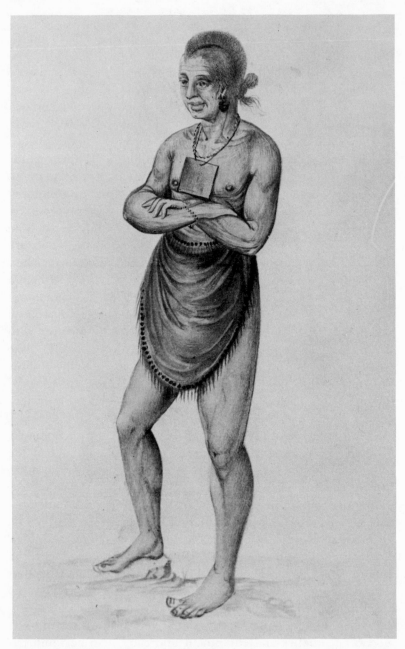

John White drawing of an Indian chief, possibly the friendly Manteo.
Courtesy of University of North Carolina Press.

take in wood and fresh water for the voyage home. The colonists
were finishing their letters and getting souvenirs ready to send
back for friends and relatives. The colony had arrived too late to
plant gardens and crops, and it was becoming increasingly
apparent that little or nothing could be expected from neighboring Indians. Some discussion (or "controversies" as White has
it) arose between the governor and the assistants as to who should
go back to England for supplies. White reports that "the whole
companie both of the Assistants, and planters, came to the
Governour, and with one voice requested him to returne himself
into England, for the better and sooner obtaining of supplies, and
other necessaries for them." He was reluctant to leave because he
feared that criticism at home would charge him with deserting
his post too soon. "Also he alleaged, that seeing they intended to
remove 50. miles further up into the maine presently, he being
then absent his stuffe and goods might be spoiled." The men and
women of the colony therefore joined in drawing up a document
ensuring White against the loss of his goods while he was gone,
"so that if any part thereof were spoiled, or lost, they would see it
restored to him." At last he agreed, and on August 27 he set sail.
After a long and almost disastrous voyage, he finally reported to
Raleigh in England on November 20.

Raleigh set about at once preparing a small ship to go to the
relief of the colony, and he also made plans for it to be followed
soon thereafter by a fleet under the command of Sir Richard
Grenville. However, a threatened invasion of England by Spain
suddenly halted all shipping. Nevertheless, even as late as the
end of March 1588, Grenville stood ready to sail, awaiting only
approval from London. This never came, and most of his ships
and supplies were used instead to reinforce Drake's fleet in the
defense of England against the Spanish Armada. White continued to make urgent pleas for ships and supplies. Some
sympathetic person in authority must have heard for in the
spring of 1588 he was allowed two small vessels, the *Brave* and the
Roe. They sailed from Bideford in April, carrying biscuit, meal,
vegetables, and other supplies. In addition, there were about

fifteen or sixteen colonists aboard who hoped to join the group already at the City of Raleigh. The captains of the two ships, however, were more interested in taking advantage of this splendid opportunity to enrich themselves through exploits in the shipping lanes than they were in relieving their fellow country-men in America. Both the *Brave* and the *Roe* captured a couple of ships from which they took whatever they wanted. After the two parted company, the *Brave*, with White aboard, was captured by a French ship. During the foray, many seamen were killed, White and three of the colonists were injured, and most of the supplies were taken. There was nothing to do but turn back, and they reached Bideford on May 22, exactly a month after sailing. Shortly afterward the *Roe* also returned.

The Spanish Armada approached England late in July, but before the end of August it had been soundly defeated, partly through the efforts of stout English ships and partly as a result of a severe storm that blew the Spanish ships into the North Sea and around to the west coast of Ireland where they broke up on the rocks. Raleigh, Drake, and Grenville were all actively involved in the battle to defeat the Spanish.

Raleigh had not been home long when a three-part agreement was signed for the purpose of sustaining the Roanoke colony. Raleigh, holding the grant from the queen, formed one-third of an organization that was set up to invest further in the colony and to share in any profits. Thomas Smythe, William Sanderson, and seventeen others who were mostly London merchants formed the second party to the agreement. John White and the assistants in the City of Raleigh formed the third unit. They all agreed to contribute money, merchandise, shipping, munitions, food, and other commodities. Unfortunately, this agreement was not reached until March 1589, and it was too late to get a large-scale relief expedition underway. Further, the new investors may have been unwilling to contribute heavily until they had additional assurance of profit to themselves.

Plans for a great privateering expedition to America were laid during the final months of 1589 by John Watts, a London merchant. Three ships were made ready to sail by January 1590, but once again all shipping was stopped because of a threat of another Spanish attack. John White suggested to Raleigh that Queen Elizabeth might permit Watts's ships to sail if he would consent to take supplies, some additional settlers, and equipment to Roanoke Island. An agreement of this kind was reached, but when the ships were ready to leave near the end of February, they refused to take any settlers or supplies, and in fact it was only with great reluctance that White was taken aboard. After spending some time at sea in pursuit of Spanish ships and later encountering rough seas, the *Hopewell* reached Port Ferdinando on August 16. Smoke was seen in the direction of Roanoke Island but it was too late in the day to go ashore. The next morning the boat taking White to Roanoke was buffeted by high seas and a strong tide. Seven men were drowned before the saddened party made its way with enormous difficulty up Roanoke Sound. As darkness drew on they saw a fire through the woods on the north end of Roanoke Island where the fort stood, and White recorded, "we . . . sounded with a trumpet a Call, and afterwardes many familiar English tunes of Songs, and called to them friendly; but we had no answere." They landed the next morning and found only the footprints of Indians surrounding the grass and rotten trees that were still burning. Near the fort, White found the letters C-R-O carved on a tree. This, he noted, "we knew to signifie the place where I should find the planters seated, according to a secret token agreed upon betweene them and me at my last departure from them. . . . in Anno 1587 I willed them, that if they should happen to be distressed in any of those places, that then they should carve over the letters or name, a Crosse ✠ in this forme, but we found no such signe of distress." The men searched the area where the houses had been, and White found that they were taken down and the site enclosed with a high palisade of trees. Near the entrance he found the name *CROATOAN* carved without the agreed upon cross above it. Inside the fort some bars of iron, pieces of lead, guns, and other heavy things were scattered about and overgrown with grass and weeds. Some of White's own chests were found hidden in the sand but their contents were either spoiled or scattered by the Indians. Night was approaching and a storm was rising, but as the party made its way to the ship White was filled with excitement at the prospect of finding the colony at Croatoan. Once aboard the *Hopewell*, the order was given to raise anchor, but the cable broke and the anchor was lost. As the storm raged, the ship was being driven ashore so fast that another anchor had to be dropped. This was the last anchor aboard. To compound their woes, the supply of food was scarce and there was little fresh water available. The weather continued to worsen until there seemed to be no choice but to abandon the search for the colony, sail to Puerto Rico to spend the winter, and plan to return in the spring. At sea the winds increased and there was so much damage to the ship that they changed course for home and reached Plymouth late in October.

The failure to find the colonists meant that they might conceivably be presumed to have survived and that Raleigh's rights would not expire in 1590 as provided in the grant if no settlement were made. Raleigh decided to make one final effort at finding an answer to the riddle of the missing colony. In March 1602 he employed Samuel Mace, "a very sufficient Mariner, an honest sober man, who had beene at Virginia twice before," to make a search. Mace and his crew sailed promptly and in due course sighted land in the vicinity of what is now Cape Lookout. They remained here for about a month gathering sassafras, roots, and bark for the London market, but by the time they decided to search for the colony, the weather had grown treacherous. Some of their equipment was lost and all of their courage, and thus the search ended in defeat. Raleigh met Mace when he landed, anxious to have good news, but of course there was none.

Queen Elizabeth died in March 1603 and Sir Walter Raleigh soon discovered that he could expect no favors from King James I, who was convinced that Raleigh had conspired with Spain to prevent his ascension to the throne of England. In November

1603, a scant eight months after the death of his patron and queen, Raleigh was found guilty of treason by the Court of King's Bench. With the loss of his freedom and his position also went all his rights to Virginia. King James now held the rights, privileges, and honors that Raleigh had enjoyed in the New World since 1584, and the king was now free to make new grants in the area.

The fate of the Lost Colony of Roanoke has probably been the subject of more speculation than almost any other event in American history. However, there has been a general tendency to overlook the information that was gathered by the earliest permanent settlers at the Jamestown colony. In the summer of 1608 Captain John Smith of the new settlement recorded that an Indian told him of people "at Ocamahowan . . . two days from Chowwonock, and 6 from Roonock, to the south part of the backe sea" who wore clothes. These people, Smith was told, had much brass and lived in houses like those built by the English. Near the end of December, Smith sent Michael Sicklemore, a gentleman and a trusted soldier, to deliver a present to the chief of the Chowanoke Indians, a tribe that was known to the Roanoke colonists. Furthermore, Sicklemore also received from Smith "directions howe to search for the lost company of Sir Walter Rawley." Early in 1609 Sicklemore returned safely but reported that he "found little hope and lesse certainetie" of the Roanoke colonists. "The river, he saw was not great," Smith recorded, "the people few, the countrey most[ly] over growne with pynes . . . but by the river the ground was good, and exceeding furtill."

Smith was not content that this closed the issue, and he sent Nathaniel Powell and Anas Todkill to search among other Indian settlements for the missing colonists. When the two men returned, Smith claimed that "nothing could they learne but they were all dead." Nevertheless, a report was dispatched to King James, and in response the king's council sent a set of instructions to the governor of Virginia in May 1609. He was told that a four-day journey south of Jamestown would take him to an Indian town, Ohonahorn, where three branches of the Chowan River come together. Here, on one of these branches, "you shall finde foure of the englishe alive, left by Sir Walter Rawely which escaped from the slaughter of Powhatan of Roanocke, uppon the first arrival of our Colonie, and live under the protection of a wiroane [chief] called Gepanocon enemy to Powhatan, by whose consent you shall never recover them, yet search into this country [as] it is more probable then towards the north." John Smith's own map of Virginia shows Ohanoack, a palisaded Indian village, on the south side of Chowan River.

William Strachey, a resident of Jamestown, wrote a *Historie of Travell into Virginia Britania* between 1609 and 1612. He was familiar with the fate of the Roanoke colonists and early in his book promised to insert an account of these "unfortunate and betrayed People," but he failed to do so. From scattered comments that appear throughout his book, however, portions of the story may be reconstructed. A short while before the English arrived at Jamestown some priestly advisers of the great chief Powhatan told the Indian leader that a nation would arise from the Chesapeake Bay that would "dissolve and give end to his Empier." Upon hearing this, Powhatan "destroyed and put to sword, all such who might lye under any doubtfull construccion of the said prophesie." When the English arrived they found "all the Chessiopeians . . . for this cause extinct." Apparently, Powhatan vented his anger not only against those of his own race, but also against the Roanoke survivors. Strachey wrote, ". . . his Majestie hath bene acquainted, that the men, women, and Children of the first plantation at Roanoak were by practice and Comaundement of Powhatan (he himself perswaded thereunto by his Priests) miserably slaughtered without any offence given him either by the first planted (who 20 and od yeares had peaceably lyved and intermixed with those Savadges, and were out of his Territory)." King James ordered that Powhatan and his chiefs be spared but that revenge be taken upon the priests "by whose advise and perswasions was exercised that bloudy Cruelty."

From an Indian named Machumps, Strachey learned that in his country at Ochanahoen people had two-story houses with stone walls, "so taught them by those English who escaped the slaughter at *Roanoak*, at what tyme this our Colony, (under the Conduct of Capt *Newport*) landed within the *Chesapeack* Bay." In this interesting community south of Jamestown Strachey also learned that "the people breed up tame Turkies about their howses." Machumps further related that "at *Ritanoe*, the Weroance *Eyanoco* preserved 7. of the English alive, fower men, twoo Boyes, and one young Maid, who escaped and fled up the River of *Chaonoke*, to beat his Copper, of which he hath certayn Mynes at the said Ritanoa." Strachey was convinced of the truth of these reports. The colonists at Jamestown, he said, would trade with the neighboring Indians only so long as these people did not "practize vyolence, or treason against us (as they have done to our other Colony at Roanoak)." He was aware of the fact that spies were posted by Powhatan and that they kept a constant watch over the small colony. Whenever a ship arrived, sailed up the James River, or departed, Powhatan was informed. This treacherous Indian, Strachey wrote, was "awayting perhaps but a fitt opportunity (inflamed by his bloudy and furious priests) to offer us a tast of the same Cuppe which he made our poore Countrymen drinck off at Roanoak." Samuel Purchase, who succeeded Hakluyt in recording the history of the time, stated unequivocally: "Powhatan confessed to Capt. Smith, that hee had beene at their slaughter, and had divers utensils of theirs to shew."

Raleigh's attempts to establish an English colony in America were costly in terms of both his own personal fortune and the considerable loss of lives. Surely those who were brave enough to risk their future in the New World hoped that what they did would be of future benefit to England, but they could not have known this with any certainty. The knowledge they gained of the natural resources of the region was of inestimable value to those who followed. Their glowing reports and encouraging promises for the future ultimately bore fruit in the 1606 charter of the

Virginia Company. Before issuing this charter, which was to establish the first English colony, King James sought the advice of men who had worked with Raleigh and who had invested their own personal funds in his ventures. Once he had assurance from these individuals that England would undoubtedly benefit from further investments in the area, he granted the new charter, under which Jamestown was planted and eventually survived.

2

ESTABLISHING THE PROPRIETARY

The vast territory that was covered by the charter granted to the Virginia Company on April 10, 1606 extended from 34° to 45° north latitude, that is, from near Cape Fear to what is now Bangor, Maine. The company, which was a private corporation, numbered among its members Raleigh Gilbert, Sir Walter's nephew, and others who had supported the earlier efforts at colonization. Of particular interest to these men was that part of their grant that had already been explored from Roanoke. In 1607 they established a permanent colony at Jamestown, not far from Chesapeake Bay where Raleigh had expected to settle his 1587 colony.

Before long, expeditions were being sent out from the colony into "Ould Virginia," as Captain John Smith called the country to the south. In 1622 John Pory, who had recently been replaced as secretary to the colony, went into the country along the Chowan River where the friendly Chowanoc Indians had earlier welcomed Raleigh's explorers. Pory's account of the great tracts of pine forests from which tall masts for ships might be acquired and his descriptions of how desperately needed naval stores—tar and pitch—might be produced to free England from her dependence upon Sweden were read with much interest at home. His report that the Indians were eager to establish trade with the English also generated considerable excitement. And surely his mention of the fact that two harvests of corn were gathered in a single season from the same ground did not go unnoticed.

These enthusiastic reports naturally focused the attention of all Englishmen, especially the Crown, on the activities of the colony. Thus, the fact that the affairs of the Virginia Company had become hopelessly entangled, with several factions struggling for control, could hardly be kept a secret. Concerned that his whims were not being regarded by the company as commands, King James ordered a writ of *quo warranto* to be issued. In the decision rendered by the court on May 24, 1624, the company's charter was declared vacated. This important legal decision had far-reaching effects not only in relation to Virginia and to the future development of the North Carolina area, but to the whole scheme of English colonization as well. The colony of Virginia, after eighteen years under the direction of a joint stock company, now came under the control of the Crown as the first royal colony in English history. When James died the following year, his successor, Charles, lost little time in proclaiming the territory to be a part of the royal demesne. The king was now free to dispose of the land as he saw fit. On October 30, 1629 King Charles granted to his attorney general, Sir Robert Heath, the territory extending from 31° to 36° north latitude, that is, the region lying from about thirty miles north of what is now the Florida state line to the southern shore of Albemarle Sound in North Carolina. Heath was the sole proprietor of this vast tract extending from the Atlantic to the Pacific Ocean. King Charles described the region as a province, and he named it Carolana for himself. The new proprietor was granted broad feudal powers equal to those formerly held by the Bishop of Durham in England, who was charged with the responsibility of protecting the country from Scottish invasion. Heath could raise and maintain an army, collect taxes, and do many other things that gave him almost regal power within his province. But Charles never let it be forgotten that he was king, and Heath was instructed to have ready in Carolana a twenty-ounce gold crown to be worn by the monarch if he should visit the province.

Heath entered into lengthy negotiations with French Huguenots and drew up detailed plans for a colony. However, his hopes of drawing colonists from among the French were dashed when the Privy Council issued an order directing that only those who acknowledged the Church of England might settle in the new province. Turning next to his own countrymen, Heath secured more than forty persons, but he was able to get them only as far as Jamestown. Here negotiations for transportation to Carolana broke down and some of the colonists immediately returned to England while others decided to remain in Virginia. Frustrated in his efforts to colonize his province and busy with legal affairs at home, Heath transferred his proprietary rights late in 1638 to Henry Frederick Howard, Lord Maltravers.

The failure to establish a flourishing colony in Carolana may well have been a reflection of affairs at home—civil war, revolution, and the execution of King Charles. Yet after 1649 the establishment of the Commonwealth, the supremacy of Parliament, and the suffering of many Royalists may have led to renewed interest in the vast unsettled region south of Virginia. Sir William Berkeley, governor of Virginia, was loyal to the Crown, and perhaps others who shared his political sympathies expected to find a welcome from him. Perhaps in anticipation of the arrival of refugees, Berkeley in 1646 sent a military expedition against the Indians to the south. A peace treaty was drawn up and within a few years Virginians were purchasing land from the Indians there. In England a number of promotional tracts were published designed to attract colonists to Virginia, to Maryland, and to Roanoke, Carolana, or South Virginia, as the unsettled but inviting region was variously called.

By the early 1650s officials in Virginia were beginning to grant land that extended far beyond the southern limits of their government. Hunters and trappers, merchants, Indian traders, gentlemen curious to explore, former soldiers, and farmers in search of better land began to appear in this area more and more frequently. Nothing in the few records they left suggests that they

were unhappy with political affairs in Virginia or that the
religious conditions there were oppressive enough to drive them
away. As a matter of fact, Nathaniel Batts, the first permanent
settler in what was to become North Carolina saw nothing at all
unusual about what he was doing; by 1655 he had a house on the
western shore of Albemarle Sound and was engaging in trade
with the Indians. The region was simply the frontier of Virginia,
and it was only natural to move out from the center of
population in search of new and better opportunities. A hunger
for land was characteristic of the people who came to colonize
the New World. Men who could afford to do so even paid the
passage of others who might not otherwise have been able to
make the journey because there was a reward for the investor of
fifty acres of land for each person he brought in. From Virginia
land records it is clear that the population of the North Carolina
area prior to 1663 already exceeded five hundred. The population had grown so large, in fact, that it had become a cause of
some concern to Governor Berkeley. In October 1662 he
commissioned Captain Samuel Stephens to be commander of the
Southern Plantation with authority to appoint a sheriff.

The interregnum following the beheading of Charles I in 1649,
during which time Parliament and the Cromwells held sway in
London, came to an end in 1660 when King Charles II ascended
the throne. This happy occasion for England was the result of
much planning, secret negotiating, and great personal sacrifice.
King Charles owed an enormous debt to those of his friends who
had remained in England during these eleven years, as well as to
those who had fled the country or who had upheld the royal
cause in the colonies. The granting of titles, positions, estates at
home, and land abroad were among the ways in which the king
demonstrated his gratitude. Eight men who had made considerable contributions to the royal cause urgently requested that they
be given a vast tract of American land over which they would be
"the true and absolute Lords and Proprietaries." On March 24,
1663 they were rewarded with a charter for the territory
extending from 31° to 36° north latitude and stretching from

ocean to ocean—the very same land that had previously been granted to Sir Robert Heath. Before long the lords proprietors discovered that the very desirable and already settled area along the northern shore of the sound, which had attracted them in the first place, was outside their province of Carolina (as King Charles, honoring himself, now spelled the name). They appealed to the king and in 1665 an amendment was made to the charter, moving the boundary of their province north to approximately where the present North Carolina-Virginia line is and south to well below the Spanish town of St. Augustine, Florida.

The charter for the province of Carolina contained many features that had a considerable and lasting influence on the course of events. For example, although the Bishop of Durham clause* was included, the charter also provided that laws should be enacted "with the advice, assent, and approbation of the Freemen of the said Province, or of the greater part of them, or of their Delegates or Deputies" in an assembly that the proprietors were to call from time to time. The history of the Carolina region throughout the proprietorship and for many years afterward shows a struggle between a democratic assembly representing the people and an appointed governor nearly always representing an outside authority. Another important feature of the charter was the provision authorizing religious tolerance. The Church of England was to be the "established church" in Carolina just as it was in England, but the proprietors had "Licence, Liberty, and Authority" to grant "Indulgences and Dispensations" to all who in their own judgment or conscience could not conform to the ritual and beliefs of the Anglican Church. For many years the proprietors said nothing about a formal establishment of the church, and as a result many Protestant groups, particularly the Quakers, flourished in freedom-loving Carolina.

---

* This provision gave the proprietors as much power in Carolina as the bishop of Durham had in England. As feudal lord of his frontier county, the bishop could collect taxes and raise an army; he was also expected to protect England from invasion by the Scots. Similarly, the proprietors were expected to manage and protect their province in the interests of England.

King Charles II. *Courtesy of the National Portrait Gallery, London.*

In other provisions of the charter King Charles demanded for himself "Faith, Allegiance, and Sovereign Dominion" from all his subjects in Carolina, one-fourth of all gold and silver mined there, and the normal customs and duties. To the proprietors belonged the right of appointing judges, magistrates, and other officials. They could grant pardons and they could establish ports through which goods would pass and customs duties would be collected. Marks of honor and favor might be bestowed so long as the titles were not the same as those in use in England. An army could be raised, forts erected, and martial law declared in order to protect the province from hostile Indians, invaders, pirates, and robbers. The colonists were also protected from the possible tyranny of the Crown and the lords proprietors by dint of the provision in the charter requiring that all laws be "agreeable to the laws and Customs of this our Kingdome of England." As native-born or naturalized citizens they would be loyal subjects of the Crown and therefore guaranteed all the rights of subjects "born within this our said Kingdome." These rights as Englishmen they might expect to enjoy "without the let, molestation, vexation, trouble, or grievance of us, our heirs and Successors." The colonists could own land and dispose of it just as Englishmen at home could, and they were free to trade with the natives. Another very important provision specifically assured them that when they were involved in legal disputes, they would be tried or their suits at law heard only in courts within the province of Carolina or in England or Wales, not in any other province or colony.

With broad feudal powers in the hands of the proprietors, and with the rights of Englishmen guaranteed to the Carolinians, there might be occasion to question the meaning of certain of the words or even general provisions of the charter. This contingency was covered: "We Will, Ordain, and Command that, at all times and in all things, such interpretation be made thereof, and allowed in all and every of our Courts whatsoever, as lawfully may be adjudged most advantageous and favorable" to the lords proprietors. Clearly, the people would have to fend for themselves, and this, the proprietors soon discovered, they were very adept at doing.

The eight men to whom the charter was granted were described in the document itself as

our right trusty and right welbeloved Cozens and Councellors Edward, Earle of Clarendon, our high Chancellor of England; and George, Duke of Albemarle, Master of our horse and Captaine Generall of all our fforces; Our right trusty and welbeloved William, Lord Craven; John, Lord Berkeley; Our right trusty and welbeloved Councellor Anthony, Lord Ashley, Chancellor of our Exchequer; Sir George Carterett, Knight and Baronett, Vice Chamberlaine of our household; And our trusty and welbeloved Sir William Berkeley, Knight; and Sir John Colleton, Knight and Baronett.

It was said of them, as it was of others who had American grants, that they were "excited with a laudable and pious zeale for the propagation of the Christian ffaith and the inlargement of Empire and Dominions." If the king actually believed this, he was badly misled. For many years the proprietors all but ignored the Christian faith in North Carolina, and they were almost totally preoccupied with their own affairs rather than with those of the empire and dominions. As soon as they thought they saw a greater opportunity for personal gain in the southern region, they began neglecting the northern portion of the province.

Two of the less prominent men among the proprietors, Sir William Berkeley and Sir John Colleton, probably were the most instrumental in securing the charter for the province of Carolina. Berkeley had been governor of Virginia since 1641, and so he most certainly knew of the present and potential value of the plantations along his southern frontier. His role in securing the charter was surely dictated by the hope of personal gain. Berkeley had a claim on the king's generosity because of the hospitality he had extended to Royalist refugees, particularly Anglican clergy, during the time of Charles's exile. Sir John Colleton—a merchant, financier, and planter of the island of Barbados—also had prior knowledge of the inviting possibilities of the region. He had investigated the area while searching for an appropriate site in which to expand his operations. During the Civil War, Colleton had enlisted a regiment, fought for the royal cause, and spent about £40,000 of his own money in the king's behalf. With the intimate knowledge of the province that these two men had, it was a simple matter to gain the collaboration of the six other men, who were certainly more influential, to bring pressure to bear on the king.

The group of eight men were in exceedingly good positions to achieve their purposes. Sir William Berkeley, Colleton, and Cooper were members of a special Council on Foreign Plantations. Cooper had invested in slave-trading expeditions to Guinea. Some of the men were members of the Company of Royal Adventurers to Africa, others were with the Hudson's Bay Company, and others held shares in the Bahama grant. Many of these men were also instrumental in formulating and executing trade policy for the nation and in directing naval affairs. In the spring of 1663, this body of men faced a three-fold task with their new province of Carolina. They had to entice more settlers into the region, they had to establish a government, and they had to make a profitable venture out of their undertaking. With the first two goals they had partial but imperfect success; with the last, they failed utterly.

Sir William Berkeley was closest to the scene of their interests and so it was to him that the other lords proprietors first turned. He was authorized to appoint a governor, but before he got around to making a choice, the proprietors acted in his stead and commissioned William Drummond of Virginia for the position. Berkeley was also authorized to appoint a council of six, and this he managed to do quickly and without intervention from the proprietors. These six officers were then to appoint various civil and military officials who were to join with the freemen or their delegates "to make good and wholesome lawes . . . for the better Government of the Collony." Berkeley was also directed to begin making land grants. Initially these grants were for very small tracts, and it was to be many years before the proprietors comprehended the vastness of their holdings and appreciated the American point of view with respect to the size of holdings in a single tract. By January 7, 1665 the proprietors had come to a clearer understanding of the form that they wanted their government to take. In a document known as the Concessions and Agreement, the proprietors announced their intention to divide Carolina into at least three counties: Albemarle would be in the northeastern section; Clarendon would be on the Cape Fear River; and another county, which was later named Craven, was to occupy what is now South Carolina.

The document very generously permitted the governor to appoint a council whose members would operate under proprietary instructions. The governor, council, and twelve representatives of the freeholders were charged with the responsibility of forming a legislature. There was promise of a much larger and representative assembly later, with far wider powers than the charter enumerated.

The details surrounding the attempted settlement of Clarendon County along the Cape Fear River provide insight into the way the lords proprietors handled the needs of their growing province. On August 14, 1662 a dissatisfied element among the Puritans sailed from Charlestown, Massachusetts, heading for the banks of the Charles River, as the Cape Fear River was then known. Under the command of William Hilton, this expedition entered the mouth of the Charles River early in October and then spent more than three weeks examining the countryside. They found the land fertile and the climate ideal; wildlife was abundant and forage for cattle was plentiful; there were no harmful snakes and only a few mosquitoes; trees of various kinds, grapevines, and wild fruit were bountiful; there was room for several towns "besides for multitudes of farms by what we see." The men were so pleased with the prospects for a colony that they decided "to purchase and buy ye said river, and ye lands about it, of ye Natives." Hilton's glowing report spurred other adventurers from Massachusetts to prompt action. Early in 1663 they set sail with their "goods," which included hogs and cattle. How many men went is not known as only a few names appear in the scattered surviving records. Something must have happened in the colony or perhaps some news of outside events disturbed the men, for by early April 1663 the new colonists were ready to abandon the settlement. For whatever cause, the colonists left suddenly and without taking their cattle with them. On a post they attached a note "the Contents whereof tended not only to the disparagement of the Land . . . but also to the great discouragement of all those that should hereafter come into these parts to settle."

Apparently unaware that the site had been abandoned, the English members of the sponsoring company, Cape Fear Company, on August 6, 1663 wrote the lords proprietors informing them of the existence of an organized group attempting to plant a colony on the Cape Fear River. On August 25 the proprietors issued "A Declaration and Proposals to All that Will Plant in Carolina." They attempted to encourage the settlement of the south side of "Charles River," and authorized settlers to fortify its mouth. Provisions were made for the appointment of a governor to serve a three-year term and for councillors and assemblymen. The assembly could make laws; "freedom and liberty of conscience in all religious or spiritual things . . . to be kept inviolably with them" was guaranteed. All of the provisions of the charter beneficial to settlers were granted, and a plan for allotting land was set forth. The Cape Fear colony had already departed for Massachusetts, but the terms offered by the lords proprietors probably would have been unacceptable anyway— chiefly the allocation of land by lot so that a man had no choice but to take an undesirable tract if it fell to him.

Exploration of the Cape Fear River region did not end with the departure of the settlers for Massachusetts in April 1663. Among the men who were responsible for securing the charter of Carolina for the lords proprietors were some who knew the island of Barbados, which was rapidly being acquired by operators of large plantations. Small landowners were being crowded out, and the abundance of land in Carolina tempted many of these people to leave their small island. On August 10, 1663 William Hilton with Captain Anthony Long and Peter Fabian, employed by the Barbadians, set out for further Carolina explorations. Two days after they sailed, a petition with some two hundred names signed to it was sent to the lords proprietors seeking permission to settle in Carolina and to have the same rights as a municipal corporation in England. This group formed the Corporation of the Barbados Adventurers, with Thomas Modyford and Peter Colleton as their spokesmen. Hilton explored along the coast south of Carolina, and then on October 16 he entered the river that he called "Cape-Fear River." For nearly two months he and his men explored both branches of the river and many small streams. Hilton described the country for the Barbadians in much the same glowing terms as he had used the year before when writing to the New Englanders who had employed him. With Long and Fabian, who were instructed to act as agents for the corporation, Hilton purchased the river and the land from the Indians again. In the following year, a thirty-four page pamphlet containing a "Relation" of Hilton's discoveries was published in London as one means of encouraging colonists to take up land along the Cape Fear River. This promotional tract also contained a series of eighteen "proposals" by which the proprietors hoped to tempt settlers even further. They dealt mostly with generous provisions for acquiring land, but a law-making assembly, free trade, and liberty of conscience were also mentioned.

One of the leading advocates of a Carolina settlement, John Vassall of Barbados, assumed leadership of a faction within the corporation that called itself "the Adventurers and Planters of Cape Feare." Vassall was delegated to correspond with the proprietors about terms of settlement, and he was given very much the same consideration as had been offered the New Englanders the previous year in the "Declaration and Proposals." Without waiting for a final understanding with the proprietors, Vassall led a colony to the Cape Fear River. It landed on May 26, 1664, and in November the lords proprietors named John Vassall deputy governor and surveyor and then appointed Robert Sanford secretary and chief register of Clarendon County. Soon other colonists arrived from Barbados, New England, and elsewhere, and the colony showed signs of prospering. The proprietors never reached an understanding with John

A Brief DESCRIPTION
OF
The Province
OF
CAROLINA
On the COASTS of FLOREDA.

AND

More perticularly of a *New-Plantation*
begun by the *E N G L I S H* at *Cape-Feare*,
on that River now by them called *Charles-River*,
the 29th of *May*. 1664.

Wherein is set forth
The *Healthfulness* of the *Air*; the *Fertility* of
the *Earth*, and *Waters*; and the great *Pleasure* and
Profit will accrue to those that shall go thither to enjoy
the same.

Also,
Directions and advice to such as shall go thither whether
on their own accompts, or to serve under another.

Together with
A most accurate MAP of the whole *PROVINCE*.

London, Printed for *Robert Horne* in the first Court of *Gresham-*
Colledge neer *Bishopsgate-street*. 1666.

One of the great many promotional tracts published during the
proprietary period.

Vassall as to the status of Clarendon County, and the appointment of his rival, Sir John Yeamans, as governor in January 1665 marked the beginning of the end of the county on the Cape Fear. With a small fleet the new governor left Barbados in October of that year, and as he reached Clarendon, his main ship ran aground and was beaten to pieces, scattering food and supplies. Desperately needed relief for the colonists of Clarendon was lost. Sir John was discouraged after a few weeks, and shortly after Christmas he returned to Barbados where he soon became involved in local affairs to the neglect of Clarendon County. With one of the small ships that escaped damage, Governor Yeamans sent Secretary Robert Sanford on a reconnoitering expedition to Port Royal, south of Cape Fear. He returned to Clarendon with enthusiastic predictions for the success of any settlement made on the river that he had discovered and named Ashley River. His excitement over the prospects of this new site contributed to the growing discontent in Clarendon.

In spite of the fact that the Clarendon leaders had laid out and settled a small town, which they called Charles Town, on the west bank of the Cape Fear River, and that the population reached a maximum of about eight hundred people living on farms scattered about sixty miles up and down the banks of the river, the lords proprietors all but ignored the settlement. John Vassall had had no clear understanding with them as to the colony's rights, and even formal pleas from the duly elected assembly brought no action. The only encouraging sign was the publication in 1666 of another promotional tract: *A Brief Description Of The Province of Carolina On the Coasts of Floreda. And More perticularly of a New-Plantation begun by the English at Cape Feare, on that River now by them called Charles-River.* Numerous privileges of colonists in Carolina were recited, and there was a special invitation for "all Artificers, as *Carpenters, Wheel-rights, Joyners, Coopers, Bricklayers, Smiths,* or diligent Husbandmen and Labourers" to remove to Clarendon. "If any Maid or single Woman have a desire to go over," the ten-page pamphlet continued, "they will think themselves in the Golden Age, when Men paid a

Dowry for their Wives; for if they be but Civil, and under 50 years of Age, some honest Man or other, will purchase them for their Wives." This effort at attracting settlers came too late, however, to save Clarendon County. Neglect from London might have been due to the Great Plague, which raged in 1664–1665, or to the Great Fire of September 1666, or possibly to the wearisome war with the French and Dutch between 1666 and 1667. Along the Cape Fear River trouble with the Indians developed. Warfare broke out and whites seized Indian children "under Pretence of instructing them in Learning the Principles of Christian Religion," but instead sold them into slavery. The arrows of the Indians were no match for English guns, but when the natives stole the settlers' cattle, they struck a very serious and painful economic blow. Whites began to leave, going back to Barbados, to Albemarle, to Virginia, and to New England.

Conditions grew desperate and Vassall wrote to London saying that £200 worth of clothing would meet the most serious need of the colony and enable it to survive another year, but even this small sum was too much for the lords proprietors. Toward the end of 1666 colonists began to depart by whatever means were available. As the early days of 1667 passed more people left, and Vassall sought just twenty men who would be willing to remain and hold the site with him. Fewer than half a dozen agreed to join him, however, and in the spring Vassall called for ships to come in and remove the last of the colonists. By the end of the summer of 1667 all had been abandoned. Charles Town, farm homes, gardens, and cleared fields were left to the mercy of the Indians and the creeping vines and old field pines. Chimneys made from brick that the colonists had so laboriously formed and baked at the site finally fell to the ground to be discovered years later by settlers who knew little or nothing of the pathetic history of the site they occupied. Instead of becoming the center of activity in Carolina, the Cape Fear section reverted to the wilderness it had been in 1524, when it was first sighted by Europeans.

The settled region of Albemarle County provides a sharp

contrast to the one at Clarendon County in that the colonists here successfully rebelled against the established authority and managed to survive despite the poor judgment of the proprietors. By early 1665 Albemarle County had its own governor and a document setting forth the form that its government should take. The first legislature met in the spring, and the territory that was later to be called North Carolina was born. The pattern of a governor and council representing the authority in London and a legislature representing the local citizens was firmly established, and it continued to exist until the Revolutionary War.

The proprietors were generally sympathetic to the requests of the Albemarle assembly, and many important concessions were thus gained by the colonists. For example, because settlers in Virginia were permitted to hold tracts more than twice as large as those allowed in Carolina, the assembly had asked that Carolinians receive the same treatment. The request was acceded to and on May Day 1668 the Great Deed of Grant containing new provisions was issued. Pleased with this and various other signs of consideration shown by the proprietors, the assembly passed a series of acts in 1669 that were designed to encourage settlement. One of these assured new settlers that they would be free from prosecution for debt during their first five years in Albemarle. Other acts made newcomers exempt from routine taxes for a year and promised that stiff penalties would be imposed upon individuals who attempted to corner the market on necessary commodities. And finally, nonresidents were forbidden to trade with the Indians—this valuable privilege being reserved for the citizens of Albemarle. At least two of these acts incurred the wrath of Virginians who saw their lucrative Indian trade threatened. They also protested that people of their own colony who were heavily in debt would flee to Carolina to escape prosecution. They very conveniently overlooked the fact that these very same laws had first been passed in their own colony in 1642; Albemarle simply patterned her legislative action on Virginia's earlier example.

The proprietors had been extremely lenient toward the people

Early settlers passing through the rivers and swamps from Virginia into Albemarle County.

in Albemarle. Because they wanted to attract settlers, their instructions for government had been very generous. However, foreseeing the danger of "erecting a numerous Democracy" in Carolina, the proprietors adopted an entirely new plan of government in 1669. Drafted by John Locke, under the direction of his friend and patron the Earl of Shaftesbury, the Fundamental Constitutions of Carolina offered the people little voice in the government. The proprietors now intended to exercise the feudal powers granted to them in their charters, and the Grand Model, as this new document came to be called, provided not only a scheme of government but a social and economic system as well. Ultimate governmental control was now in the hands of the proprietors, who planned to grant titles of nobility that carried with them large tracts of land and special privileges. Freeholders who were beneath the nobility, could still own land and hold Negro slaves, but they were to be permitted to play only a limited role in government. Leet-men, who were bound to the land, would be tenants of the nobility. The Grand Model provided for an established Anglican Church, with a considerable measure of toleration accorded to those "of different opinions concerning matters of religion." The supreme agency of government was to be the Palatine's Court, composed of the eight proprietors. A Grand Council was to exercise executive, legislative, and judicial powers, while another agency, the Parliament, was to be the assembly for the province. Both proprietors and freeholders would be represented in the Parliament.

The Grand Model was designed to provide a government not for the existing social order but rather for a society that the proprietors expected would develop in Carolina in the future. Consequently, the officials in Albemarle were instructed to apply only those features of the document that were considered workable under present conditions. But even the application of limited parts of the plan required significant changes in the government. Under the Fundamental Constitutions the assembly lost, at least for a time, its power to initiate legislation and the governor lost both his authority and his prestige. On the other hand, the council gained considerably in prestige and authority.

Although the Constitutions were proclaimed "The Sacred and Unalterable Form and Rule of Government," they were revised at least five times between 1669 and 1698 and never were fully put into effect. They finally were abandoned after 1700 by the lords proprietors, but before then violence and confusion were commonplace. Many of the disorders in Carolina had their origin in the form of government that provided the people with no legitimate channels for initiating change. Factions that had existed in the colony almost from the time of the arrival of the first settlers began to strengthen. Leading the antiproprietary or popular faction were the precharter settlers George Durant, John Jenkins, John Harvey, Richard Foster, John Willoughby, and Valentine Bird. They felt that they owed nothing to the proprietors, and they certainly did not appreciate proprietary meddling in local affairs. Those who had come to the county since 1663 generally had a different point of view and they formed the proprietary or prerogative faction. Frequently, these were men who were indebted to the proprietors for their position in Carolina. Thomas Eastchurch, who was at one time speaker of the assembly and later appointed governor, was among their leaders, as were Thomas Miller, Timothy Biggs, and John Nixon.

Conditions became almost unbearable in Albemarle County. Illness, hurricanes, drought, excessive rain, the loss of livestock for various unspecified reasons, and the scarcity of shipping all combined to dishearten the people. The colony lacked good ports and the shifting sands of the Outer Banks, and the changing inlets kept ocean-going commerce away. Produce from the colony often had to be shipped through the ports of Virginia, where excessive entry and clearance fees were charged. It would seem that the Carolinians were certainly industrious enough. They planted corn and tobacco and tended cattle and hogs; during the off-season they engaged in whaling. Yet in spite of their "industrie labour and paines" their work was not profitable. "It hath pleased God of his providence," one official noted, "to inflict such a generall calamitie upon the inhabitants . . . that for Severall yeares they had nott injoyed the fruitts of their labours which causes them generally to growne under the burtyn of poverty and many times famine."

In 1672 the council in desperation arranged to send Governor Peter Carteret to England to plead with the proprietors for relief. He was to seek a reduction in quitrents (so called because they "quit" the landowner from any further obligation, which the proprietors, as feudal lords, might have demanded), aid in defense of the colony, grants of land for children when they came of age, and a reduction of the fees that were charged for Carolina goods passing through ports in Virginia. Carteret met with absolutely no success in London and, in fact, the proprietors completely disavowed any responsibility for the unfortunate conditions in Carolina. They even complained that Carteret had left his government in "ill order and worse hands" but this was simply not true. To serve as acting governor, he had appointed the very capable John Jenkins, but this individual was an old settler and a member of the antiproprietary party. The proprietors further charged that Carteret's government was at fault for not encouraging the New England trade and for discouraging the extension of settlement to the southern shore of Albemarle Sound. The proprietors refused to recognize that their own actions had created these conditions, and instead they attempted to place all the blame on the local government. The rift between the people of Carolina and the proprietors widened as successive petitions for aid and guidance were met by stern rebuffs. That they soon were involved in heated disputes and open revolt should have been no surprise to the lords proprietors. The people recognized that after the settlement of Charles Town in the southern part of the province of Carolina in 1670, the proprietors readily shifted the focus of their interest to that new area because it seemed to offer more hope of quick profit. With a clear reference to this virtual abandonment of the older settlement, a citizen of Albemarle wrote the proprietors: "You have not been out as yet any thing upon that County in the Province called

Albemarle, yet the inhabitants have lived and gott Estates under your Lords there by their owne Industry and brought it to the capacity of a hopefull Settlement and . . . had your Lords smiles and assistance [been] but a tenth part of what your Southern parts have had, it would have been a Flourishing Settlement."

Because Carolina ports were inadequate for large vessels and because of Virginia's excessive fees on Carolina commerce, the people of Albemarle were forced to turn to smuggling as the answer to their commercial problems. Coastal traders from New England, using shallow-draft vessels that could slip through the inlets, opened a profitable but illegal trade with Carolina planters. In violation of British navigation acts, Carolina tobacco was finding its way to Scotland, Ireland, Holland, France, and Spain without first passing through England. The Plantation Duty Act of 1673 required ships clearing one colonial port for another to pay customs duties, and customs collectors in the colonies were to be directly responsible to the commissioners of the customs in London. The governor of Albemarle was obliged to appoint customs collectors, but the only men available for the job were local inhabitants and they were not diligent in performing their duties. The proprietors favored the Plantation Duty Act because they believed that it encouraged direct trade with England and that this would prove beneficial to their colony. Citizens of Albemarle, they felt, could buy English goods at more reasonable prices if they dealt directly with England than if they went through New England traders. They also feared that open violation of the law might endanger the life of their charter.

Albemarle citizens realized that enforcement of the English navigation acts would deny them a free market outside England and that heavy duties on tobacco would keep northern merchants from sending their ships to Albemarle to buy. Therefore, when Thomas Miller, the newly appointed deputy governor and customs collector, arrived he was met with a show of force by those who objected to his instructions from the proprietors to enforce the navigation acts. It was only with the assistance of the militia that he was able to assume office. When Miller called for the election of a new assembly, he attempted to disfranchise his opposition, and then he had warrants issued for the apprehension, dead or alive, of some of the most prominent men in the colony. At the same time, he increased the size of the militia by adding a "pipeing guard," which he claimed was necessary for protection against the Indians who were reacting to attacks against their neighbors and friends in Virginia during Bacon's Rebellion. Miller's enemies objected to the expense of this special guard for the governor as well as to the unmistakable hint of class distinction that it lent to his office. Miller also employed the ship captain who had recently brought him to Carolina to stop and search vessels in the waters of Albemarle Sound for contraband.

Miller's arbitrary use of power infuriated the citizens of Albemarle, who had long been accustomed to a less formal and less repressive government. Friends of John Jenkins, who had been governor before Miller's arrival, urged resistance. An opportunity for action finally presented itself in early December 1677 with the arrival of a New England ship under the command of Captain Zachariah Gillam. On board the *Carolina* was a supply of arms, a good stock of merchandise to meet winter needs, and rum to add cheer to a dreary life. When Gillam went ashore to present his papers to Miller, the governor insisted that he pay duty on tobacco that he had taken out of the colony the year before. Gillam refused, saying that he had paid the tax in England, whereupon Miller seized his papers, ordered his crew confined, and arrested Gillam and placed him under a £1,000 bond for breach of the navigation acts. When Governor Miller learned from Gillam's papers that George Durant, the principal exporter of tobacco in Carolina, was a passenger aboard the ship, he went out to the *Carolina*, anchored in the Pasquotank River. Approaching Durant with a brace of cocked pistols, he thrust one of them to Durant's chest and arrested him as a "Traytour." The crew of the ship called his bluff, however, and Miller was soon in close confinement.

During this time two old citizens of Albemarle, Richard Foster

(who was one of the proprietors' deputies) and William Crawford, rowed out to the ship to consult with their friend, Durant.
What plans they laid no record survives to tell, but the events
of the next few days suggest that they were carefully made
plans.

Word spread rapidly throughout the county. Valentine Bird
and John Culpeper, a firebrand recently arrived from Charles
Town, were in command of a group of men under arms, and they
were soon joined by Durant, Foster, and Crawford. Captain
Gillam refused to be intimidated by Miller, especially after he
received the support of many people who begged him to remain
and give them an opportunity to trade. To the cause of popular
government, lax customs officials, and free trade, Captain Gillam
contributed guns and cutlasses from his store in the hold of the
Carolina. Within a week the antiproprietary faction was in firm
control of affairs and Governor Miller and his supporters were
under arrest and being held in isolation in one or more log jails.
The rebels found the seal of the colony hidden among Miller's
possessions, and they used it liberally to lend an air of authority
to their documents. They called upon voters to elect delegates to
an assembly, and this was readily accomplished. In one precinct,
however, the voters threatened to become even more independent than their leaders had anticipated. They raised voices against
lords, landgraves, and caciques (the latter two were the titles of
nobility authorized by the Fundamental Constitutions) and
insisted that they would "fly to the King's protection." Richard
Foster, recognizing the danger in such threats, quieted them, but
they ended the occasion by directing their representatives to
secure for them freedom in the tobacco trade and the right to
ship it "where they pleased and how they pleased." Thomas
Miller, they also demanded, must be brought to trial.

When a freely elected assembly finally met at George Durant's
house it named a speaker and council. At the same time, six
members were chosen to sit as a court to try Miller. There is no
evidence, however, that a governor was chosen. Probably John
Jenkins, who had been displaced by Miller, simply and quietly

just resumed office. As Miller's trial was getting underway, word
arrived that Thomas Eastchurch, the man for whom Miller acted
as deputy governor, had reached Virginia and was on his way to
take up his appointed post as governor of Albemarle. He issued a
proclamation ordering the colonists to end their rebellion and to
send a delegation to him in Virginia to explain their recent
action. His directives were ignored, but when Carolinians
appealed to the governor of Virginia for advice and guidance,
they were told that any question about the government of
Albemarle should be submitted "to the proper place in England." The colonists persisted in their resistance and even sent an
armed force from Albemarle to the Virginia frontier in the hope
of preventing Eastchurch from entering the colony. The matter
was finally resolved in February 1678 when Eastchurch suc-
cumbed to an illness he had contracted in Virginia. Miller later
escaped from jail and fled to England.

Culpeper's Rebellion, as this affair has been called, was one of
the earliest popular uprisings in the American colonies against a
government that the people considered to be unjust. It succeeded
in providing a stable government for the colony, one under which
taxes and other duties required by law were faithfully collected.
The only one of the rebels who happened afterward to go to
England was Culpeper, and there he was promptly arrested and
charged with high treason. However, the proprietors, perhaps
again out of concern for their charter, convinced the court that
no legal government had existed at the time of the alleged
rebellion and that therefore Culpeper could have been guilty of
nothing more serious than rioting. With the restitution of lost
royal revenue, the matter was officially forgotten.

On the whole, the lords proprietors made every effort to meet
this crisis wisely, but they had heard so many tales from so many
messengers that they found it impossible to distinguish truth from
falsehood in the reports from Albemarle. They could not tell the
innocent from the guilty and were unable to pronounce judgment with impartiality. What they wanted most of all to
accomplish was a restoration of peace and law in their province.

Diorama depicting the 1677 uprising in Albemarle County known as "Culpeper's Rebellion." *Courtesy of the Museum of History, Raleigh, North Carolina.*

Toward this end they chose Seth Sothel to be the new governor. He was a man they were confident would represent neither faction. Sothel, who had recently become a proprietor by purchasing Edward Hyde's share, would presumably be above local squabbles while maintaining a position of double authority, that is, as governor and as a proprietor. En route to Carolina following his commissioning, Sothel was captured by the Turks and taken to Algiers where he was held in prison for about five years. During this period a succession of local men in Albemarle served as governor, and in the main they acted very capably; customs duties were collected and a tax was even levied and collected to make good the revenues lost during the rebellion. In 1683 Sothel escaped from the pirates and managed to make his way to Carolina where he soon proved to be one of the most arbitrary and corrupt governors in any of the English colonies. He completely disregarded instructions from the other proprietors, illegally appointed officials, acted contrary to all of the documents of government, accepted bribes, jailed his opponents without trial, illegally seized several estates that he, as governor, was responsible for settling, and in numerous other ways generally outraged the people. By 1689 Sothel's tyranny could be endured no longer and the assembly finally put him to trial. He was found guilty of thirteen charges, banished from the colony for a year, and declared ineligible forever to hold office. When the proprietors discovered what had actually occurred in their colony during Sothel's administration, they apologized to the people for the wrongs they had endured.

The lords proprietors were slow to come to an understanding of the mistakes they had made in their bumbling efforts to govern Albemarle. Insurrection, rebellion, and revolution subsided only when they ceased all their efforts to enforce any of the provisions of the Fundamental Constitutions. The government of the colony then returned to the familiar pattern of governor, council, assembly, and courts. What had occurred in Albemarle, however, was only one aspect of similar movements against unpopular governments that swept Britain and the colonies.

The Glorious Revolution of 1688 had rid England of Roman Catholic James II, the last of the Stuarts, and with him went the final remnants of the theory of the divine right of kings. The government in Britain became more responsive to the popular will with the accession to the throne of William and Mary. In the American colonies a series of armed uprisings from Massachusetts all the way down the coast into Carolina went far toward securing the country from fear of Roman Catholic domination and from the Crown's attempts to unify the New England colonies into one dominion to which Pennsylvania, Maryland, and Virginia might have been added. In all the colonies representative assemblies were assured. There were many instances of close cooperation among the various colonies during these little local wars.

The New England colonies, of course, were in constant communication with each other. But in addition, many men in Massachusetts also played key roles in the Albemarle commotions. Men from Albemarle participated in Bacon's Rebellion in Virginia, and some Virginians, in turn, involved themselves in Albemarle during the troubles in 1677 and afterward. Virginians also participated in the religious and political difficulties in Maryland during 1689 and 1690. The combined results of all these struggles prevented the Crown from unifying the American colonies into one or perhaps several administrative units. Each colony remained independent, and the government of each was more responsive to the will of its people than it could possibly have been if their citizens had sat quietly by and permitted enforcement of the navigation acts or if they had said nothing while their charter rights were nibbled away by officials in London.

3

GROWTH AND CONFLICT UNDER THE PROPRIETORS

The expansion of North Carolina outside the bounds of the original Albemarle County was a natural movement of people in search of new land and opportunities. Probably in anticipation of settlement that was to follow, Seth Sothel took out a patent in 1681 for twelve thousand acres of land along the Pamlico River. So many people had moved here by 1696 that Bath County was formed to include most of the peninsula between Albemarle Sound and the Pamlico River. At about this same time, a "great Mortality" among the Indians, possibly caused by an epidemic of smallpox, opened up desirable land for occupation. Some French Huguenots moved into the area about 1704 or 1705. They came from Manakin Town on the James River in Virginia where apparently crowded conditions and word of good land on the Pamlico had induced them to leave. The new county was named for John Granville, Earl of Bath, one of the lords proprietors, but it was also known for a time as Pamlico, the Indian name for the river. The four original precincts of Albemarle County (Chowan, Pasquotank, Perquimans, and Currituck) enjoyed the "ancient privilege" of electing five representatives each to the assembly, but Bath County was permitted only two. This set a precedent by which all newly formed counties had fewer representatives than the older sections of the colony. Discrimination between the old and the new counties was to cause considerable controversy throughout the remainder of North Carolina's history as a colony. The differences between the sections grew as the colony expanded, but these disparities were not exclusively political in nature. Geographical factors and their direct influence on economic development also contributed to conflicts between the counties.

The lords proprietors were anxious to have towns established in the counties as convenient centers of trade and tax collection. In addition, towns would provide mutual protection and perhaps even serve as an outward sign of progress and growth. By 1705 there must have been a sufficient concentration of population on the Pamlico River to suggest a town, and so at the junction of two creeks not very far from their mouth in the Pamlico River, a site ideally suited for convenient water transportation and for protection against any enemies who might approach by land, Surveyor-General John Lawson, Joel Martin, Sr., and Simon Alderson, Sr., proceeded to lay out a new town. It was called Bath in honor of the man for whom the county was named, and on March 8, 1706 the assembly passed an act formally incorporating the town. Land was reserved for a church, a market, and some other public buildings. Also set aside was a glebe for the use of the minister at the church and a town common (land reserved for public use as a pasture, wood lot, and other purposes designed to be of benefit to the entire community). This particular town, though it continued to exist (and in fact still exists today and is the oldest town in the state), never really flourished; a dozen or so houses were about the maximum of which it could ever boast, but St. Thomas Church, erected there in 1734, is the oldest surviving church building in North Carolina. The county as a whole, however, held enough promise for future growth so that in 1705 it was divided into Wickham, Pamptecough (or Pamlico), and Archdale precincts. These three names were changed in 1712 to Hyde, Beaufort, and Craven, and they continue to exist today as counties in North Carolina. The confidence placed in Bath County was justified, and before long it was a serious contender with the old Albemarle section as the center of activity in the colony.

St. Thomas Episcopal Church in Bath, built in 1734, the oldest standing church in North Carolina. *Courtesy of the Travel and Promotion Division, Department of Natural and Economic Resources, State of North Carolina.*

Among the earliest people to move here were some more of the French Huguenots from Manakin Town in Virginia. In 1707 or 1708 they settled at the mouth of the Trent River in several family groups. John Lawson described the people as being "much taken with the Pleasantness of that Country, and, indeed, [they] are a very industrious people. At present, they make very good Linnen-Cloath and Thread, and are very well vers'd in cultivating Hemp and Flax, of both which they raise very considerable Quantities; and design to try an Essay of the Grape, for making of Wine." Not all of the Huguenots remained on at Trent River. In 1711 one of the pastors of the group, the Reverend Claude Philippe de Richebourg, moved with some of his adherents to the Santee River in South Carolina.

Before long, Swiss and German colonists would be joining the English and French settlers already established in North Carolina. As early as 1703, and perhaps even before then, some Swiss had become interested in the possibility of colonization projects in Carolina. Franz Ludwig Michel of Bern was in Carolina in 1703 and wrote a glowing letter to his brother suggesting how profitable a colony would be. Several Swiss merchants and businessmen formed a joint-stock company, George Ritter and Company, and by early 1705 detailed plans for a colony were drawn up. These set forth the duties and privileges of the colonists and specifically covered various religious, political, and financial questions. A few years later, Baron Christoph von Graffenried, one of the members of the Swiss company, happened to be in England where he met John Lawson. The surveyor-general, who was in London seeing about the publication of his book, *A New Voyage to Carolina*, undoubtedly painted a glowing picture of the Neuse River area, where he had acquired 640 acres and built a house for himself. Lawson had much to do with the final decision that established a colony there under the sponsorship of the Swiss company.

At the same time that these plans were developing in Switzerland, events were taking place elsewhere in Europe that had an important bearing on the outcome of the projected colony at Neuse River. Thousands of Germans were moving out of the upper Rhine (or Palatinate) and the neighboring provinces. A variety of causes brought about this mass movement: a prolonged series of wars over the years had left the region devastated and impoverished; taxes were burdensome; disagreements among various Protestant sects gave rise to a good deal of unrest; and the cry of Roman Catholic persecution was raised, but this was probably the weakest of the factors contributing to migration. The immediate cause for the exodus was provided by the incredibly harsh winter of 1708–1709. Severe Arctic cold swept through central Europe, freezing the rivers until well into April. Grape vines and fruit trees, the source of livelihood for most of the people of the region, were killed. The planting of grain was delayed, and the price of bread soared. Agents from the proprietary colonies of Pennsylvania and Carolina went among the suffering and distributed printed information about the bountiful land in the New World that so desperately needed settlers. It was even hinted that Queen Anne would assist them in securing transportation to America.

Soon after the late spring thaw a thousand refugees a week were making their way up the Rhine to Rotterdam, and thence to London. Large numbers were sent to Ireland and to New York, where it was expected they might produce naval stores for Britain. The lords proprietors of Carolina, recognizing the potential for new settlers, sought assistance from the Board of Trade in providing transportation for Palatines who were between the ages of fifteen and forty-five. The proprietors said they would give each of these persons one hundred acres of land free of quitrent for ten years. Before an arrangement could be concluded with the Board of Trade, the Swiss promoters solved the proprietors' problem for them. The Swiss had at first sought land in Virginia, but Virginia was a royal colony and the queen was unwilling to accept diminished royal sovereignty by granting them the extensive control they sought over the land and the settlers. Carolina was different, however; it was a proprietary colony and the lords proprietors were quite willing to enter into negotiations with the Swiss whereby they might acquire land and limited sovereignty over it. The proprietors agreed to sell ten thousand acres between the Neuse and Cape Fear rivers for £10 per thousand acres and to allow a twelve-year option on additional land. They also agreed that the title of landgrave would be bestowed upon anyone of the Swiss company who purchased five thousand acres. Christoph von Graffenried, on August 4, 1709, paid £50 for five thousand acres and a few days later was given a coat-of-arms and invested "in Robes of Scarlet interlaced with Gold, To be by [him] worne on all great and solemn occasions."

Graffenried then assumed direction of the Swiss company and proceeded with plans for the establishment of a colony in North Carolina. He made a deal with commissioners in London to transport 650 Palatines to America if they would pay the passage. In turn, the company agreed to set aside 250 acres for each family, furnish provisions for a year, and provide certain other necessities. The lords proprietors directed Christopher Gale, one of their officials in North Carolina, to furnish the colonists with whatever provisions he could, and it was agreed that the Swiss company would repay the proprietors a portion of their value. Before the end of 1709 the company began purchasing additional land and when negotiations were concluded on January 1, 1710, Graffenried and his associates held 17,500 acres. It was clear that they needed more settlers, and so they turned to the many German refugees in and around London. Graffenried selected "healthy, industrious people" with assorted qualifications and provided them with tools and what was believed to be ample food. Crown commissioners inspected and approved the ships, and before the end of January the colonists, led by Lawson, departed. Graffenried remained in London to complete plans for a colony of Swiss to follow shortly.

Officials in Bern, Switzerland, cooperated with Graffenried and his company because they saw an opportunity to rid the country of some undesirable people: paupers and a troublesome religious element composed of Baptists, Anabaptists, and Mennonites. The religious contingent of deportees, however, never made it to America. Some of their number were released even before leaving Switzerland because of age or sickness. The remainder were rescued at the Dutch border by sympathetic dissidents who managed to prevent the forcible deportation of their Swiss brethren. Only the one hundred paupers were permitted to pass to England. Accompanied by Graffenried, they finally sailed in July and reached Hampton, Virginia, in September. There followed a tiring voyage up the Nansemond River and then a trip by wagon overland to the Neuse River.

When they finally reached the site of the colony, Graffenried heard distressing tales of death and suffering from the Palatines. Winter storms at sea had delayed them and they were thirteen weeks in crossing. Lack of adequate supplies, salty food, and close confinement had taken a heavy toll. Then, in the mouth of the James River, they were boarded by French privateers and plundered. When they finally reached North Carolina in desperate need of assistance to make their way overland to Neuse River, they called at the home of Thomas Pollock, who charged dearly for supplies. Finally, at journey's end, the Palatines discovered that Lawson and Gale had actually made no provisions at all for them at the site chosen for their settlement. The people were too weak to carry on the necessary work, and in fact many had been reduced to such low circumstances that they had to sell some of their clothes to their English neighbors for food. When Graffenried arrived he sent to Pennsylvania for flour and to Virginia for other supplies. The arrival of food renewed the hopes of the people, and they faced the winter with a good bit of certainty that conditions would improve.

Graffenried had already paid the lords proprietors for the land he claimed, but as a step toward insuring peace he also paid the Indians for whatever claim they might have on the same acreage. He was to complain later that he had also been obliged to pay John Lawson for some of the land to which the surveyor-general claimed a prior right. Having paid three times for much of his land, Graffenried undoubtedly felt that he was justified in

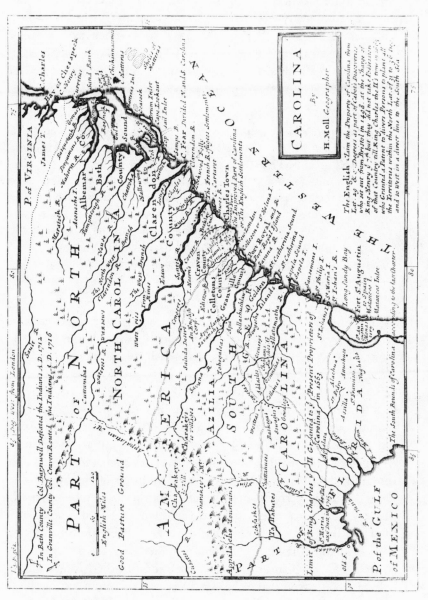

Herman Moll's map of Carolina, 1729.

bemoaning the fact that Lawson had not completed his part of
the bargain. Certainly land should have been cleared and some
kind of shelters erected before their arrival. It was now late
summer and the settlers would have to manage as best they
could, but Graffenried decided to lose no time in having the
surveyor-general proceed with plans to lay out the new town. In
his account of the event, he described the instructions he gave
Lawson:

Since in America they do not like to live crowded, in order to enjoy a
purer air, I accordingly ordered the streets to be very broad and the
houses well separated one from the other. I marked three acres of land
for each family, for house, barn, garden, orchard, hemp field, poultry
yard and other purposes. I divided the village like a cross and in the
middle I intended the church. One of the principle streets extended
from the bank of the river Neuse straight on into the forest and the
other principle street crossed it, running from the Trent River clear to
the Neuse River. After that we planted stakes to mark the houses and to
make the first two principle streets along and on the banks of the two
rivers. . . .

Graffenried recorded that the new town was named for the
river on which it was located and for his home city in
Switzerland: Neuse-Bern. To the English this sounded like New
Bern and before long that is what the place was being called.
Only twenty of the families actually lived right in the town;
Graffenried commented "artisans are better off in a city than on
plantations." Therefore, he established the locksmith, mason,
blacksmith, tailor, miller, butcher, weaver, potter, tilemaker,
carpenters, shoemakers, and other tradesmen in the town. The
remainder of the colonists were settled on farms of 250 acres each
along the nearby rivers and creeks. A market was to be operated
in New Bern once a month, and there was to be an annual fair
after the European custom. There was no church, but during the
first year an Anglican clergyman visited the town, where he
preached in English and French and administered communion.
The Palatines and the Swiss acclimated themselves quite well

in their new surroundings, and as the end of their first year neared Graffenried boasted that his colony had made more progress in that limited time than the English had made in four years. The town of New Bern held promise of being the important trading center that the lords proprietors had so long desired to see established in Carolina. Lots were marked out and reserved for the governor and council, and it was even reported that many people from Pennsylvania and some from Virginia purchased lots in the new town. Graffenried was so proud of the town's development that he even spoke of the desirability of shifting the seat of government from Little River in Albemarle, where the assembly had met a number of times, to New Bern. On Little River, he wrote, "we were badly lodged and had no security," whereas he believed the new town was fortified and could be easily defended. Graffenried exercised almost total control over the life and government of his little colony. The people owed allegiance to him and he owed them protection. In this single instance in North Carolina the feudal ideals set forth by the lords proprietors in the Fundamental Constitutions came nearer taking effect than they did anywhere else. But, unfortunately, this interesting experiment on the American frontier did not survive long enough to receive a true test. Less than two weeks after the Swiss marked their first anniversary on the Neuse River a near-fatal blow to the whole colony was struck by the Tuscarora Indians and their confederates.

From the outset of settlement the Indians had many grievances against the whites, the most important of which were: encroachments on the land and hunting grounds of the natives; the enslavement of Indians, particularly women and children; the "sharp practices" of white traders; and the contemptuous attitudes of many whites toward the Indians. The natives had long resented white settlement on their hunting grounds, correctly believing that it would not be long until the newcomers would take possession of all their lands. To heighten the apprehensiveness of the Indians, when the settlers acquired land—by treaties, purchases, and deeds—they frequently cheated the natives. And it cannot be forgotten that their unscrupulous practices extended even into the trade they conducted with the Indians. Almost every contemporary writer commented on the "irregular" practices of white traders who "dealt too hard" with the natives and cheated them in various ways. For the furs and skins of deer, beaver, bear, and other wild animals brought in by the Indians, the whites exchanged rum, trinkets of many kinds, cloth, powder, lead, and guns (despite legislation against the sale of firearms to natives). The early settlers of the Neuse-Trent region "were quick to grasp the fact that money could be made by exchanging cheap goods for many times their value in skins." "Fire water," usually rum, and firearms were the two articles most highly prized by the Indians. As Lawson wrote, they were never "contented with a little [rum], but when once begun, they must make themselves quite drunk."

Most of the contemporary accounts that spoke of the friendly relations between the two races were written by individuals who sought to attract new settlers. For obvious reasons their promotional pamphlets and books tended to play down the hostilities that existed between the whites and Indians. But the deep-seated conflicts arising out of the white man's shabby treatment of the natives could not long be ignored. Lawson, who perhaps understood the North Carolina Indians better than anyone, wrote: "They are really better to us than we have been to them." To this observation he added the significant and prophetic comment, "The Indians are very revengeful, and never forget an Injury done, till they have received Satisfaction." Thomas Pollock, who was president of the council and later became acting governor during the Tuscarora War, declared at first that the Indians struck in 1711 "without any cause that we know of," but he later admitted that "our own divising hath been the cause of all our troubles."

As early as 1701, the Indians of the Pamlico River area complained to Lawson that the settlers on Indian land "were very wicked people and that they threatened the Indians for hunting near their plantations." In 1703 the Coree Indians staged a minor uprising and were declared "public enemies" by the local government. In 1706–1707 Thomas Pollock marched against the Meherrin Indians along the Virginia border, seized thirty-six members of the tribe and imprisoned them for two days without food or drink, wrecked their cabins, and threatened to destroy their crops if they did not surrender their lands. When North Carolina officials appealed to Virginia authorities to take some action concerning the Meherrins in that colony, Governor Spotswood and the Virginia legislature refused to do anything because they considered the whites to be the aggressors in this conflict and claimed that North Carolina was "the author of its own misery." In 1707 it was reported that settlers along Pamlico River "expected ye Indians everyday to come and cut their throats." Just a few days before the massacre of September 22, 1711, the Indians complained directly to Graffenried "that they had been badly treated and detained by the inhabitants of the Pamtigo [Pamlico], Neuse, and Trent Rivers, a thing which was not to be longer endured." He declared that the whites "cheated the Indians in trading, and would not allow them to hunt near their plantations, and under that pretense took away from them their game, arms, and ammunition," and that "these poor Indians, insulted in many ways by a few rough Carolinians more barbarous and unkind than the savages themselves, could not stand such treatment much longer, and began to think of their safety and vengeance, what they did very secretly." Colonel William Byrd of Virginia, writing about the traders of North Carolina, said, "These Petty Rulers don't only teach the honester Savages all sorts of Debauchery, but are unfair in all their dealings and use them in all kinds of Opression." He declared that the traders had abused the Indian women and mistreated the men "until the Indians grew weary and tired of the Tyranny and Injustice with which the whites treated them and resolved to endure the bondage no longer."

The final action by the whites that led directly to the outbreak of the Tuscarora War was the settlement of New Bern in 1710.

The arrival of more than four hundred new settlers within a few months was serious cause for alarm among the Indians. These newcomers gobbled up the most desirable land along the Neuse and Trent rivers and along some of the large creeks flowing into these waterways, and they often began farming so near an Indian village that they blocked the path to the water. The Indians observed their new neighbors very closely and were aware of the divisive influence of recent religious and political disputes among the whites. They noted that many of the settlers were "outlanders" and not English, and they knew that this generated a certain amount of discord. Further, the Indians were surely not unaware of the refusal of the large Quaker element to bear arms in time of trouble. Perhaps, the Indian leaders must have reasoned, all of the differences and the disagreements that they witnessed, combined with a recent yellow fever epidemic and other causes of suffering, presented them with an ideal opportunity, and possibly the last one, to clear the white man out of the country. Thus, at the end of a hot, dry summer when crops had been bad and the harvest poor, the Tuscarora joined forces with the Coree, Pamlico, Machapunga, and Bear River Indians. As William Byrd expressed it a few years later: "Then it was that all the neighbor Indians, grown weary of the tyranny and injustice with which they had been abused for many years, resolved to endure their bondage no longer but entered into a general confederacy against their oppressors of Carolina." Dawn on September 22, 1711, shortly after the first anniversary of the arrival of the Swiss, was the date set for the attack.

No one among the settlers expected that anything out of the ordinary was about to happen. It was fine autumn weather and Lawson, as an official of the colony, planned a little expedition to find out first, how far upstream the Neuse was navigable and second, how far away he was from the mountains. Early in September 1711 he and Graffenried, accompanied by two friendly Indians and two Negro slaves and equipped with provisions for fourteen days, set out on a trip up the river. Two or three days later they were captured by "60 armed Indians, seized, plundered, and hurried through the forest" to the Indian town of Catechna, where they were carried before King Hancock of the Tuscarora. After long deliberation by a council presided over by Hancock, it was decided that the two distinguished prisoners should be released. But the next morning, as Lawson and Graffenried were preparing to resume their journey, other chiefs arrived and demanded the privilege of questioning the white captives. As a result of a quarrel that broke out between Lawson and Cor Tom, one of the chiefs of Coree Town, a council meeting was held after dark and both prisoners were condemned to death. Early next morning, a third council of chiefs was held and it was decided to spare the life of Graffenried, whom the Indians mistakenly identified as Governor Hyde, but to kill Lawson, who was summarily executed. There are several conflicting accounts of his death. Some Indians later told Graffenried that the threat was made to cut Lawson's throat with his own razor, and Graffenried's Negro slave confirmed this. But others reported that Lawson was executed by hanging, and still others claimed that he was burned. The story that is most commonly believed is that "exquisite torture" was inflicted upon John Lawson, the Englishman in Carolina who best understood and sympathized with the Indians.

The day after Lawson's cruel death, "the notables of the village" revealed to Graffenried their plan for a large-scale war in North Carolina, to be directed especially against the white residents along the Pamlico, Neuse, and Trent rivers and Core Sound. The attack began at daybreak on the morning of September 22, when a total of five hundred painted and screaming warriors did their bloodiest deed against the whites ever seen in North Carolina. Except for the little town of New Bern, which was spared, the isolated settlers along the Neuse, Trent, and Pamlico rivers and in the Core Sound region reeled under their blows. Christopher Gale wrote in early November of some of the treacheries that were known to him.

The family of one Mr. Nevill was treated after this manner: the old gentleman himself, after being shot, was laid on the house-floor, with a

Graffenried's drawing of himself, John Lawson, and their Negro servant during their captivity by the Tuscarora Indians.

clean pillow under his head, his wife's head clothes put upon his head, his stockings turned over his shoes, and his body covered all over with new linen. His wife was set upon her knees, and her hands lifted up as if she was at prayers, leaning against a chair in the chimney corner, and her coats turned up over her head. A son of his was laid out in the yard, with a pillow laid under his head and a bunch of rosemary laid to his nose. A negro had his right hand cut off and left dead. The master of the next house was shot and his body laid flat upon his wife's grave. Women were laid on their house-floors and great stakes run up through their bodies. Others big with child, the infants were ripped out and hung upon trees. In short, their manner of butchery has been so various and unaccountable, that it would be beyond credit to relate them. This blow was so hotly followed by the hellish crew, that we could not bury our dead; so that they were left for prey to the dogs, and wolves, and vultures, whilst our care was to strengthen our garrison to secure the living.

The Indians took 20 or 30 prisoners, mostly women and children. They had killed between 130 and 140 whites; the Swiss and Palatines accounted for about half the dead. Those who survived were "forc'd to keep garisons and watch and Gard, day and Night."

Early attempts to retaliate were futile, and the colonists suffered even more losses. Their feeble efforts were poorly organized and they lacked strong leadership. This encouraged the Indians to think that they had succeeded in weakening the whites beyond recovery.

The people in New Bern took refuge in houses outside the town that they hoped might somehow be fortified. William Brice had previously built a fort on his plantation and many people gathered there. When Graffenried returned after his release by the Indians, a few again expressed a willingness to follow him, but most of the Swiss and Palatines were suspicious of a man who refused to make war on the Indians. This, however, was a stipulation to which he agreed as a means of securing his own release and to save New Bern from attack. Many of the group became so dissatisfied with his position that they openly opposed him and drew up a list of twenty articles accusing him of malfeasance. Graffenried was powerless to unite the settlers behind him. Brice and his followers set out to seek revenge on the Indians and in so doing they violated the agreement Graffenried had made to save New Bern. When Brice's men captured a chief of the Bay River Indians and roasted him alive over an open fire, the Indians were no longer obliged to spare Graffenried's people and after a brief rest they renewed their attacks. More people were killed, houses burned, livestock stolen or driven away, and fields of corn destroyed. Bath County was nearly depopulated. Ruin and desolation were widespread and the few that were left finally called on Albemarle for assistance. Plantations along the shore of Albemarle Sound were fortified, but the Quakers, who made up a large portion of the population, refused to take up arms. Governor Hyde, the council, and the assembly called on Governor Spotswood of Virginia for assistance. Spotswood offered to send a trader down to the Tuscaroras with goods to ransom some of the prisoners, but he said that he could dispatch Crown troops under his command only if North Carolina guaranteed provisions for them. Hyde had only limited funds at his disposal and the season had been so bad that little food was available for the local population, much less an army. No help, then, was forthcoming from Virginia.

Turning next to South Carolina, Christopher Gale took a plea for aid to Governor Robert Gibbes. The governor quickly submitted Gale's request to the assembly, and in a generous act of intercolonial cooperation the members resolved "that the inhabitants of North Carolina in their present deplorable circumstances should be aided and assisted by this Government." They voted to raise and send to North Carolina "a Sufficient number of warlike Indians. . . ." An appropriation of £4,000 was also voted to finance the expedition; a five-man committee was appointed to gather supplies; John Barnwell was put in command of the troops, and a small vessel was also provided to keep officials in Charles Town posted on the course of the war.

In North Carolina such supplies as could be gathered were distributed to those who needed them. To help meet the

Christopher Gale, several times chief justice of North Carolina from 1714 until his death in 1734.

immediate demands for funds to arm and provision a military force to take to the field against the Indians, £4,000 in bills of credit was authorized. This was the first emission of paper money by the assembly and it marked the beginning of a serious problem that was to plague North Carolina during the remainder of the colonial period and even over into statehood, when the difficulty of redeeming paper money became critical.

Colonel John Barnwell (later known as "Tuscarora Jack") recruited thirty-three white men and nearly five hundred friendly Indians, chiefly Yamassees, and divided this force into three companies. Marching across three hundred miles of uncleared land through forests and swamps, the army reached the Neuse River on January 29, 1712. From here Barnwell set out in haste, hoping to surprise the Indians at Narhantes, their chief town, but he found that the natives actually lived on many scattered farms with no more than four houses grouped together. He also found that a chain of nine forts had recently been erected for defense. Barnwell elected to attack the strongest fort, which he took with some difficulty. Thirty prisoners were captured and fifty-two scalps taken. Indians under Barnwell's command took many slaves and much plunder. The Tuscarora were so frightened by the attack that they fled, abandoning their forts. They continued to retreat during the next few days as Barnwell passed through half a dozen of their towns and destroyed nearly 375 houses and two thousand bushels of corn. All along this trail of devastation he found much property that had been taken from the white settlers. Barnwell's force was then considerably weakened by the desertion of a large number of the South Carolina Indians who ran off as soon as they had loaded their backs with booty. The one company that did remain was assured by Barnwell that no more offensive movements would be made until they were joined by troops from North Carolina. Marching to Bath, the reduced army passed through an area in which they reported various signs of Indian atrocities. On February 10 they finally reached Bath where they were welcomed with such signs of joy and relief that it brought tears to the eyes of Barnwell's men. The march had been successfully made in the face of great hardships, but it had accomplished much for North Carolina.

At the end of February, reinforced by some North Carolina troops, Barnwell again marched against the Tuscarora. His first target was to be Hancock's town, but upon reaching his destination, he found that the Indians had constructed a strong fort in an excellent position. Moving forward, "within 10 or 12 yards of the fort they were met with a withering fire from the Indians" which so frightened the raw North Carolina troops that they panicked and fled. Barnwell severely berated them as a "country base, cowardly crew," but they refused to return. The attack had to be temporarily abandoned. During the night those Carolinians who had remained steadfast to Barnwell dug trenches and threw up breastworks near the fort overlooking the Indians' canoes and source of water. With the rising sun the Indians saw what had taken place in the night and they attempted to flee. However, the fire of Barnwell's men managed to keep them contained within the fort. Under cover of guns from the fort, the Indians sent some of their white prisoners for water while at the same time they began to torture others who were still inside the compound. North Carolinians with Barnwell had relatives inside the fort and they begged Barnwell to come to terms with the Tuscarora. All things considered—the shortage of ammunition and supplies, the unreliability of the North Carolinians under fire, the many wounded, and the fact that the Indians might be able to hold out for a long time—Barnwell agreed to withdraw if the dozen captives inside the fort were released and canoes provided to return them to New Bern. Before the end of the month twenty-two more captive settlers were to be released along with twenty-four Negroes who were also being held. A time was set for a meeting to discuss terms for a general peace. The army then marched to New Bern, arriving on March 12, where a number of the white men became ill and several Indians died. For this reason they were unable to march again until the end of the month. Barnwell was himself so sick that he could not keep the appointment with the Indians to discuss peace, but rather than sacrifice the opportunity he sent in his stead Colonel Francis Michel, who had come to New Bern with Graffenried. No Indians appeared for the conference.

The assembly was distressed that Hancock's fort had not been taken, and renewed efforts were made to get more supplies for Barnwell. At Graffenried's suggestion some cannon and other heavy pieces, together with shells and shot, were sent to the small army. Barnwell, now recovered from his illness, established a garrison across the river from Bath to keep communications open between the Pamlico and the Neuse, and then he set up a base for his baggage and horses on the south side of the Neuse near the Trent. On a bluff overlooking the Neuse River some twenty miles up from New Bern and about seven miles from Hancock's fort he built the triangular Fort Barnwell. A breastwork protected the weakest side of the fort and he constructed huts and collected provisions for his troops. Early in April, when he had been joined by Colonel Thomas Boyd with 70 North Carolinians and some friendly Chowanoc Indians, Barnwell moved against Hancock's fort with 153 white men and 128 Indians. The siege continued for ten days in an engagement that Barnwell said "for variety of action, salleys, attempts to be relieved from without, can't I believe be parallelled against Indians." Attempts to take the fort were unsuccessful, however, and all efforts to burn it failed. On April 17, pleading shortage of supplies, Barnwell ignored a directive from the assembly of North Carolina and signed a treaty of peace with the Indians. Apparently the Tuscarora chose to surrender rather than risk defeat and certain death at the hands of their enemies.

The terms of the treaty required the Indians to deliver immediately to Fort Barnwell all white and Negro captives who were being held in the fort, while all other captives were to be returned within ten days. King Hancock and three "notorious murderers" were also to be turned over to Barnwell. They were to give up all of the horses, skins, and plunder by turning over immediately whatever they had in the fort and by delivering the rest, which they had elsewhere, to Fort Barnwell within ten days. To ensure compliance with the terms of the treaty three hostages (two brothers of Hancock and a brother of the chief of the Corees) were to be left with Barnwell. All of the corn in the fort, which turned out to be very little, was to be taken by Barnwell's South Carolina Indians for use on their way home. In the future if the Indians had any complaints about the action of whites, they were to register them with magistrates of the government of North Carolina. The Tuscarora were to confine themselves to the land along the Neuse River and Contentnea Creek and to stay off of the land between the Neuse and Cape Fear rivers; that region was to be reserved entirely for hunting and fishing by South Carolina Indians. Any other Indians found there were to be treated as enemies. To symbolize the victory of the whites, the Indians were ordered to demolish their fort, and they were forbidden from ever building any more forts in the colony. As a sign of their subservience to the English, the Tuscarora were required "To come yearly to the Governor in March and pay Tribute." Twenty days after Barnwell negotiated this peace, the Indians were to call upon the governor to sign these and any other articles that were agreed upon. In return for agreement to comply with the terms of the treaty, the Indians in the fort were permitted to depart unharmed, a provision Barnwell strictly enforced.

Hancock, it was discovered, had fled to Virginia and most of the goods that had been taken from the colonists had already been sold to Virginia traders, in some cases for ammunition despite Governor Spotswood's directive to the contrary. Hancock was later taken by the forces of Tom Blount, leader of the Tuscarora in the northern part of the colony who remained neutral or friendly to the whites. Once Hancock was in the hands of the whites he was promptly executed.

Barnwell, convinced that he had accomplished his objectives in North Carolina, abandoned Fort Barnwell and returned with his remaining troops to New Bern. Marching back to South Carolina at the very end of June, he was seriously wounded in the legs, apparently by someone under his command. Since Barnwell was unable to mount a horse, he sent to Charles Town for a sloop to transport himself and his wounded back home. It has been said that Barnwell, unhappy over North Carolina's apparent indifference to him and his forces and angry over the failure of officials to promptly deliver resolutions of thanks from the assembly, seized some Indians to be sold as slaves. This was a false charge spread abroad by friends of former governor Cary and perhaps also by Governor Hyde, who may have been feeling a bit jealous over the handling of the Tuscarora affair. After all, it was Barnwell from South Carolina who put down the Indian uprising that Governor Hyde, as commander-in-chief, should have quelled. An objective examination of the records shows that the Indians who were to be sold into slavery actually were seized after Barnwell had boarded the sloop in the lower Cape Fear area.

The Tuscarora were offended by the seizure of these Indians and they insisted that the whites had violated the terms of the truce. So with justification they resumed their attacks in the summer and fall of 1712. North Carolina was again in a desperate plight, a situation worsened by another yellow fever epidemic that took many lives, including that of Governor Hyde. The acting governor, Thomas Pollock, immediately called on South Carolina for aid and received a favorable response, in spite of North Carolina's ingratitude to Barnwell. In November 1712, Colonel James Moore with 33 whites and about 1,000 "friendly Indians" marched to the Neuse and, cooperating with Pollock's forces, won a "glorious victory" at Fort Nohoroco on Contentnea Creek on March 25, 1713. Pollock reported his and Moore's losses as 57 killed and 82 wounded; "Enemies Destroyed is as follows—Prisoners 392, Scolps 192, out of ye sd. fort—and att least 200 kill'd and Burnt in ye fort—and 166 kill'd and taken out of ye fort." The total loss to the Indians was 950 men, women, and children killed or captured. Moore, who suffered 22 white men killed and 36 wounded, had dealt a fatal blow to the Tuscarora Indians of North Carolina. An undetermined number of Indian prisoners were sold as slaves, and those of the tribe who were not engaged in this final battle fled westward toward the head of the Roanoke River.

In view of the ruined condition of North Carolina, Pollock gave up any idea he might have had of completely wiping out the warring faction of the Tuscarora and turned instead to the writing of a peace treaty. About the middle of April 1713 a preliminary treaty was signed with Tom Blount, who was recognized as "the King and Commander in Chief [of] all the Indians on the south side of Pamptico River under protection of this government." Blount agreed to return all the captives and all the livestock and other possessions that had been taken from the whites. A formal treaty was signed before the middle of May and it brought to an end the threat of massive Tuscarora slaughter of whites in the future. Pockets of resistance remained, however, and roaming bands swept out of the swamps between the Pamlico and Neuse rivers to attack various farms. Colonel Moore remained in North Carolina to reduce these scattered bands, and when he departed he left some of his most faithful Indians to complete the task. It was not until February 11, 1715, that a secure peace returned. On that day the bellicose Indians signed a treaty by which they agreed to live peacefully on a reservation near Lake Mattamuskeet.

Many of the Tuscarora abandoned North Carolina for New York where they joined relatives among the Five Nations. From time to time small parties returned to visit North Carolina where they managed to alarm the whites. Their main purpose, however, was not to do battle; they came instead to convince first one community and then another of the Tuscarora to join them in New York. Although the Tuscarora of North Carolina had by that time been accepted as friendly neighbors, their reservation lands in Bertie County were continually being taken over. As a result, they finally left in 1803.

North Carolina had hardly concluded the February 1715 treaty when trouble struck South Carolina. On Good Friday, April 15, 1715, the Yamassee Indians, many of whom had accompanied Barnwell and Moore into North Carolina, killed a number of white traders. Creeks and other tribes did likewise, spurred on by unfair trading practices and general abuse of the

Indians. Trouble soon spread and North Carolina had to send two companies to aid her recent benefactors. The outcome of the Yamassee War was the removal of any threat of Indian trouble in the region along the Cape Fear River in the far southern corner of North Carolina. In addition, Colonel Moore succeeded in preventing the Cherokee and Creek Indians from uniting against South Carolina, a move which very likely would have proved fatal for the whites there.

Although the greater portion of manpower used to crush the Tuscarora was contributed by Indians from South Carolina, North Carolina's involvement in both the Tuscarora and Yamassee wars put considerable strain on her limited financial resources. According to Pollock, the public debt was greater "than we will be able to pay this ten or twelve years." Altogether £36,000 in revenues from taxes and other sources were not adequate to retire these bills. In 1729, £10,000 was still outstanding, and the paper currency had depreciated so rapidly that it was soon passing for as little as five to one. Continued depreciation caused the lords proprietors to refuse the acceptance of bills of credit in payment of fees and quitrents. But there was also a bright side to the picture. The removal of the Indian menace and the consequent opening up of vast tracts of land that would soon be occupied by white settlers, the separation from South Carolina (begun in 1689 and formalized in 1712), and the virtual elimination of personal factions made Pollock's leadership effective. And with the strengthening of governmental authority, the way was prepared for an era of growth and progress. By the time Pollock was succeeded by Governor Charles Eden in May 1714, the colony was about to enter a period of "peace and quietness."

4

EXPANSION AND CONSOLIDATION

The legislature of 1715 did much to usher in an era of progress
when it revised and codified "the ancient standing laws of this
government" and passed some sixty new laws that were designed
explicitly to promote the peace and welfare of the province.
Some of these were aimed at stimulating legitimate trade and
others were directed at checking smuggling and piracy, which
were so prevalent that the colony had acquired an unsavory
reputation. As early as 1683 the English lords of trade complained of the "harboring and encouraging of Pirates in Carolina
. . . to the great damage that does arise in his Majesty's service."
It was charged that Governor Seth Sothel had issued commissions "to Pyrates for rewards," and that Governor John Archdale
had "sheltered them." Spurred to action by a 1684 order from
the Privy Council, the lords proprietors issued instructions in
1685 "for restraining and punishing" those who committed
"Treasons, Felonyes, Pyracyes, Robberyes, Murders or Confeder-
acyes" at sea or in any "Haven, Creek, or Bay" over which they
had jurisdiction. Residents of Carolina were forbidden to "know-
ingly entertaine, conceale, trade or hold any correspondence by
Letter or otherwise with any . . . Pyrates." Those who did so
were liable to arrest and prosecution as "Accessory and Confederates." This action had little or no effect, and in February 1697
the English Board of Trade warned the lords proprietors that the
"entertainment given to Pyrates in Carolina had occasioned
many ill minded persons, seamen and others to desert their

habitations, and apply themselves to such wicked and destructive courses to the great weakening and dispeopling of the Colonies so abandoned by them, and to the great dishonour of the English nation."

It is not difficult to understand why there were so many pirates operating along the coasts of the English colonies. British navigation acts and other trade laws were extremely unpopular in the colonies, and it was considered smart, proper, and certainly profitable to evade them. Piracy was not thought to be a very serious evil; in fact, many of the pirates were regarded as respectable members of the community, and sometimes they were protected and sheltered by the people. Smuggling and piracy were not discouraged by the settlers because desirable goods could be purchased at a better price from pirates than from established merchants. Pirates also helped to keep out French and Spanish vessels, thus enabling England to expand her own trade with the colonies. The fact that England was at war with France and Spain from 1689 to 1697 (King William's War) and again from 1701 to 1713 (Queen Anne's War) tended to encourage smuggling and privateering. The borderline between piracy and privateering is a slender one, and the history of colonial piracy reveals that many men began their thieving careers in a legal manner as privateers, but then, when the war ended, these men continued to prey upon the commerce of the enemy, as well as on that of England and the colonies, as pirates. Of course, there were other reasons for the prevalence of these "sea robbers" during the Golden Age of Piracy (1689–1740): the yearning for adventure; the possibility—seldom realized—of getting rich quick; unemployment and the desire for profitable occupation, even an illegal one; and the weakness, inefficiency, and even collusion of port and other officials.

Still other factors made the North Carolina area particularly appealing to pirates and thus account for the concentration of these men along the coast. The Outer Banks, the shallow inlets, the sand bars, and the islands near the mouths of some of the rivers made excellent hiding places for their ships. The pirates could conceal themselves easily and then dart out suddenly into the Atlantic to catch heedless merchant vessels. They could also, of course, hide quickly in the same places if pursued. Pirate ships often were smaller and faster than the ships they attacked and thus they could enter an inlet and take cover in a sound where ocean-going vessels could not follow. Another very important factor contributing to the thriving piracy business was the isolation of North Carolina from her neighbors. This made rapid communication difficult, and pirate activity could be begun and completed before any form of defense could be summoned. Also, the weak and unstable government of the colony assured that no sustained policy of law enforcement was likely to be established. Numerous officials were active in the government for their own personal benefit, and pirates often found friends in high places who would protect them in return for a share of the profits. Piracy flourished and there seemed to be very little that could be done about it. Between 1717 and 1721 it was reported that nearly forty vessels were seized by pirates off the Carolina coast.

Several of the most notorious pirates operated for a time from New Providence in the Bahamas, Port Royal in Jamaica, and other islands in the West Indies. In 1717 Captain Woodes Rogers was appointed governor of the Bahamas, and he was given strict instructions to clean out the nest of pirates. At the same time, King George I reissued an old proclamation offering a pardon to all pirates who would take an oath of loyalty and become law-abiding citizens. Some took advantage of this opportunity to resume their places in the community and avoid prosecution, but others, who found the excitement of their former life too much to give up, ignored the offer and persisted in their old ways. Driven out of their old havens on the islands, many pirates found the coast of North Carolina to be just as secure and convenient and soon took to the sea from their new bases.

The most notorious of the colony's pirates were Edward Teach (alias Thatch), better known as "Blackbeard," and Major Stede Bonnet, called "the gentleman pirate." Blackbeard, "a swaggering, merciless brute," was a native of Bristol, England, a seaport town from which many American adventurers set out. Teach's earliest experience at sea was gained as a seaman on a merchant vessel, but during Queen Anne's War he saw service for a time on a privateer sailing out of Kingston, Jamaica. After the war he followed the practice common to many seamen of signing on a pirate ship, and he sailed out of New Providence Island in the Bahamas. When the British authorities drove the pirates from that island in 1718, the "whole remnant of the scoundrels" transferred their operations to the Carolina coast. Blackbeard located at Bath, where he boasted, probably with truth, that he could be invited to any home in North Carolina. From his new base of operations, Blackbeard seized many ships along the coast, including English and colonial vessels. When the king offered pardon to all pirates, Teach promptly grabbed at the opportunity. Within a few weeks, however, he was back at his old trade. It was at this time that the British expedition headed by Woodes Rogers set out to round up the pirates and put an end to their activities. It failed, however, to capture either Blackbeard or Bonnet.

Stede Bonnet, a man of wealth and education, had retired from the British army as a major and settled on the West Indian island of Barbados, where he had a fine home and a good reputation. For some reason he joined Blackbeard's gang; later he went into piracy on his own and maintained headquarters along the Lower Cape Fear. His ravages against South Carolina shipping were so destructive that Governor Robert Johnson fitted out an expedition, headed by Colonel William Rhett, to put an end to the pirate's activities. After a furious five-hour battle in the mouth of the Cape Fear River, Bonnet was captured. He was taken to Charles Town where, along with twenty-nine other pirates, he was tried, convicted, and hanged on December 10, 1718. During November and December of that year, no fewer than forty-nine other Carolina pirates were hanged. A few weeks after Bonnet's capture, Governor Alexander Spotswood of Virginia, hearing that Blackbeard was off the North Carolina coast with a prize, sent out two sloops under the command of

Edward Teach, the pirate, better known as "Blackbeard."

Lieutenant Robert Maynard of the Royal Navy, in quest of the notorious pirate and his famous ship *Adventure*. Encountering Blackbeard off Ocracoke Inlet on November 22, Maynard and his men, in fierce hand-to-hand combat, killed the pirate and half of his crew of eighteen; the other nine seamen were taken to Virginia where they were tried, convicted, and hanged. There were a few sporadic outbreaks of piracy after this, but the heyday of the pirate had come to a close.

With the ending of piracy and the elimination of hostile Indians, the settlers began once again to show an interest in expanding their farming, hunting, and trading into regions farther and farther from the older centers. It should be noted that some moves toward expansion had in fact been attempted during the troublesome period of the first two decades of the eighteenth century. For example, by 1710 South Carolina, in the hope of ensuring the safety of her citizens, claimed the right to control Indian affairs as far north as the Cape Fear River. In the face of proprietary instructions to the contrary, that government also took upon itself the privilege of granting land along the river. Thomas James received grants on August 17, 1714 for three tracts totaling more than twelve hundred acres on the west side of Cape Fear River. John Hughes and Enoch Morgan already held land adjacent to James. In September 1714 more than thirty-one hundred acres nearby were granted to Price Hughes, a native of Wales and a man of some wealth and ability. He was interested in the establishment of a Welsh colony in the area. Unfortunately, the plan for the proposed settlement was abandoned when Hughes was killed the following year by Indians while he was exploring around the mouth of the Alabama River on the Gulf of Mexico. Unlike these four men, most of the colonists in both Carolinas were deterred from adventuring onto the land along Cape Fear River during this period because of the presence of hostile Indians and the fact that many pirates frequently used the river for careening their ships and as a place of refuge. Once these threats were removed, many settlers recognized the inviting possibilities of the land along the river.

The lords proprietors were reluctant to authorize the granting of land in this region, but people began to move in anyway. George Burrington became governor of North Carolina in January 1724 and one of his greatest concerns was the Cape Fear country. He spent the winter of 1724–1725 there and was convinced of the importance of reliable settlers in this area for the advancement of North Carolina. In spite of the fact that the proprietors had not authorized grants of land to be made here, and in the face of South Carolina's claims that the Cape Fear River marked the boundary between the two colonies, Governor Burrington began to issue grants in the spring of 1725. Maurice Moore, Roger Moore, Eleazer Allen, and John Porter received the first grants for a total of almost nine thousand acres of land. These men had close ties by blood and marriage. Before long quite a few substantial planters were also moving in from South Carolina, where unsettled conditions and the threat of Spanish invasion from the south encouraged many people to leave. By 1727 the rumor was being spread that a new province, which would be independent of both Carolinas, was to be created at Cape Fear. The wealth of the Moores, the political maneuvers of Burrington (who was removed as governor by the proprietors in July 1725, but who remained in North Carolina until the proprietors sold their rights to the Crown), geography, and other factors made this a real possibility. The town of Brunswick was established on the west bank of the Cape Fear in 1725, and the stage apparently was set for the creation of a third colony in Carolina. The last governor that the proprietors were to appoint was Sir Richard Everard, and while in office he issued numerous grants for land in the Cape Fear area. Many prominent families, including some that had been very active in the settlement of Albemarle, removed to Cape Fear. Edward Moseley and John and Samuel Swann were among them. Members of the Harnett, Vail, Ashe, Smith, and Jones families, many of whom were destined to play important roles in the development of the region, were also among the early arrivals.

In 1729 the proprietors yielded to the demands of the Crown

that they sell their rights in Carolina.* The colony had not been properly managed by the proprietors for many years, and local affairs had reached such a state of confusion that drastic action became necessary. In the interests of good government, intercolonial harmony, and imperial affairs, the Board of Trade recommended that all corporate and proprietary colonies be acquired by the Crown. After several years of negotiations, the proprietors finally consented to sell.

Burrington hastened to England to convince Crown officials to appoint him governor, but it was not until 1731 that he took over his former office and became the first royal governor of North Carolina. His outstanding contribution to North Carolina was a road extending across the eastern part of the colony from Virginia to Cape Fear. With some Indian guides and some white men to mark the road, he spent seven weeks laying out the route. It is unlikely that more was done than the clearing of some trees, but even this opened up the Cape Fear to easier settlement and more frequent communication than had previously been possible. Burrington's record of achievement was seriously flawed, however, by his uncontrollable temper and the wrath he displayed in governing the people. This caused a great deal of trouble for the colony because it gave rise to various irreconcilable factions among the settlers. Burrington submitted so many ill-natured reports to the Crown that he clearly revealed his weaknesses for the position. He was relieved in 1734 and was succeeded by Gabriel Johnston.

The physical expansion of North Carolina during the eighteenth century was paralleled by its growth in population. At the close of the proprietary period, the colony was more sparsely

---

* Seven of the eight shares were sold; the Carteret heir, soon to become Earl Granville, retained his rights. Some years later a line surveyed through the middle of North Carolina marked the southern limit of the Granville district, which comprised one-eighth of the total territory in Carolina in 1663. By this time the district consisted of the most thickly settled and the wealthiest part of the colony, and Granville's control of land rights there caused considerable trouble until his rights reverted to the state of North Carolina in 1776.

settled than any of England's other mainland settlements, with about 36,000 inhabitants, one-sixth of them black. During the next four decades, however, the population increased almost ninefold: 45,000 in 1749, 120,000 in 1765, and some 300,000 on the eve of the Revolution. By then, North Carolina was the fourth most populous colony, exceeded only by Virginia, Pennsylvania, and Massachusetts. Most of this extraordinary growth in numbers was the result of a steady influx of immigrants from other colonies and from Europe, filling the Cape Fear Valley and spilling over into the backcountry.

Around 1730 some people of Welsh origin began to take up land along the west bank of the Northeast Cape Fear River. They settled farther inland than their predecessors from South Carolina a dozen or more years earlier. The new arrivals came from Delaware and Pennsylvania, and perhaps also a few moved in from South Carolina. No single large tract was acquired; instead, individuals came on their own initiative and took out land for themselves. There was a sufficient concentration of settlers, however, so that the region they occupied by 1733 between the Northeast Cape Fear and the Cape Fear rivers came to be called the Welsh Tract, a term that was still in use as late as 1775. Hugh Meredith, a printer who had worked with Benjamin Franklin, visited the Welsh Tract in the fall of 1730, and reported quite accurately on the geography of the country, the economic conditions that he found, and the prospects that he foresaw for the region. Meredith's report to Franklin, which was published in two installments in the *Pennsylvania Gazette,* may very well have been a deciding factor in helping others make up their minds about moving to Cape Fear. Franklin commented that the settlement had "for these 3 or 4 Years past, been the Subject of much Discourse, especially among Country People." He printed the observations sent to him by Meredith because he said "great Numbers" of people from Pennsylvania and neighboring provinces had already been down to look over the site, but none had written about it. Around 1740 Malatish Hamilton laid out a town on what is now Washington Creek to serve as a center of trade for the Welsh Tract. By 1756, when the Presbyterian missionary Hugh McAden visited the area, many families of other than Welsh origin could be found living there. McAden claimed that there were enough people "to form a congregation sufficiently large to invite the services of a minister."

Migration from Scotland to America began in the 1730s and soon centered in the Cape Fear section of North Carolina. For a long time severe economic depression had plagued the Highlands, where changes in the agricultural system resulted in increased rent and even eviction for countless numbers who lived off the land. Another factor that brought considerable pressure to bear on the Highlands was the growth of the population. This resulted in large measure from the reduction of deaths, which was made possible by the use of smallpox inoculation and by the curbing of starvation through the introduction of potatoes and kale. Changes in the clan system and its resulting paternalism combined with the other problems to force people to seek a new life elsewhere.

James Innes of Caithness, in the far north of Scotland, received a grant in January 1732 for 320 acres located about eighty miles up the Cape Fear River in what was soon to become Bladen County. A little over a year later he received an additional 640 acres. In April and May 1733 Hugh Campbell and William Forbes secured grants of 640 acres each. These three men were the vanguard of hundreds of Highland Scots who were to fill up the Cape Fear Valley during the next forty years. Innes soon secured two more grants of the same size as his first, and Campbell received one more. Crown regulations authorized 50 acres for each person taken into the colony, so the amount of land these men held suggests that they were responsible for the transportation of seventy people.

The arrival of Governor Johnston in 1734 marked the beginning of the development of large communities of Highlanders in southeastern North Carolina. Between 1734 and 1737 numerous land grants were issued; the smallest was for 299 acres while the largest was for 640 acres. Some of the people settled as

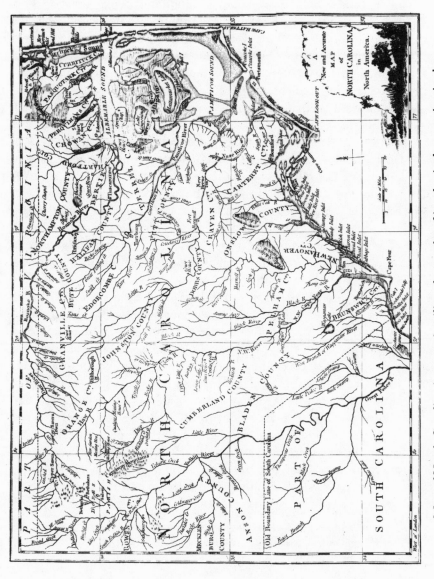

Map of North Carolina in 1779, detailing the results of its physical expansion in the eighteenth century.

far as a hundred miles above Wilmington, a new town established about 1733 as a rival to Brunswick. Others were as close as
sixty miles. Governor Johnston encouraged the immigration, and
in 1740 a single group of 350 Highland Scots arrived. The
governor supported a legislative proposal that such people be
exempt from public taxes for ten years as a means of encouraging
still more settlers to come. New Hanover County had been
formed in 1729 before any Highland Scots are known to have
arrived; but as these people filled up the backcountry, Bladen
County was created in 1734, followed by Anson in 1750 and
Cumberland* in 1754. About 1760 a town was established up the
Cape Fear at the head of navigation as a center of trade for the
Scots. It was named for a natural feature that attracted much
attention: Cross Creek where the water of two streams appeared
to mingle and cross. In 1762 the town of Campbellton was
established quite nearby, and in 1778 the two were combined. In
1783 the name was changed to Fayetteville. Letters written from
North Carolina to friends and relatives in the Highlands spurred
an almost continuous flow of newcomers until the movement was
stopped by the Revolutionary War.

In the Highlands most of the Scots had been extremely poor,
living in sod or stone houses without windows and with dirt
floors. A hole in the roof let out smoke from a fire in the middle of
the room—often the only room. Livestock sometimes shared this
meager shelter. Once they reached North Carolina, however, the
living conditions of the Scots improved rapidly. A plentiful
supply of wood made it easy for them to build rather substantial
houses and to have more furniture than they could ever have
dreamed of enjoying in Scotland. Each house had a chimney,
and windows were not uncommon. Customary dirt floors were
acceptable at first, but the comfort of wooden floors was soon
discovered. Vast tracts of longleaf pine invited the production of

---

* It is ironic that the name Cumberland should have been selected, as it
honored William Augustus, Duke of Cumberland, who unmercifully slaughtered Highlanders after they had already been defeated at the Battle of
Culloden in 1746.

naval stores for which Parliament offered a bounty. Forest resources also led the people of the Cape Fear region to produce lumber, barrels, and other wood products. Corn and other grains including some rice were also produced, and together with livestock these added further to the income of the people.

Most of these people continued to speak their native Gaelic for a long time. Their ministers—most of the Scots were Presbyterian—preached in Gaelic, and a printing press established in Fayetteville before the end of the eighteenth century produced tracts and pamphlets in their native tongue. A tourist in 1828 commented that so many of the people in Fayetteville and "for four and twenty miles round" understood only Gaelic, "that they are obliged to have a clerk in the Post Office who can speak Gaelic." An innkeeper who spoke English also spoke Gaelic "tolerable and understands it perfectly, having been in the habit of hearing it all his life."

Kilts and other forms of typical Scottish dress were denied the Highlanders at home as a part of the punishment meted out to them by the victorious English after the Battle of Culloden. In North Carolina, however, Scottish plaid may have been seen for a time along the Cape Fear. James Murray, a merchant in Newton (as Wilmington was first known), wrote to James Rutherford on September 4, 1739, ordering some merchandise for his store. Among other things, he asked for "Scots plad about 18^d or 20^d p^r Ell, brown Linnen from 3^d to 18^d p^r Ell, Coarse and Midling Diaper, these fit for ye Summer and Winter. Galacheils Gray [a cotton fabric for dresses] at 6^d or 7^d Ell to be here in Sepr or October for Winter only. What you buy by ye Scotts Ell, let it be measured by an exact 3 foot allowing a thumb, and y^t Measure put on ye Piece."

Soon after the first Highland Scots arrived in the early 1730s plans were being made in Ireland for the departure of another group of colonists. Arthur Dobbs of Ireland and Henry McCulloh, a London merchant, sought a grant of land near the head of the Northeast Cape Fear River on which they intended to settle 120 people ("poor Protestant families") from Ireland. They were expected to carry on the potash trade, raise hemp, and produce naval stores. McCulloh also had plans for sending some workmen ahead to build houses for the colonists. The request was granted, and by 1736 the people were settled on Black River in what is now Duplin County.

Several efforts were made to procure Swiss colonists for North Carolina, but they met with little success. In 1736 Samuel Jenner, who described himself as "Agent for the Switzers who propose to settle in North Carolina," asked for a grant of six thousand acres of land lying west of the Roanoke River. Governor Burrington, who was in London at this time, urged the Board of Trade to take favorable action on this request. He pointed out that Swiss settlers could teach others in the colony to grow hemp and flax, to make silk and potash, and to plant vineyards and produce good wine. While the Board of Trade was hearing Jenner's request, it was also considering Henry McCulloh's petition for grants in the Cape Fear River Valley of seventy-two thousand acres in one tract and sixty thousand in another. Hearings in both cases dragged on until finally McCulloh's request for the two tracts of land was approved. Jenner's name, however, simply drops from the record.

McCulloh succeeded in enticing forty-two Swiss who had earlier settled in South Carolina to move to his land in North Carolina. James Murray, the Newton merchant, wrote to McCulloh on November 6, 1736: "Last week I was up to the North East [Cape Fear River] to the lower part of your land setting the Carpenter to work to finish two houses there (I mean at Camp Innes) for the reception of the Swiss Messrs Hutchinson and Grimke have sent in. They [the Swiss] were here about 3 days, during which time his Excell^y our good Govr took a great deal of pains to provide for them and to assure them they should have every thing to their satisfaction till they were settled. With which they went up last Tuesday very well pleased." McCulloh had also become involved in a plan, which was sponsored by Murray Crymble and James Huey, to bring six thousand settlers from Switzerland to North Carolina. In anticipation of these newcomers, Murray wrote McCulloh again in January 1737 and assured him that the Swiss families now inhabiting the settlement were doing well. He remarked, however, that the people were concerned that their land had not been surveyed, but he was quick to add that the surveyor had just returned from a trip and would "settle their bounds next week."

Silence followed; at least no records survive to tell the story. In March 1744 the governor and council of North Carolina complained to the Crown that McCulloh's land in the midst of a growing area was unoccupied. He did import some Swiss colonists from South Carolina, they said, "but 'tis true, he used them so ill and had so little Regard to his contract with them, that they have left the land." The Swiss may have returned to South Carolina, although they were unhappy with the swampy site assigned them there. Possibly they found more friendly sponsors in North Carolina.

The Cape Fear River, North Carolina's best outlet to the commerce of the world, was well settled before the middle of the eighteenth century and the stage was set for the important role it would play in the development of the entire colony. With the settlement of this area where the dividing line between North Carolina and South Carolina remained unsurveyed, numerous controversies arose involving, for example, the enforcement of criminal laws, the execution of judicial directives, the collection of taxes, service in the militia, and the handling of Indian affairs. Private interests were also involved, and conflicting claims to land along the border often led to disorders, riots, and bloodshed. Several times during the years after 1729 commissioners met to discuss the question of the common boundary of the two colonies. They reached an agreement that the line should begin at the Atlantic Ocean thirty miles southwest of the mouth of Cape Fear River and run not closer than thirty miles to the river until it reached the 35th parallel. From there it was to run straight west to the South Seas. If this westward line approached land occupied by the Cherokee or the Catawba Indians, it was to be run to the north of them, afterward returning to the 35th parallel. Commissioners from the two provinces agreed to this arrangement, but many years were to pass before the line was to be completely surveyed. In 1735 only about a hundred miles of the boundary, the straight northwest line parallel to the Cape Fear River, was delineated. The surveyors actually made an error in locating the exact position of the 35th parallel, and they stopped too soon. From this wrong point, however, the line was carried on to the Catawba villages in 1764. Eight years later the survey was resumed, running west to the mountains where a Cherokee boundary line had been marked in 1767. None of these lines followed the prescribed 35th parallel; the first portion was south of it and the second portion, west of the Catawba villages, was north of it.

The Cape Fear region was not the only site in North Carolina that saw new settlers moving in during the 1730s. At this same time two streams of population, flowing mostly from Pennsylvania and to a lesser degree from New Jersey, Maryland, and Virginia, were pouring into Piedmont North Carolina. The earliest, largest, and most widespread of these two population elements was the Scotch-Irish; the other was composed of immigrants of German descent, commonly, though erroneously called Pennsylvania Dutch. The term Scotch-Irish is geographical and not racial; it does not mean a mixture of the two national stocks. It refers to Scots, chiefly Lowlanders, who differed in many significant particulars, including language, from the Highland Scots. The story of how James I of England planted the nine escheated counties of North Ireland with Lowland Scots is well known. Leaders of six clans in the north of Ireland were defeated by English forces and fled the country; in 1607 their lands in the nine northern counties were declared escheated to the Crown. An elaborate plan of colonization was developed, and Scottish Presbyterians were encouraged to move to Ulster Plantation, where some had already settled several years earlier. From them it was hoped that civilization might spread throughout Ireland. They would teach industry and thrift to the "wild Irish" and bring the land into cultivation. A few Highland Scots, some English, particularly poor Londoners, and a few Irish "natives of good merit" joined the Scots in forming Ulster Plantation. Here in the north of Ireland the people found more freedom than they had ever known before. They were near enough to Scotland so that Presbyterian ministers were available to them, and their church flourished with its democratic government. In the decade after 1709 more than thirty thousand Lowlanders settled in Ulster where they drained swamps, cleared forests, and began the manufacture of linen and woolen cloth, not only for their own use but also for exportation to England.

In Ulster the Scotsman had a variety of experiences and developed several characteristics that were to serve him well when he came to America. In Ireland he lived in the midst of an unfriendly native population, and sometimes force had to be used to protect his property. When similar conditions faced the Scotch-Irishman on the American frontier he knew how to meet them. The new freedom that he experienced in Ireland, wherein a man could move about from place to place and select an occupation to his own liking, prepared him to face something similar but on an even larger scale in America. In Ulster the Scotsman lived among English, Irish, and French neighbors. Consequently, getting along with people of different nationalities in America presented no problem to him. In Ireland he was exposed to more advanced methods of farming, which had been introduced from England, than he had known on the tradition-bound Scottish farm, and the skills he developed certainly served him well in America. It was the practice of his Presbyterian church to teach boys to read and write so that they might read the Bible and study their catechism. In one group of more than three hundred Ulstermen in America, it was discovered that 96 percent of them could sign their own name, an unbelievably high literacy rate for immigrants. Their women had no rights, owned no property and were generally uneducated. It was their duty to manage the house and children and to help in the field when needed. These were necessary tasks that they had no difficulty performing in America. Most important among his qualities and characteristics was the Scotch-Irishman's adaptability. This made it possible for him to fill the American frontier up and down the Atlantic seaboard and to push the frontier farther and farther west.

By 1700 all that the Crown had expected of the Scots in Ulster had been accomplished, and their competition with English industry was beginning to be felt. Repressive measures such as the Woolen Act were passed, and these together with economic depression set the stage for the mass movement of the Scotch-Irish to America. The demand of English landlords for higher rents, increased tithes, rough and excessively cold winters, failure of the potato crop, disease among their sheep, and other catastrophes triggered the emigration. The first of many mass movements started in 1717 and lasted a year. In spite of officials in Ireland who tried to slow the exodus, other very large groups followed in 1725–1729, 1740–1741, 1754–1755, and 1771–1775. Some of these people found places for themselves in New England, but Pennsylvania and Maryland were most hospitable.

Only an insignificant handful from the first two waves reached North Carolina. Some of the Scotch-Irish could not pay their own way to the New World, so they bound themselves out to serve a master in return for their passage. At the end of their period of service they were free to move out and make a place for themselves, and it was some of these who led the way into North Carolina. The fourth wave found good encouragement to come to North Carolina from Arthur Dobbs, a native of Ulster who had become governor of North Carolina in 1754. A few ships sailed directly to the Cape Fear and a few more went to Charles Town, but the great majority disembarked their passengers at Philadelphia. Those who could find suitable land in Pennsylvania or Maryland did so. Frequently the sons in a family would remain with their parents until they came of age, and then they would move down into the Shenandoah Valley of Virginia where they could afford to buy land. From there the natural course led others farther south until the valley opened into the Piedmont, North Carolina. Those who chose to move directly from Pennsylvania or Maryland into North Carolina followed the Great Wagon Road, from Philadelphia over to Lancaster and to York, southwest to the site of Winchester, Virginia, down the valley across the Fluvanna River, to the Staunton River and along it through the Blue Ridge, south across the Dan River below the mouth of the Mayo River and south to near the Moravian settlement at Wachovia, on to the Yadkin River, and finally to Salisbury. Later it was extended into Mecklenburg County.

The Scotch-Irish came into North Carolina in great numbers only after Pennsylvania, Maryland, and Virginia no longer offered suitable land at a price they could afford to pay. Their arrival coincided with the awakened interest in the backcountry on the part of the officials and wealthy men, and in many cases it was these individuals who paid the passage of the Scotch-Irish. Between 1735 and 1750 such large numbers reached North Carolina that several new counties were created. Many of these inhabitants came by way of Wilmington and Charles Town and settled on the frontier along the western edge of the Piedmont. All of the new settlers, of course, were not Scotch-Irish, but undoubtedly they accounted for a majority. The Scotch-Irish in North Carolina became good substantial farmers, seldom planters. About 75 percent of them had farms of between one hundred and five hundred acres; 5 percent had fewer than one hundred acres; and 5 percent held over a thousand acres. That they proved to be good farmers and respectable citizens is suggested by the following journal entry made by an observer in the 1780s:

This part of the country is very thickly inhabited; the land is not very productive, yielding corn and some grain. Along the Haw River you may see some good settlements, especially the Haw Fields, which abound very plenteously with fine corn fields, wheat, rye, oats, and barley. The inhabitants here and about Guilford Court House are chiefly [Scotch-] Irish, being very courteous, humane, and affable to strangers, as likewise are the inhabitants of the counties of Mecklinbourg and Roan, over the River Yatkin, the latter being remarkable for being true friends to their country on this present critical occasion, which no other parts about here can boast of.

At the same time the Scotch-Irish were filling up the vacant lands in Pennsylvania, they were facing competition from newly arrived Germans. An English writer a few years later observed that the Scotch-Irish "not succeeding so well in Pennsylvania as the more frugal and industrious Germans, sell their lands in that province to the latter, and take up new ground in the remote counties in Virginia, Maryland, and North Carolina." Not all of the Germans reaching North Carolina were from the Palatinate, although they were generally spoken of as Palatines. A large portion of them were from northern Germany, and actually a number of Swiss were included within their settlements. Wills and other records from Rowan County show that some of these people came from Holstein, Wuertemberg, Lorraine, and Brunswick; from the cities of Coburg, Hamburg, and Helmstedt; and from various places around the Black Forest.

The earliest recorded Germans to enter North Carolina after Graffenried's colonists (1710) must have arrived in 1747 or 1748. Governor Dobbs wrote in 1755 that some land he held had been settled seven or eight years before by "22 families of Germans or Swiss, who are all an industrious people." He praised his tenants highly, continuing: "they raise horses, cows, and hogs with a few sheep, they raise Indian Corn, wheat, barley, rye and oats, make good butter and tolerable cheese, and they have gone into indigo with good success, which they sell at Charles Town, having a waggon road to it, tho' 200 miles distant . . . they sow flax for their own use and cotton, and what Hemp they have sown is tall and good." Many Germans settled in what is now the area of Alamance, Guilford, and Orange counties. Between 1747 and 1750 the so-called Pennsylvania Dutch began to arrive in the western Piedmont. Within the next few years great numbers arrived to take up land in the territory now in Davidson, Rowan, Cabarrus, Stanly, Iredell, Wilkes, Catawba, Lincoln, and other more western counties. Cabarrus came to have the heaviest concentration of Germans, followed perhaps by Rowan County. In reporting the population growth along the frontier, colonial officials made little or no distinction between English, Scotch-

The Michael Braun House, built in Rowan County about 1765 by a
German settler from Pennsylvania. *Courtesy of the Travel and Promotion
Division, Department of Natural and Economic Resources, State of North Car-
olina.*

Irish, or German residents. Local records, however, indicate that the greatest influx of Germans occurred in the 1760s and afterward. The close of the French and Indian War meant it was safe once again to take up land in isolated spots along the frontier. In 1765 it was reported that a thousand wagons passed through Salisbury. Germans continued to move into North Carolina even into the final years of the eighteenth century. Many of them were the sons and even grandsons of families who had come to Pennsylvania from Germany many years before.

With the arrival of large numbers of Germans in North Carolina the colony for the first time contained citizens who did not speak English or who had no interpreter ready at hand. There were, of course, some bilingual emigrants among the Germans, but pride kept their native language alive for well over a century. The language began to weaken only when business transactions had to be negotiated and when it became necessary to have terms for things not previously familiar to the Germans. By 1790 the first generation of children had reached adulthood and most of them used both English and German. Not surprisingly, isolated rural areas continued to use German exclusively for a much longer period than did the people who lived near Salisbury and other towns. There was never a German newspaper in North Carolina for these people, but a printer in Salisbury and one in Virginia provided almanacs, religious tracts, and other small printed pieces for them. The problem of unfamiliar personal names among the Germans in a community of English and Scottish caused some concern. On occasion a slight change in spelling, frequently to conform with English attempts at pronunciation, gave the Germans new and acceptable names. For example, Johannes Steigerwalt became John Stirewalt, Michael Guthmann became Michael Goodman, Johannes Eckel became John Eagle, and Franz Oberkirsch became Francis Overcash. In instances where a German name could be translated, that method served well enough in providing a suitable English surname. For example, Zimmermann became Carpenter, Schneider became Taylor, Weiss became White, and Stein became Stone. There is an interesting example in which the descendants of a German named Klein changed and translated their family name in a variety of ways: among them were Peter Klein, John Kline, Jacob Cline, John Small, George Little, and William Short.

An entirely separate group of German-speaking people moved into Piedmont North Carolina soon after the middle of the eighteenth century. They were members of the Unitas Fratrum (United Brethren). Known as Moravians, this Protestant body originated in Bohemia (now Czechoslovakia) among a body of Christians who had fled from nearby Moravia. In 1722 members of this church moved to Saxony where they settled on the estate of Count Nicholas Zinzendorf at Herrnhut and attracted numerous followers. The Moravian Church was patterned on the simple ways of the primitive Christians, and the villages that they occupied operated on a communal scheme. Each person contributed according to his ability and shared according to his need. The emphasis, however, was on a way of life rather than on doctrine. Elders of the church watched over every phase of life both spiritual and secular in the community. A "choir system" operated in which the people were divided into groups according to age, sex, and marital status. In 1733 the Moravians established a mission station in the West Indies to work among the slaves. The following year a small party of them moved to the infant colony of Georgia where they had a grant for land. In 1735 August Gottlieb Spangenberg, a bishop in the Moravian Church, led a second group to Georgia, and within five years they had paid the sum they owed for their land as well as the cost of their transportation. Georgia lay on the frontier between the English and Spanish possessions in America, and when war broke out between the two countries, the Moravians were expected to bear arms. This was not only against their religious principles, but it also violated an understanding their leaders had had with the trustees of Georgia. The Moravians abandoned their outpost in Georgia and moved to Pennsylvania in 1740 where they established two towns, Bethlehem and Nazareth.

The Moravians had been good citizens in Georgia and in Pennsylvania, and word of them reached John Carteret, Earl Granville, in England. He was the proprietor who had refused to sell his share of Carolina to the Crown in 1729, and he was now looking for reliable colonists to settle his land in North Carolina. Spangenberg visited North Carolina in 1752 to look over possible sites for a Moravian community. With a party of five men who came with him from Pennsylvania, Spangenberg began his search at Edenton. He talked with Granville's agent, purchased tents and other equipment, and became acquainted with some of the laws and customs of the colony. He set out on September 18 but his men soon fell victim to chills and fevers, and within a month two of them had to return to Pennsylvania. At a cabin near the present location of Hillsborough the Moravians met a hunter named Perkins and Granville's surveyor, William Churton. These two men joined the party as it made its way into the Blue Ridge. Although Spangenberg was impressed with the wild isolation of the mountains, that was not the type of location he was seeking. Turning back toward the east in the midst of harsh winter weather, Spangenberg found the spot that seemed ideal to him. The tract, he said, was "full of springs, rivulets, and creeks, well timbered for the greatest part, good for agriculture and cattle raising."

In early January of 1753 Spangenberg decided that a tract of just under one hundred thousand acres in the hilly Piedmont would serve his people quite well. In August the site was purchased for £500 down and an annual quitrent of slightly less than £150. In the fall, after harvest time in Pennsylvania, fifteen unmarried men set out from Bethlehem for Wachau, as the new place was called. It was named for an ancestral estate of the Zinzendorfs, but it soon came to be called Wachovia, from two German words meaning meadow-stream. Each of the fifteen men was a specialist, including among others a minister, a doctor, a shoemaker, a tailor, a baker, a tanner, a gardener, three farmers, and two carpenters. On November 17 the party reached the site of the present Bethabara. Soon they began to clear the land and

Earl Granville.

prepare the site for the arrival of other Moravians. In the spring they planted corn, potatoes, flax, cotton, tobacco, barley, rye, oats, millet, buckwheat, turnips, pumpkins, and a carefully tended vegetable garden. Fruit trees were purchased from persons who had settled nearby earlier, and some livestock was also acquired. Many neighbors, particularly the Scotch-Irish, came to see what was going on here for the services of the various specialists among the Moravians were much in demand. Before long the settlers opened a store and Bethabara came to be a center of commerce. More and more men and women joined the advance party at Wachovia and the German speaking Moravians soon had a large, thriving settlement of several congregations, including one that was established at the town of Salem in 1766. Yet they remained a close-knit group, making no attempt to influence their neighbors. They emphasized community cooperation and common ownership of property. Not until 1849 did the congregation abandon its supervision of business, and the Moravian Church continued to use the German language officially until 1856. They sent wagons to Campbellton, to Wilmington, and to Charles Town to sell their wooden wares, pottery, clay pipes, farm and dairy produce, and other goods. They brought back whatever the community needed but could not produce, as well as stock for the store. Goods in the Moravian store attracted customers from many miles outside the Wachovia tract.

The Moravians were a very methodical and hard working people who saw to it that tasks were assigned so that everybody in the community would be busy. Soon after the new town of Salem was laid out in 1766 engineers among the group established a system of waterworks by which water was piped into the homes through oak pipes from a source about a mile outside the town. The Moravians were also careful keepers of records. From the time of their arrival daily diaries and annual summaries of events were kept, and now these provide an excellent source for information about their own activities as well as about all of North Carolina. Their contacts in various places, together with

The Moravian town of Salem, founded in 1766. *Reproduced by permission of the Archives of the Moravian Church, Bethlehem, Pennsylvania.*

the fact that many people of importance visited the Moravians, meant that they were well aware of what was going on over a wide area. In contrast with other groups in colonial North Carolina, the Moravians tended to segregate themselves from other settlements, though they had more visitors than any other community in the colony.

The filling up of the Piedmont forced men who were seeking land to venture into the valleys of the Blue Ridge. In seeking the source of mountain streams rushing down to join the Yadkin River or the Catawba River, they were led higher and higher into the foothills and finally into the mountains. Matthew Rowan, acting governor in 1753, reported that he had been "up in the Country that is now Anson, Orange, and Rowan" in 1746 and had found not more than a hundred fighting men. Now, just seven years later, he claimed to have found at least three thousand "and dayley increasing." Most of the people in these "three fruntire Countys," he reported, were "Irish Protestants, and Germans brave Industerous people." Among the earliest residents of the mountains were George and Jacob Shook (or Shuk), who moved from Pennsylvania in 1749 to that part of Rowan County that later became Burke. Not quite so far west but perhaps in a more mountainous region was Christopher Gist who, also in 1749, had a house on the north bank of the Yadkin River. Another new resident was sixteen-year-old Daniel Boone, who accompanied his parents in 1750 to the region that was soon to become Rowan County. In the same year, Andrew Lambert, who was granted six hundred acres in newly founded Anson County, occupied land that the Indians had not yet abandoned. He found traces of roaming Indians on his land and in his corn, and he knew that they had killed and eaten some of his cattle. "He called his dogs which he used for bear hunting, some 8 or 10 in number," an acquaintance wrote a little while later, "and with his rifle in hand, he drove them out like sheep before him and thus rid himself of the nuisance." Not all new residents succeeded, however; in some cases the Indians not only robbed people of their stock, but "even killed some of them." It was also reported that "if they enter a house and the man is not at home they become insolent and the poor woman must do as they command."

When the Moravians crossed the Blue Ridge in 1752, they became the first white men from North Carolina to penetrate so far west. Soon, however, the barriers in North Carolina were being crossed with great frequency. As president of the council and acting governor, Nathaniel Rice wrote the Board of Trade on August 1, 1752: ". . . the Country enjoys great quietness, and is in a flourishing condition, the western parts settling very fast." Rice's enthusiasm was certainly well founded. Within two years nearly all of the vacant land, except in the back settlements near the mountains, had been taken up. Settlers were arriving there "in hundreds of wagons from the northward." People seeking this land either sent an agent in advance to select land for them, or they persuaded some friend already at the site to do so. These newcomers were described as very industrious people who settled down quickly to begin producing hemp, flax, and corn, and to breed horses and other stock. Some of those who took up vacant land actually were not aware of its precise location. Edmund Pendleton in Virginia, for example, reported that he and John Taylor obtained a patent in 1756 for three thousand acres on Reedy Creek, a branch of Holston River, under the impression that it was in Augusta County, Virginia; but when the North Carolina-Virginia boundary line was extended, they discovered that their land was actually in North Carolina.

The French and Indian War was concluded in 1763, and the threat of French interference on the frontier was removed. A royal proclamation issued in October was designed to prevent clashes between whites and Indians in the future. No white settlements were permitted beyond the crest of the mountains— "beyond the Heads or Sources of any of the Rivers which fall into the Atlantic Ocean from the West." If any North Carolinians had yet taken up land this far west, there certainly were not many of them. In fact, those who had even approached this point before 1754, withdrew during the war. Within two years, however, the push of white settlements to the mountains was again underway. Toward the end of the summer of 1765 John Stuart, England's agent for dealing with the Indians in the South, reported that in North Carolina lands had been granted "as far back as the Mountains and deprived the Indians of the Lower Cherokee Towns of the most valuable part of their hunting grounds." He warned of the dangers of such action, mentioning the possibility of "perpetual Broils" if it continued. "The Inhabitants of those back Countries are in general the lowest and worst part of the People and as they and the Indians live in perpetual Jealousy and dread of each other so their rooted hatred for each other is reciprocal." By the next spring Stuart's prediction seemed about to be realized. "I had much trouble by the imprudent behaviour of our back Settlers behind this, and the other Provinces," he wrote on March 31, 1766, "and the Cherokees have only been restrained from taking Revenge for the murder of eight of their Countrymen in Expectation of Obtaining Satisfaction from the Justice of Government, which in truth is not Strong enough to Operate with necessary vigour among such People."

The line established by the royal proclamation of 1763 was generally ignored. Daniel Boone set out in 1767 for the Kentucky country and then returned to his Rowan County home with tales of fertile land and ample game. Between 1769 and 1771 he made numerous trips in which he led large bands of colonists through the mountains into Tennessee and Kentucky. The Wedgwood potters in England heard reports of a desirable white clay that could be found in the North Carolina mountains, and in 1767 they sent Thomas Griffiths into the forbidden Cherokee country past the crest of the mountains to bring them several tons of the desirable material. By 1768 the Holston Valley Settlements in southwestern Virginia had grown so large that they extended into North Carolina. A treaty with the Indians made in 1768 opened a strip of land beyond the crest of the mountains to white settlement, and in the following year a Virginian moved west of the mountains. In so doing, William Bean became the first permanent settler in what was later to become Tennessee. Others soon followed him and before long there was a thriving community on the Watauga River. By 1772 the need for protection against horse thieves and outlaws prompted the people to form a government, known as the Watauga Association, and to set down what has been described as "the first written constitution by native Americans."

Governor William Tryon in June 1767 led some commissioners, troops, Indian guides, and interpreters on an expedition into the mountains of southwestern North Carolina. It was his intention to run a dividing line between the western frontiers of the province and the Cherokee hunting grounds. After surveying for fifty-three miles, the team concluded that the obstacles of the mountains were too great to permit them to continue marking the line; from their final marked trees it was simply agreed that the line should continue in a direct course to a known point in Virginia. The line, of course, was of little effect. Before the end of the year seven hunters from Charles Town penetrated sixty miles beyond it, and early the following year two hunters from Maryland explored the far side of the mountains from Maryland to east Florida. All of these men were simply a part of a movement to explore the mountains in an informal and personal way. The mountains, of course, still provided a formidable hindrance to mass western movement. By the end of June 1773 more than 120 families from the "back parts" of Virginia and North Carolina had made their way to Point Coupee on the Mississippi River. Near the end of 1773 it was reported in New Bern that a sloop had sailed from there with a number of passengers who also intended to settle on the Mississippi. Information was sent back describing the fertile soil and the good crops that could be produced with ease. Maps of 1770 and 1775 show roads ending at the mountains, but transportation by water solved the problem of many who wanted to take up land beyond the end of the road.

By the summer of 1776, "a Great number of Families wishing

to avoid the calamities of a rancorous Civil War" had migrated to the new frontier "to seek bread and peace in those remote desarts." With the adoption of the Declaration of Rights in December 1776, preliminary to the adoption of the first state constitution, North Carolina's leaders did not forget her citizens on the western frontier and urged that the boundaries of the state be carefully determined. The charter of King Charles II describing the province of Carolina as extending from sea to sea was cited, but the revolutionary patriots of 1776 decreed that this should "not be construed so as to prevent the establishment of one or more Governments Westward of this State, by consent of the Legislature." Thus, the idea that the American union was capable of indefinite expansion through the creation of new states had already begun to take root.

5

THE QUEST FOR POWER UNDER
THE CROWN

When North Carolina was purchased by the Crown in 1729, the governor, council, assembly, and courts, as well as the various local agencies remained as they had been before. Thus the people could envision no immediate or serious changes taking place in their government; the Crown merely replaced the lords proprietors as the immediate source of power. There was, however, a definite change in the spirit and efficiency of the government. A strong executive capable of sustained policy succeeded a weak and constantly changing leadership, and this made possible a stability of purpose, promptness of action, and a strength of administration that had been impossible heretofore.

The direction of affairs in North Carolina now became the concern of the Board of Trade, which in turn made recommendations to the Crown. A firm colonial policy evolved, applying to all the royal colonies, that sought to preserve and strengthen political dependence on the mother country. In addition, the policy was aimed at binding England and the colonies together in an economically self-sufficient empire. To facilitate the realization of these goals, members of the Board of Trade and other officials in London sought to make the governments of the colonies as much alike as possible. In doing this, the provisions of colonial charters frequently were ignored. By placing governors, judges, and other officials on fixed salaries and freeing them from dependence on the legislatures, they became more independent and tended to favor the Crown more than the people of the colony. Judges, the Board of Trade decided, should hold their commissions during the king's pleasure. This meant that the judges were not subject to election by the people, that they could not be removed from office except by the Crown, and that they might, in effect, expect to serve for life if they did not offend the Crown. The Crown, as the source of authority in the colonies, began to exercise the royal prerogative, which was actually a convenient way of arbitrarily dictating what might and might not be done. London used this vague right as a means for extending her control over the governing of the colony. For example, the royal prerogative was invoked to decide the question of what constituted a quorum in a colonial legislature; it was used in calling, adjourning (proroguing), and dissolving sessions of the legislature; and it was used not infrequently to veto laws. Under this same right the Crown also expanded the application of the navigation acts, which had already caused considerable trouble in North Carolina, and strengthened the powers of enforcement officials.

Policies imposed by the royal prerogative were met with vigorous opposition in North Carolina, where the conflict between the authority of the Crown on the one hand and the privileges of the people on the other grew increasingly bitter. The Crown acted on the theory that its authority in colonial affairs was absolute, and it undertook to conduct the colonial government through instructions that it held to be binding on both the governor and the assembly. After their experience of long years of very independent action under the indifferent lords proprietors, the colonists were not accustomed to following this line of thinking. The people maintained that the power of the Crown was restricted by the Carolina charter just as the power of the proprietors had always been curbed in that way. As the people saw it, the Crown simply replaced the proprietors and was still bound to administer affairs in the colony in accordance with the provisions of the charter.

The Crown, intent on the larger affairs of the empire, ignored the claimed rights and interests of the colony while North Carolina, very naturally, considered its own affairs to be paramount and never tried to understand or to sympathize with the royal policies. The result of this clash of ideologies and interests was inevitable. The governor struggled to uphold the prerogative of the Crown while the assembly championed the rights and privileges of the people. Controversies between the two marked the entire political history of North Carolina as a royal colony. There as elsewhere in the colonies the view was held that a legislature was a "little parliament," not subordinate to but comparable in powers with the House of Commons in England. It is true that many of the questions that caused the most concern were actually rather inconsequential, but some did involve basic constitutional issues. Underlying the conflict was the very important question of whether the colonial assembly should be a real legislative body, representing the will of the people and having the power of independent judgment and action, or whether it should be merely an organ of government designed solely to register the royal will.

The men appointed by George II and George III to govern their royal province of North Carolina were not so much favorites of the court as they were good, deserving Whig party members who were recommended for the post by some lesser official with influence. A colonial governorship was not a very important reward and seldom attracted successful and influential Britishers. The official salary in North Carolina was small and often uncertain of collection; the chance that fringe benefits might be derived from the office was slight and the opportunities for speculation were scanty. However, a governor might indeed benefit from fees authorized for certain of his duties, and many of the men who held the office helped themselves to vast tracts of land. Yet North Carolina did have several very capable governors during this period. Three of the five royal governors, Johnston, Dobbs, and Tryon, were colorful personalities who well understood the point of view of the people and even sympathized with them on many occasions in the face of royal instructions to the contrary. Even if these men had been free of all self-interest and filled with great ability as statesmen, they still would have aroused antagonism in North Carolina because of the nature of the British colonial scheme. The governors were often in combat with various groups and factions that tried to control provincial affairs.

George Burrington, the first royal governor of North Carolina, arrived in February 1731, the second year after the purchase of the colony by the Crown, and was given an appropriate ceremonial reception. As governor of the colony under the lords proprietors in 1724–1725, Burrington had allied himself with the so-called popular party on many occasions, and it was the leaders of this group who hastened to welcome him when he returned. They soon discovered, however, that proprietary Governor Burrington and royal Governor Burrington were quite different.

In the new governor's instructions the Crown offered to remit to the people the unpaid quitrents if the following two conditions were met: first, the assembly was to require the registration of all land held in the colony so that an accurate rent roll could be provided for the Crown; and second, all quitrents and officers' fees, which had previously been acceptable in some of the rated commodities of the country or in provincial currency, were to be paid in the future in proclamation money (an assortment of coins from a great many countries, circulating at a value set by royal proclamation). When the assembly met in April 1731, Burrington, by executive order with the approval of the council, had already fixed the officers' fees in proclamation money, and he had even prepared a bill for the assembly relating to the question of quitrents. But the assembly proved unexpectedly independent. The members resolved that in the future all payments of quitrents should be made as they were in the past, that is, "in some valuable commodities, or in the bills now current in the Province at proper rates." They also informed the new governor that the assembly alone had the power to regulate officers' fees.

Burrington replied that the king's instructions giving the

governor and council power to regulate and settle fees had effectively repealed all laws declaring that fees should be received in other forms. This alarmed the assembly, and its members became concerned over their rights. They reminded the haughty governor that the Carolina charter of 1663 granted the people "all Liberties, Franchises, and Privileges" enjoyed by the people of England; and they declared that among their rights was the guarantee "that they shall not be taxed or made lyable to pay any sum or sums of money or Fees other than such as are by law established." They demanded that the governor forbid the collection of fees in proclamation money "until such time as the Officers' Fees shall be regulated by Authority of Assembly."

Burrington, attributing all of this opposition to Edward Moseley, who was not only speaker of the house but also public treasurer, was determined to destroy this formidable adversary. The combination of these two offices occurred in almost every colony, and it seriously encroached upon the governor's patronage powers. Burrington opened his campaign against Moseley by producing two additional instructions: the first prohibited the expenditure of any public money except upon warrant of the governor, and the second directed that all commissions issued during the proprietary period be withdrawn and that no public office be held except by a commission from the king. Burrington laid these instructions before the assembly together with a declaration of his intention to appoint "a fitt person" to serve as treasurer. The assembly, smarting under this fresh attack, countered Burrington by ruling that no public money should be disbursed except as directed by the assembly, and then it went on to express the opinion that the other instructions about commissions did not apply to officers who were appointed by act of the assembly, as was the treasurer, but only to those who held commissions from the lords proprietors. They reminded Burrington that a perfectly suitable treasurer, appointed by themselves, was then in office and that the governor need not trouble himself to try to appoint another.

Burrington promptly dismissed the assembly and did not call it again for two years. In the meantime he had his instructions confirmed from London and in July 1733 he announced that the Crown was standing by the original instructions. He claimed to be especially forbidden to accept quitrents and fees in any form other than proclamation money. This was money acceptable in London, while provincial currency or the rated commodities of North Carolina were worth little outside the immediate area. Not surprisingly, the assembly liked Burrington's superior manner no better than they liked his instructions. In a caustic response they said that they, too, had consulted the source of their power, the people, and had been advised not to burden the province with any such payments in proclamation money. A quarrel flared up and neither side would yield. The governor called an assembly three times, but it refused to pass even a single bill. The elected representatives of the people refused to obey the king's instructions, and the governor would agree to nothing short of complete submission. Burrington on one occasion explained his intransigency when he said, "If the King's Instructions are contrary to some Laws of the Province, the Governor must act in Obedience to the King's Commands, therefore you must not be Surprized [that] whatever your law directs contrary to my Instructions is not taken notice of [by] me."

Several heated debates followed in which the governor showed himself to be abusive, insolent, and dictatorial. Because the rights, the duties, and the very dignity of the assembly were at stake, the house was resolved to uphold them at all costs. Burrington's opponents continuously filed complaints against him to the Board of Trade, but their charges probably contributed less to his downfall than did his own official reports, which in violent and unreasonable language revealed all too clearly his unfitness for office. In the summer of 1733 the board advised that he be recalled and that Gabriel Johnston be appointed to succeed him. Burrington's response was that no governor could have carried out his instructions in North Carolina and at the same time have kept peace with a people "who are subtle and crafty to admiration, who could neither be outwitted nor cajoled,

who always behaved insolently to their governors, who maintained that their money could not be taken from them save by
appropriations made by their own House of Assembly, a body
that has always usurped more power than ought to be allowed."

Gabriel Johnston took the oath of office at the town of
Brunswick in November 1734. A Scotsman of good birth and
education, he was at thirty-five superior in almost every way to
his fifty-three-year-old predecessor. During his eighteen-year
administration there was never a mention of scandal, and he
gave no cause for personal complaint. He did, however, manage
to play politics in a very shrewd way, and in so doing he showed
just as little consideration for the assembly and as much regard
for the king's prerogative as Burrington had. But Johnston
proved a great deal more successful in carrying out royal
instructions.

Johnston not only maintained all the positions taken by
Burrington on the quitrent question, but he also insisted that the
king had the right to fix the places of collection. It would be
collected at "specified places" and not at the taxpayer's home, as
had been customary. He also said that the quitrents should be
paid in "gold and silver" or in bills circulating at a rate of
exchange fixed by the council. The governor even set up a Court
of Exchequer to collect rents by distress if necessary. He
maintained that there was "a general submission to his orders."
In the fall of 1735 he reported quitrent collections of £1,200
sterling and predicted that this figure would double the next
year. He appointed a new rent collector or "receiver general" for
North Carolina, although the one at Charles Town in South
Carolina was supposed to serve both colonies.* The new collector
was even instructed by the governor to "distrain" or seize
property for nonpayment if necessary. The shock of such a
possibility brought a general compliance from the people during
the tax collector's first rounds. But general murmurs of opposition soon began to be heard, and before long loud protests and

---

* In 1754 the sheriffs were made the tax collectors on a basis of 10 percent for
themselves and 5 percent for their deputies.

threats of violence were being made. Treasurer Edward Moseley even refused to pay his own quitrent, and he urged others to follow his example.

Complaints were sent to the assembly accusing the collectors of demanding payment in currency at rates of seven or eight for one of sterling. In addition, it was alleged that the collectors threatened to add extravagant charges if they had to seize property for payment. The assembly opposed Johnston's actions and appealed to "the Ancient Laws and usage" of the colony. But Johnston, backed by the council, said they could not pay "any regard" to the "Ancient Laws," which were all "null and void." Having protested in vain, the assembly then took its cue from the governor's own actions, and the sergeant-at-arms was ordered to seize tax collectors.

At this point Governor Johnston, resorting to what he called "management," displayed a capacity for tact and cunning that was far superior to that shown by Burrington. He played politics extremely well and thus managed to reach a compromise. Recently Johnston had taken issue with the assembly over the validity of blank patents for land. These were printed forms signed by the proper officials, but with the date, name of the patentee, location of the land, number of acres, and amount of the purchase money left blank. Such patents, estimated to have involved 150,000 acres, had been used by many people to take up land for themselves after the lords proprietors had closed their Carolina land office. They simply filled in the blank spaces to apply to unsettled land that they found. Governor Johnston maintained that all of these were worthless; he had no record of them for tax purposes.

Finding himself checked in the quitrent controversy, Johnston proposed to yield his position on blank patents if the assembly would yield on quitrents. A bargain was promptly reached. The governor agreed to confirm titles for land held under these questionable documents, and the assembly consented to prepare a rent roll and to limit the number of places where quitrents could be paid. The governor also consented to accept certain rated commodities or their value in provincial money, which would be fixed from time to time by a commission made up of the governor and representatives of the council and of the assembly. In 1739 a bill embodying these provisions passed the assembly and was promptly signed by Johnston. The governor and the assembly congratulated themselves over the solution to the controversy, but before a year had elapsed word arrived from London disallowing the bill. Although Johnston realized that the four years he had spent in securing it were wasted, this did not dampen his enthusiasm for political maneuvering.

From time to time Johnston played politics in the province by embroiling the Albemarle and the Cape Fear sections in controversy. His extravagant land dealings and obvious favoritism toward residents of the Cape Fear region increased the considerable tension that already existed between the sections. Johnston even promoted the growth of what was to become the town of Wilmington on the Cape Fear River, and it was here that he often called the assembly to meet. The northern counties held their lands under the old Great Deed of Grant of 1668, which gave them better terms than the Crown had allowed in other more recently formed counties. Also, each of the older counties of the Albemarle region elected five members to the assembly, while the newer counties were permitted only two or three each. This gave the Albemarle section a majority. The governor, aware of the ill feelings generated by this inequity in representation, called the assembly of 1741 to meet in Wilmington, anticipating that few if any Albemarle delegates would come to a session so far from home. Enough did attend, however, so that he was unable to bend the assembly to his will. Consequently, it was prorogued after four weeks. The next three sessions were held in New Bern, but they too failed to provide the satisfaction the governor was seeking. Finally, in November 1746 he tried Wilmington again, and because of very bad weather not a single member came to represent the northern counties.

The Albemarle members felt secure that the assembly would not transact any business without the presence of a quorum, which was understood for many years to mean a majority of the members. What they failed to realize was just how bitterly the southern members resented the larger number of delegates elected by the northern counties. They also misjudged how anxious the southern counties were to have a more centrally located capital. Speaker Samuel Swann of Onslow County, a "middle" county, was willing to agree to the directive in the governor's instructions that fifteen members of the lower house should constitute a quorum. The assembly thereby surrendered a precedent that it had held since its establishment—one granted by the proprietors and permitted by the Crown. In England the House of Commons had determined its own quorum since 1641, but in the Carolinas royal governors attempted to deny this right. Two important laws were passed by this divided assembly. The first limited representation in the assembly to two delegates per county and one per borough town and recognized fourteen members plus the speaker as being a quorum for the transaction of business by the house. The second act fixed the seat of government at New Bern and regulated certain courts and court action.

Johnston dissolved the assembly when it had finished its work and issued writs for the election of a new house in accordance with the new law. Inhabitants of the Albemarle section, declaring that they would not obey the new law until it had been confirmed by the Crown, insisted that their sheriffs certify five members per county as they had always done. When the new assembly convened in New Bern in February 1747, the northern counties sent their accustomed number of delegates. A resolution introduced in the house declared the elections in the Albemarle counties to be null and void "and that his Excellency the Governor be addressed to direct the Clerk of the Crown to issue Writts to elect Members for the said several Counties to represent the said freeholders in General Assembly." Albemarle refused to submit, and that portion of North Carolina was not represented in the assembly for more than seven years. The great schism which the action of the governor had precipitated was a long time in healing.

Another factor contributing to the widening split in North Carolina was the demand from the Cape Fear region that greater quantities of paper currency be issued. Albemarle merchants found it almost worthless in their dealings with Virginia wholesalers, who often refused to accept it. People elsewhere in North Carolina, however, were quite content to use it when they bought goods from Albemarle merchants. Later they also found it perfectly satisfactory in paying for forts erected along the frontier as protection from Indians. Relations between the sections deteriorated still further when the assembly of 1748, in return for the governor's support in its attempts to reform the basis of representation, passed an act providing for the preparation of a rent roll. The act contained several obviously biased provisions aimed at the Albemarle section, and the Board of Trade recognized them.

Leaders from the Albemarle counties had sent two attorneys, Thomas Barker and Wyriott Ormond, to London to present their case to Crown officials. They cited a number of early instances in which reference to five representatives per county had been made in official instructions concerning them. They also noted that the fact that a majority was required to constitute a quorum in the assembly was also well documented. Before resting their case, they very earnestly questioned the right of the assembly to fix the basis of representation. These were all serious questions, and Governor Johnston's own agent in London, James Abercromby, applied "skilful delaying tactics" to any decision. Both sides were heard, and the Board of Trade then called for more information. A decision by the Privy Council was delayed until 1754. It was agreed that the governor had a right to call a meeting of the legislature at any time and place he might choose. An absolute majority of members of the House of Commons was not necessary to conduct business. The question of representation was covered in the conclusion reached by the Board of Trade in 1750 in its advice to the slow-acting Privy Council. The acts in question, they said, "appear to have passed by Management Precipitation and Surprize when very few Members were present and are of such nature and Tendency and have such effect and Operation that the Governour by his Instructions ought not to have assented to them, tho' they had passed deliberately in a full Assembly, and we are of opinion that they are not proper to be confirmed."

Governor Johnston died in 1752, at the halfway point between the report of the Board of Trade and the decision of the Privy Council. The whole period from 1746 until 1754 was one of great unrest and near anarchy. Governor Johnston wrote Agent Abercromby in 1750: "I have nothing more to trouble you with only to tell you how uneasy every body here is to have an account of the Determination of that tedious affair of the five Members which has now for four years compleat kept this Poor unhappy Province in inexpressible confusion; If it is not soon to be decided I don't see how we can long keep up the face of Government." Bishop Spangenberg was in North Carolina during this schismatic period and he commented on the conditions that he observed. From Edenton in the Albemarle on September 12, 1752, he wrote in his diary:

If I am to say how I find things in North Carolina I must admit that there is much confusion. There is discord between the Counties, which has greatly weakened the authority of the Legislature, and interferes with the administration of justice. The reason is this, as I hear it from both sides: When the Colony was still weak the older Counties were permitted to send five men each to the Assembly. After a long time the Colony increased in size, and new Counties were formed, but were allowed only two representatives each. That continued until the newer Counties were numerous enough to have the majority in the Assembly; then before the older Counties realized what was being done, an Act was passed reducing the representation of the older Counties to two each also. This irritated the older Counties, and they refused to send any one at all to the Assembly, but dispatched an agent to England to try to regain from them their ancient rights, and meanwhile they declined to respect any Act passed by the Assembly. So in some respects anarchy reigns in these older Counties: there are many cases of murder, theft, and the like, but no one is punished. The men will not serve as jurors, so when Court is held for the trial of criminal cases no one is there. If a man is imprisoned the jail is broken open; in short 'fist law' is about all that is left. But the County Courts are held regularly, and matters within their jurisdiction are attended to as usual.

After Johnston's death the government was administered first by the president of the council, Nathaniel Rice, and then by his successor, Matthew Rowan. Finally, at the end of October 1754 the new governor, Arthur Dobbs, reached New Bern. He was a Protestant Irishman who had long had an interest in vast tracts of land in North Carolina. The assembly, which he called in December, was the first one since June 1746 in which all of the counties were represented. The northern faction of the popular party succeeded in electing John Campbell as speaker, but both sides, aware of the impending French and Indian War, assured the new governor that they would cooperate to make his administration smooth. This conciliatory attitude did not last long, however, as the same old questions that had plagued earlier governors once again emerged. The assembly refused to follow London's instructions to accept fifteen members as a quorum; nothing less than one-half of the house, which would have been thirty or thirty-one, was ever recognized by them.

A great debate between the assembly and the governor also arose over the qualification and tenure of judges. It was conceded that the appointment of a chief justice during the king's pleasure was a right of the Crown. Attorneys were usually sent over from England for this office, but they were usually men whose personal character and legal training failed to measure up to the dignity and responsibility of the office. They owed their appointment and tenure to the Crown, and they were apparently often subject to executive influence in North Carolina. In the hope of limiting this influence as much as possible, the assembly arranged the circuits so that the chief justice could not attend more than half the courts. In addition, they passed an act providing for associate or assistant justices. In the absence or disability of the chief justice, these men were to have full jurisdiction. While these

Will Hoare Pinxt.   Ja.M.Ardell Fecit.

His Excellency, Arthur Dobbs Esq.

Captain GENERAL and GOVERNOVR in Chief & Vice Admiral of the PROVENCE of
North Carolina in AMERICA.

Royal Governor Arthur Dobbs. *Courtesy of Mangum Weeks, Alexandria, Virginia.*

associate justices were to be appointed by the governor, the assembly formulated the qualifications for the post in such a way as virtually to exclude all nonresident attorneys, and they secured the independence of these judges by giving them tenure during good behavior.

Crown officials considered this court bill a violation of the royal prerogative. It was disallowed, and Dobbs was instructed not to consent to any such arrangement in the future. The disagreement over judges reached a crisis in 1760 when the assembly was called into special session to vote aid to the Crown for military purposes during the French and Indian War. Members obstinately refused to consider an aid bill unless the governor would consent to their court bill. The contest became rancorous, but the explosions it gave rise to apparently cleared the air and led the way to a compromise. In return for appropriations, the governor agreed to sign the court bill, provided it included a clause specifying that unless approved by the king its duration would be limited to two years. Needless to say, the king's approval was never given, and the only reward Dobbs received for his efforts was a stinging rebuke from his superiors in London.

Closely tied in with all of these controversies was the problem of executive and judicial salaries. During most of the colonial period officials had to serve two masters—one from whom they received their commissions and the other from whom they hoped to receive their pay. Under the Crown the governors were instructed to procure definite salaries for executive and judicial officials. Both Burrington and Johnston tried, but the assemblymen merely replied that if the king wanted such salaries fixed he could pay them out of his own pocket. The Board of Trade took the hint and set the governor's salary at £1,000, but for many years the collection of quitrents to provide funds depended upon proper legislation, which the assembly refused to pass. Quitrents in North Carolina were so irregularly collected that Burrington's salary was never paid, and Johnston, at the time of his death, had not been paid for thirteen years. Governor Dobbs, in contrast to his predecessors, made arrangements before leaving England to receive £1,000 sterling annually from revenue in the Leeward Islands and Barbados. The assembly, nevertheless, from time to time used its power over the public purse to force from all of the executives various concessions that they considered important.

Throughout this period of bitter wrangling over questions involving royal prerogative, the legislature operated under the sincere conviction that it was fighting the battles of constitutional, traditional, and representative government. By constitution, it meant the Carolina charter and the practices that had grown up under it. Steadfastly, the legislature held to the belief that the provisions of the charter had not been affected by the transfer of the colony to the Crown. As late as 1761 Dobbs wrote that the assembly contended that the charter was still in force and that it bound the king as well as the people. He summed up the assembly's case when he said, "The Assembly think themselves entitled to all the Privileges of a British House of Commons and therefore ought not to submit to His Majesty's honorable Privy Council further than do the Commons in England, or submit to His Majesty's instructions to His Governor and Council here." Dobbs appealed to the king to strengthen his hand so that he might more effectively "oppose and suppress a republican spirit of Independency rising in this Colony." How clearly Dobbs foresaw the coming break between England and her American colonies is uncertain; but, to be sure, his warning voice was completely ignored in London.

6

A COLONY IN THE EMPIRE

Throughout the royal period the colonies found themselves surrounded by threats of attack. Until Georgia was settled in 1733, the Carolinas formed a buffer region between the English and Spanish, but now there was the constant danger of Spanish invasion from Florida. Enemy Indians, in league with the French or the Spanish against the English, were poised menacingly all along the frontier. White settlers who approached the mountains of North Carolina, where there were numerous French trading posts among the Cherokee Indians, had good reason to fear attack because the French generously provided arms and encouragement for Indian raids on English settlements. The Atlantic Ocean was another source of danger; the colonies were perilously vulnerable to attack from French and Spanish ships. Before long the colonists became involved in fighting England's battles with Spain, France, and, of course, the Indians. Although this involvement gave rise to numerous conflicts within and among themselves, the colonies gained some very important benefits that would serve them well in the next few decades. First and probably most important, participation in England's wars brought the colonies out of isolation and into contact and cooperation with one another, thus giving rise to a sense of shared destiny; second, the colonists gained invaluable military experience.

North Carolina played a significant role in two intercolonial wars. The first of these was the War of Jenkins' Ear (1739–1744), which began as an Anglo-Spanish conflict but then expanded into the War of the Austrian Succession (known in America as King George's War, 1744–1748) in which England and Austria allied themselves against France and Prussia. It was during this conflict that the king for the first time called upon the colony for men and money to support a military campaign. King George "demanded [troops] in so Gracious and condecending a manner," Governor Johnston informed the assembly on February 5, 1740, "that I cannot make the least doubt of your ready and cheerfull complyance." The troops were requested to join an expedition against Spanish outposts in the New World. No quota was established for North Carolina because His Majesty did not want to "set Bounds to [the people's] zeal for our service . . . we doubt not in the least but they will exert themselves upon this occasion as far as the circumstances of the Colony will allow being assured they cannot render a more acceptable service to us and to their Mother Country nor do anything more essential for their own Interest." The instructions to the governor required the colony to provide victuals, transportation, and other necessities, except clothes, tents, arms, and ammunition, from the time of enlistment until the men joined the British expedition. To help pay for this, the assembly suggested that more paper money be issued. Johnston refused to agree to this, whereupon the assembly came up with an elaborate scheme for levying and collecting a special tax of three shillings for every tithable in the province. This tax was to be paid in "commodities of the country," including rice, tobacco, beeswax, skins, and other produce. Governor Johnston estimated that this would provide £1,200, a sum sufficient "to equip and subsist four companies of 100 men each until they could join the army in Jamaica when they would be put on the payroll of the Crown."

In the northern part of the colony three companies of one hundred men each were raised, and a company of more than a hundred was enlisted in the Cape Fear region. "I have good reason to believe that we could have easily . . . raised 200 more," Johnston said, "if it had been possible to negotiate the

Bills of Exchange in this part of the Continent." On July 20, 1739 the *Virginia Gazette* reported that a ship was ready to sail in April for Carolina with seventy cannon, a large quantity of ammunition, and arms for three thousand men. Johnston later revealed that he had actually been unable to find any ship captains who were willing to accept North Carolina currency in exchange for the necessary transportation. "I was therefore under a necessity of making use of His Majesties secret Instruction to me and hire four Vessels here [Edenton] and one at Cape Fear and have drawn upon the Commissioners of the Navy in Consequence of that Instruction." By November 5, 1740 he was able to report that North Carolina had recruited "about 400 men . . . who are now embarked and just going to put to Sea."

No roster of the men enlisted for this campaign has survived, and the names of a few officers are known largely by chance. Captain James Innes of Wilmington, who spoke Spanish, commanded the Cape Fear company, and his lieutenants were Archibald Douglass and William Pringle. On November 15 the Cape Fear company sailed aboard a transport for a rendezvous in Jamaica with the British navy and foot troops. Captain Innes had letters of marque giving him leave to attack enemy shipping on the way. The *South Carolina Gazette* for November 24, 1740 reported that the men "were in general brisk and harty, and long for Nothing so much as a favorable Wind, that they may be among the first in Action." From all the colonies there were thirty-six companies of one hundred men each; only New Hampshire, Delaware, South Carolina, and Georgia provided no troops. South Carolina and Georgia did, however, apparently supply forces to protect the southern frontier against the possibility of a Spanish movement overland from Florida. A fleet sailed from England with fifteen thousand sailors and twelve thousand foot troops, and they met the colonial expedition in Jamaica late in 1740. North Carolina troops were the last to arrive, and they were placed under the command of Colonel William Gooch of Virginia. Admiral Edward Vernon was commander of the fleet and Brigadier General Thomas Wentworth commanded the troops. Neither Vernon nor Wentworth was a leader capable of the task before him, and the whole campaign was badly managed with an excessive loss of life.

The most serious phase of the campaign took place during the attack on Cartagena, New Granada (now Colombia), on the mainland of South America. General Wentworth called for troops, but Admiral Vernon delayed from April 2 to April 6, 1741 in landing a detachment. What was intended as a predawn attack was delayed by bungling until sunrise, when it was discovered that the ladders for scaling the walls of the Spanish fort were too short. The English invaders were subjected to a deadly fire, and they suffered a loss of about 50 percent before retreating. In the tropical climate a host of unfamiliar diseases also took a devastating toll among the troops. The loss of life was almost unbelievable. Of the five hundred soldiers from Massachusetts, only fifty lived to reach home again. In January 1743 only about twenty-five of the one hundred men from the Cape Fear company returned, and there is no record that any from the other three companies survived, though they may have. Of the thirty-six hundred Americans on the expedition not more than six hundred survived.

While North Carolina troops were in the Caribbean, Spanish ships played havoc with the colony's shipping. In the spring of 1741 several Spanish privateers began to operate off the coast. From a tent town established as a base at Ocracoke Island, the Spanish were able to control shipping through the good inlet there as well as shipping on coastal waters. They apparently intended to remain for a time. They alarmed the "bankers," as the residents of the Outer Banks were called, burned some houses, and destroyed cattle. From this secure harbor the Spanish used smaller vessels to patrol the sounds. In less than two weeks in late April and early May, the Spanish captured six ships, including two from Edenton, "before they had been an half hour at sea." The Spanish were fearless and operated so close to shore near the inlets that a Pasquotank ship owner and county official, James George, "had the Mortification to see his Vessel and

Cargo taken before his face as he stood on the shore." One still Sunday morning early in July the Spanish boarded a becalmed sloop about thirty miles up the sound from Ocracoke and captured its crew. Captain Thomas Hadley, however, managed to escape and make his way to the Cape Fear where he reported the troubles in that district. Merchants and ship owners there became alarmed and secured the assistance of an English privateer who happened to be in port.

Captain George Walker of the ship *Duke William* with twenty guns had put to sea from England under letters of marque soon after war was declared "to reap what advantages thereof might accrue." In the Cape Fear he learned of the work of Spanish privateers and that the North Carolina coast was "at present unprotected by any of his Majesty's Fleet." Offering his ship to local leaders "for the government's service, to act in the defence of their coasts, and for the protection of their trade," an agreement was reached under which the crew was placed on wages "as in the king's ships," while Walker, "tho' commander, entered himself a volunteer." The ship's complement was increased by the volunteer services of "several gentlemen of the country." The *Duke William* set out on a four months' cruise from St. Augustine to the Virginia capes. Walker reported that the coast was soon cleared of Spanish privateers, "Spanish ships . . . having quitted their cruise, as we supposed, upon receiving some intelligence of our fiting out." On Ocracoke Walker found that the invaders had erected a fort, which he destroyed together with the battery and other fortifications, "so that the Spaniards never returned during our stay on that station, which intirely broke their plan of privateering in those seas." The cruise was over, but Walker apparently had made so favorable an impression upon the gentlemen of Cape Fear that they offered him a sixty-five hundred acre tract if he and his crew would settle in their midst. With regret and a bit of wonder at what "posterity" would think of his not accepting such an offer, Walker departed and left the patrol of the coast to a royal ship that had just recently arrived.

The War of Jenkins' Ear had cost North Carolina a goodly

number of men, some serious losses in shipping, and a considerable amount of money and supplies. This relatively poor colony was learning that being a member of the British Empire was expensive. But there was no peace yet. The War of Jenkins' Ear merged into King George's War, which arose, at least in part, over a conflict between France and England concerning colonial boundaries in northern New England and in the Ohio Valley. War was declared in March 1744, and the northern colonies were soon fighting the French. After the capture of Louisburg in the spring of 1745, an attack on Quebec was planned by a joint army of English and colonial forces. A small army was raised in North Carolina, but for this colony the return of the Spanish posed a far more serious threat than did the activities of the French. Apparently North Carolina learned a lesson from her involvement in the War of Jenkins' Ear, for this time she gave some thought at the outset to the question of protection at home. In 1745 the assembly passed an act authorizing the erection of a fort on the lower part of Cape Fear River.* Another move toward assuring protection at home was the passage by the assembly in June 1746 of "An Act for the Better regulating the Militia of this Government." This legislation required the service of all freemen and servants between the ages of sixteen and sixty, with the exception of Anglican ministers, members of the council and assembly, and a few others. The governor was authorized to call up the militia in case of an invasion or of a military expedition. In a broad gesture of intercolonial cooperation the act also specifically stated that if Virginia or South Carolina were invaded, "so many of the Forces of this Government as shall be thought necessary to give proper relief . . . shall . . . march . . . to their Assistance, at the Expence of the Province desiring such Assistance."

Though the members of the assembly were beginning to recognize that the future of the colony was dependent, at least to

---

* A second act, which was passed in 1748, carried an appropriation to get the work underway, but the fort constructed below Brunswick and named Fort Johnston was not completed until 1764.

some extent, upon contact with the other colonies, not all the settlers shared this attitude. In Northampton County on March 5, 1746, an Independent Company under the command of Captain Robert Hodgson was mustered into service for the defense of South Carolina. So many men deserted, however, that on May 30 Governor Johnston felt compelled to issue a proclamation against giving refuge to these deserters "on Pain of being fin'd and punished with the utmost Rigour of the Law." Any deserters who voluntarily surrendered within forty days "shall be kindly receiv'd and pardon'd; but those who shall neglect so to do, if they are taken, may depend on being dealt with as the Act of Parliament, for preventing Mutiny and Desertion, directs." Captain Hodgson sought the assistance of "all Gentlemen, as well as those who consider that the Strength of a Frontier Province is a great Addition to the Security of their own" in getting his men back.

This problem of desertion was not unknown in other companies. Captain Kenneth McKenzie's company from Brunswick County was camped at Williamsburg, Virginia, in July 1746 when Dudley Delks and two other soldiers fled with their weapons. Lieutenant Governor Sir William Gooch of Virginia advertised for their return and offered a reward for their capture. England was at war with France between 1744 and 1748, but certainly the most serious period of conflict in North Carolina occurred between 1747 and 1748 during what was called "The Spanish Alarm." In June 1747 a band of Spanish privateers sailed fearlessly into Beaufort, captured several vessels that they found in port, and quickly departed after two days. Having met no serious opposition on this visit, the Spanish returned on August 26, at which time they landed. Colonel Thomas Lovick of the county militia called out his troops, and they remained on duty until the town was abandoned by the invaders three days later. At the end of that time the militia divided into groups and rotated watches until about the middle of September. The total cost to the province for officers' and soldiers' pay and for the powder was just over £103.

Spanish activity in North Carolina during the summer of 1747 was described by Governor Johnston in his remarks to the Board of Trade in the spring of 1749. He told them that,

several small Sloops and Barcalonjos, came creeping along the shore from St. Augustine full of armed men, most Mulattoes and Negroes, their small Draught of water secured them from the attacks of the only ship of war on this station, they landed at Ocacock, Core sound, Bear Inlet, and Cape Fear, where they killed several of his Majesty's subjects, burned some ships and several small Vessels, carried off some Negroes, and slaughtered a Vast number of Black Cattle and Hogs, these Practices were continued all the summer 1747 and enraged the People to the highest degree.

The incident in the Cape Fear was more serious than the governor's very brief reference probably suggested to the Board of Trade. Early on Sunday morning, September 4, 1748, two Spanish privateers appeared in the Cape Fear River opposite the defenseless little town of Brunswick and announced their arrival by opening fire. Almost at the same moment the town was invaded by Spaniards who had been landed a short distance downstream. The citizens were terrified and saw no alternative but to flee. Several ships that were anchored in the harbor stood ready to be plundered as did the hastily evacuated town. As soon as they could recover their composure, the people sounded an alarm that spread throughout the region. A messenger rode off to Charles Town to seek the aid of British naval vessels, and Captain William Dry organized as many of the militiamen as he could round up. A muster called for Monday was attended by too few men, and action had to be postponed until Tuesday. By then the Brunswick men were joined by others from the area, some sailors who had escaped from the ships in the harbor, and several Negro slaves. About eighty men were on hand but there were arms for only sixty. Most of those who had fled the town on Sunday morning left their guns at home. Twelve men led the way back into town and found the Spanish, full of confidence, moving about unhurriedly and stealing from the houses whatever they found to their liking. The invaders were taken by surprise and fled in great haste to the security of one of their ships. The men of Brunswick killed about ten Spaniards and captured thirty more, but they could do nothing other than take cover as the privateer began shelling the town. Unexpectedly and for no known reason the privateer suddenly caught fire; almost immediately after the smoke was sighted from the shore she exploded. Some ninety men, including the captain and all of his officers were killed, and the few that survived were taken prisoner. Only about thirty minutes elapsed from the time the citizens returned to Brunswick until the privateer lay at the bottom of the river.

This was not, however, the end of the affair. The Spanish still held in their possession a New England ship that they had captured earlier in the harbor, and their other privateer, which had gone up the river, now returned and began shelling the town. Seeing that he was accomplishing nothing, the captain sent a messenger ashore under a flag of truce offering to cease firing if allowed to leave with the New England ship. Captain Dry agreed that they might leave, but only if all stolen property were returned and all prisoners released. Having no ship to prevent their departure, Dry was in no position to enforce his decree. The Spanish simply gave up the fight and sailed down the river with their prizes. Riding at anchor off Smith Island the next day, the Spanish commander sent word that he would exchange prisoners, but he gave the colonists only until three o'clock. When no Spanish prisoners appeared by the appointed time he sailed away. The total complement of the two Spanish vessels had been about 260; approximately half of them had been killed and 40 taken prisoner. Most of the plunder they had seized was lost when their first ship exploded. Although the colonists suffered only 2 men wounded and a few taken prisoner, their property damage was enormous.

After the Treaty of Aix-la-Chapelle was signed in October 1748, France took advantage of the lull in hostilities to begin reinforcing her string of military outposts just beyond the mountains all the way from Canada down to the mouth of the Mississippi. They were garrisoned by trained troops who would move at a single command from Quebec. England, on the other hand, could do nothing to secure this kind of military unity. She possessed thirteen separate colonies, each one of which felt itself to be independent of the others. Troops could be enlisted and funds appropriated for the common defense only when thirteen separate legislatures were convinced of the wisdom of such action. Except for the generally ineffective instructions that came from Crown officials in London, there was no broad directive for action. There were few forts in existence, the militia was carelessly recruited and poorly trained, and military supplies were scarce.

Late in 1753, anticipating the struggle with France, Great Britain asked colonial officials in seven northern colonies to confer with the Iroquois Indians in an effort to gain their support against the French. In June commissioners from five of them, together with representatives from Connecticut and Rhode Island (not originally invited) convened in Albany, New York. After reaching an understanding with the Indians, the Albany Congress then turned its attention to the question of uniting for the common defense. Largely as proposed by Benjamin Franklin, a plan of union was drawn up for consideration of each of the colonies and by Crown officials. The Albany Plan for a voluntary union envisioned a president general appointed by the Crown and a Grand Council of Delegates appointed by the colonial assemblies. In addition, the plan contained provisions for this union to control Indian affairs, including the power to declare war and negotiate treaties, regulate trade with the Indians, and levy taxes for the purposes of raising and maintaining armies. Various other provisions for the common welfare were also described in the plan, which was sent to the governor of each colony for presentation to his legislature. A few days before Christmas Governor Dobbs laid the recommendations before the house "for your Consideration that you may Concurr with them or alter and amend the plan." He reminded the members that it was King George's desire "to promote a happy Union among the provinces for their General Union and Defence." Late in the

afternoon of the day before Christmas the house resolved that the
plan be referred to the next session and that in the meantime
copies be printed and sent to each member. There is no evidence
that copies were ever printed or that the matter was ever again
mentioned in the assembly. There apparently was no interest in
the proposal in any of the colonies because it infringed on their
independence. No other colony indicated its approval and
neither did the Crown, which saw it as an encroachment on the
royal prerogative. Benjamin Franklin made the apt comment
that "everyone cries, a union is absolutely necessary, but when
they come to the Manner and Form of the Union, their weak
Noodles are perfectly distracted." The matter was dropped,
perhaps lost in the troubles of a war that lasted nearly ten years.

On the eve of the French and Indian War, North Carolina,
with her interior region just beginning to be settled, was in a
particularly weak position to be facing another military conflict.
The colony had made no provisions for defense, and in many
cases settlers were pushing perilously close to Indian lands. With
an almost careless abandon the newcomers put hunting grounds
to the plough and thereby enraged the increasingly hostile
Indians. On February 20, 1754, the assembly heard the president
of the council, Matthew Rowan, describe an urgent message that
he had received from Governor Robert Dinwiddie of Virginia
informing him that "the French have formed, and gone considerable length in executing a design to encroach on our Settlements
to the Westward." Rowan continued, "You know too well
gentlemen the Importance of the Western Territory to these
Colonies to sit still and tamely see a formidable foreign Power
possess themselves of it." The assembly expressed surprise that
the French would violate the treaty of peace and that they would
engage the services of a "merciless and rapacious Nation of
Indians" to assist them. An appropriation of £40,000 was made
for defense; this sum was to cover the expenses of raising and
equipping troops that were to be sent to the aid of Virginia,
supplying arms and ammunition to the frontier counties of North
Carolina, and strengthening Fort Johnston. A special tax was
levied to raise this money.

Washington's defeat at Great Meadows on May 25, 1754, prompted North Carolina to recruit a regiment of 750 men. It was expected that the cost of this expedition would be maintained by Virginia once the men passed into that province. When it was learned that North Carolina would have to maintain the regiment herself, the number was reduced to 450. These troops, under the leadership of Colonel James Innes, may well have been the first raised by any British colony in America to fight outside its own borders in behalf of a common cause and in the general defense. For their support the troops were obliged to use North Carolina currency, which was frowned upon outside the province, but they also drove with them herds of livestock to be sold to raise additional money for their maintenance. Unfortunately the demand was off, and they were unable to secure the necessary funds from this source. Some of the troops had to be dismissed and sent home because there was no way to support them. A company under the command of Caleb Grainger, however, saw service in New York and apparently suffered a few wounded. Major Edward Brice Dobbs and Captain Thomas Arbuthnot also commanded companies of North Carolina soldiers in service in New York. In these cases the colony of New York contributed funds for a portion of the support of these units.

Early in June Colonel Innes was placed in command of all the forces in Virginia. When Washington returned from the frontier, some of the men from North Carolina and some from Virginia filled his ranks, and under Colonel Innes the regiment was ordered again to the frontier. At Wills Creek, near the headwaters of the Potomac, Innes built Fort Cumberland. In a letter of September 4, 1754, to Captain Archibald Douglass, James Murray commented on conditions in the army: "You will have been informed e'er this, that our old friend Col. Innes has the chief command of the American forces along the Ohio, where he has an enemy alert in their preparations and notions, well supported, and only a few ragged men from these discontented colonies without money or provisions to oppose them. Thus he is like to gather few laurels on these mountains. He had better have stayed at home to gather lightwood."

Innes's Fort Cumberland was the point of rendezvous in 1755 for troops under Major General Edward Braddock, who had succeeded Governor Horatio Sharpe of Maryland as the British commander-in-chief of all forces in America. An attack was planned against Fort Duquesne on the Ohio River. With British troops reinforced by Americans, including some North Carolina Rangers and a company of eighty-four men under Major Edward Brice Dobbs, son of the new governor, Arthur Dobbs, Braddock marched rather slowly for nearly ten days. Finally Washington was able to persuade him to drop off some of his heavy baggage, reduce his force somewhat, and move faster. Growing overconfident, Braddock neglected to take adequate precautions against surprise, and his carelessness proved fatal. Trapped in a withering fire before reaching his destination, Braddock was mortally wounded, and many of his officers were killed and his force routed. The army retreated to Fort Cumberland, leaving the entire American frontier in the control of the French who immediately began courting the Indians for their support against the English. The British army did not make a very favorable impression on the Americans. James Murray said that by Braddock's conduct before the encounter with the French, he had shown himself to be "a bird ready for the snare." Another merchant, Henry Laurens of Charles Town, South Carolina, had some telling comments to make in a letter to a British friend on August 20, 1755:

Our Ministry would do well to prosecute a War in America with Americans. Only they are not frightened out of their wits at the sight of Indians which by our Accounts was the case with your English Veterans. We wish they had staid at home as the advantage the Enemy have gain'd by their shamefull behaviour will put us to ten times the inconveniency in this part of the World that their coming has been of service. We hope our other Commanders, Generals Shirley, Pepperhil, and Johnson will do something to counter ballance this mishap or it is much to be fear'd we shall loose our Interest with most of the Indians on the Continent which would extreamly embarass us and half ruin our Colonys, particularly this to support a War against them. The Creeks are very much courted by the French and seem to listen too attentively to their proposals. The Cherokees indeed have forbid them coming to them but as Indians are very fickle in their Minds we should fear if the French gain'd ground that they would become nutrals if they did not take up the Hatchett in their favour.

In 1754 the assembly had provided funds and authorized Governor Dobbs to recruit forces to protect the frontier of North Carolina. Since that time, Indian alarms along the frontier had become so threatening that the law had to be strengthened. Citing "horrid Cruelties and unparalleled Barbarities," the assembly appropriated additional funds in 1755 to help maintain "Forces for his Majesty's Service," to construct forts along the frontier, and to provide three companies of fifty men each for service in the northern colonies. In 1756 two companies for the protection of the North Carolina frontier were authorized. The practice became established, and one of the first acts of the assembly each year through 1761 was to provide funds for defense.

To construct a fort on the frontier a very young but capable man, Hugh Waddell, was chosen for the task. A site in the wilderness that would be of convenient access for families living along the farthest frontier of Rowan County was selected. The fort was begun late in 1755 and completed the next year. Named Fort Dobbs in honor of the governor, it was located near a tributary of the Yadkin River a few miles north of the present city of Statesville. It was described by an inspector for the assembly in 1757 as

a good and Substantial Building of the Dimentions following (that is to say) The Oblong Square fifty three feet by forty, the opposit Angles Twenty four feet and Twenty-two in height Twenty four and a half feet. . . . The Thickness of the Walls which are made of Oak Logs regularly Diminished from Sixteen Inches to Six, it contains three floors and there may be discharged from each floor at one and the same time about one hundred Musketts the same is beautifully scituated in the fork of Fourth Creek a Branch of the Yadkin River.

Heavy attacks by Indians, who were being urged on by the French, took place through the Shenandoah Valley in Virginia and along the Catawba River in North Carolina. Indians other than those native to the region were often responsible for the raids; Shawnees and Delawares frequently were recognized among the attackers. Throughout the region so many people were slain and taken prisoner that much of the frontier was abandoned. In Rowan County the number of taxables dropped from an estimated fifteen hundred in 1756 to just eight hundred three years later. Most of those who fled took up residence on the east side of the Yadkin River. In Salisbury when Chief Justice Peter Henley was holding court a group of heavily armed Catawba Indians entered the courtroom and "insulted" the judge. On another occasion several Indians came to William Morrison's mill, which was located several miles west of Fort Dobbs, and "Attempted to Frow a pail of water into his Meal Trough, and when he would prevent them they made many attempts to strek him with their guns over his head." Other people in the same area complained that Indians frequently stole meat, bread, meal, and clothes. "His method of making war is never open and manly," one witness wrote. "He skulks in ravines, behind rocks and trees; he creeps out in the night and sets fire to houses and barns; he shoots down, from behind a fence, the ploughman in his furrow; he scalps the women at the spring, and the children by the roadside, with their little hands full of berries."

In the spring of 1757 William Pitt assumed a new position of leadership in the British government and immediately began formulating plans to change the course of the war, which clearly had been going against the British. He reorganized the army and helped develop a new strategy for the war. An important feature of the plan for America included the capture of Fort Duquesne, and this objective was given to Brigadier General John Forbes. The expedition, fitted out in the spring of 1758, was nearly three times as large as Braddock's had been; it consisted of 1,200 Highlanders, 350 Royal Americans, 2,700 Pennsylvanians, 1,600

Virginians, 250 Marylanders, and 300 North Carolinians, some of whom were Indians. Roads were cut through the wilderness and several new forts constructed. In November the British forces were encamped at Loyal Hannon, about forty miles southeast of Fort Duquesne, and here they paused to debate whether to attack or go into winter quarters. General Forbes offered a reward of £500 to anyone who would capture an Indian with information as to conditions at Fort Duquesne. According to a report by Governor Dobbs, Major Waddell, who was in command of the contingent from North Carolina, "had great honor done him, being employed in all reconnoitering parties, and dressed and acted as an Indian." One of Waddell's men, Sergeant John Rogers, captured an Indian who had the much needed information. The French advantage had been considerably diminished by the loss of some positions to the north and by severely depleted supplies. In addition, the uncertainty of the intentions of the British had affected them, and their manpower was weakened by the desertion of many of their Indian allies. General Forbes determined to press on immediately, and at his approach the French blew up their fort and fled. The English constructed a new fort on the site and named it Fort Pitt; the town that grew up around it later became Pittsburgh.

The French made a final desperate effort to turn the Indians against the English, and they again succeeded in inflicting considerable damage on the North Carolina backcountry. The terms of a treaty between the French and the Cherokees, which had originally been drawn up in December 1756, were to be put into effect when the French thought proper. The time obviously had come after the loss of Fort Duquesne. One of the provisions of the treaty noted:

The English having declared War against the French for no other reason than that the French want to protect and defend the red Men their Children brethren and Allies, Cherokees ought to look upon the English as their Enemies; the more so as they themselves have all to fear from the English, who propose to build forts on the Territories with no other view than to make themselves Masters of them more easily, and to make Slaves of them, their Women and Children as well as their Old Men.

The Cherokees who signed the treaty agreed "that upon their return home, they will force all the English that may be there, to withdraw from off their Lands, and will destroy the House of Force they have already built there."

Before the end of 1758 roaming bands of Cherokees had driven a number of colonists off land they had settled years earlier along the Catawba River, and then in the following year they killed some people in Rowan County. Several "ranging companies" were engaged in patrolling the frontier, and an expedition against the Cherokees was carried out. Undaunted by the colonists' efforts, the Indians persisted in their raids. At the end of February 1760 Fort Dobbs was attacked by a party of at least sixty or seventy Indians who had been roaming about the fort for several days. The Moravian communities of Bethabara and Bethania were centers of refuge from Indian attack, particularly in 1760. Bethabara had a stockade that offered some protection, and approaching Indians were often frightened away by the ringing of a bell for religious services. The Wachovia diary for 1760 recorded that the Indians had a large camp about six miles from Bethania and a smaller one less than three miles away. Spies were seen in the neighborhood every night. It was reported in March that more than fifteen members of the community were slain; later the Moravians were told that an unsuccessful attempt had been made to take some of their neighbors prisoners. Apparently the watchman's horn frightened the kidnappers.

South Carolina officials called upon Major General Jeffery Amherst for aid in putting down the Indian troubles. Two regiments of British regulars from Pennsylvania under the command of Lieutenant Colonel Archibald Montgomerie arrived in Charles Town on April 1, 1760. Setting out on April 23 with his 1,200 regulars, 40 Catawba Indians, and about 450 South Carolina troops, the expedition destroyed five Indian towns on the way to the frontier. When the Cherokee ignored Montgomerie's call for a peace conference, he reluctantly

The fortified Moravian town of Bethabara, established in 1753. *Reproduced with permission of the Archives of the Moravian Church, Bethlehem, Pennsylvania.*

marched on the middle towns. In June the Cherokees ambushed the British army near Echoe in the southwestern corner of modern North Carolina. Even though their casualties were heavy, they were able to drive the Indians away. The burden of wounded men was so great, however, that the English were unable to pursue the fleeing enemy. After burning Echoe the army returned to the security of Fort Prince George on the South Carolina frontier. Montgomerie's exploits were considered most unsatisfactory by the South Carolinians who denied that he had accomplished anything other than stirring up the Cherokee. Montgomerie returned to Charles Town and then prepared to sail for New York in August. Reluctantly he left behind four companies for service in the west.

Neither the South Carolinians nor the Cherokees could agree on the best policy to follow. Some of the colonists wanted to try to make peace while others sought to achieve a decisive victory before negotiating a settlement to the hostilities. Some of the Cherokees were willing to seek peace, but others distrusted the whites. The government in Charles Town finally reached a "long laboriously labored answer." They called for more troops. James Grant, a veteran of Culloden and a capable soldier, was assigned the task with sixteen hundred regular troops. His orders were to remain until the Cherokees were defeated. Arriving in January 1761, he was soon joined by a regiment of South Carolinians and six hundred mounted rangers. He marched in the spring to Fort Prince George where he increased his force by the addition of about four hundred North Carolinians, some Virginians, and fifty Catawbas. Early in June, Grant entered the Cherokees' mountain stronghold and advanced to within a few miles of the battlefield where Montgomerie had been ambushed the year before. Here his force withstood a vigorous attack and succeeded in driving away the Indians. Pushing ahead, Grant burned fifteen Indian towns and destroyed nearly fourteen hundred acres of growing corn. After about a month of chasing Indians and driving them into the remote mountains, Grant returned to Fort Prince George to await the signing of a treaty of peace. After

much debate preliminary terms were agreed upon and signed on
September 23, 1761; final terms were signed on December 18 in
the name of all the colonies, but especially North Carolina and
Virginia.

With the end of the French and Indian War in 1763, France
ceased to be a menace in America. Spain, an ally of France near
the end of the war, relinquished her power in the New World
and ceded Florida to Great Britain. In March Lord Egremont,
who as secretary of state for the Southern Department supervised
the American colonies, wrote Governor Dobbs that he feared the
removal of the French and Spanish would alarm and increase
the jealousy of the southern Indians. He urged that steps be
taken to assure them that England had no "Design of extirpating
the whole Indian Race." King George III directed that the
governors of North Carolina, South Carolina, Virginia, and
Georgia meet as early as possible with his Indian agent at
Augusta, Georgia (or at any other convenient place) for a
conference with the Creeks, Choctaws, Cherokees, Chickasaws,
and Catawbas. The king also announced that he was sending
between £4,000 and £5,000 worth of goods that he intended
should be given to the Indians as a token of his goodwill and
friendship. The Indians were to be made to understand that the
king had forced the French and Spanish to move beyond the
Mississippi so that Englishmen and Indians could live in peace.
All past offenses of the Indians were to be forgiven because, as the
king insisted, he was confident the natives had been misled by
the French. A great trade was now to be opened up between the
English and their new friends, the Indians. As one means of
maintaining the peace, the king issued a proclamation on
October 7, 1763, which, among other things, declared that "all
the land and territories lying to the westward of the sources of the
rivers which fall into the sea from the west and northwest" should
be reserved for the Indians. Purchase of land or settlement
without prior royal approval was prohibited "on pain of our
displeasure." This document has been called "one of the most
important instruments of British policy concerning North America during the eighteenth century."

Dobbs and the other governors and John Stuart, Indian agent, met at Augusta with some seven hundred Indians representing the various tribes throughout the South. At the congress, which lasted from November 5 through November 10, 1763, lengthy discussions were held about various matters that had led to differences in the past. At the next session of the assembly Governor Dobbs reported that he had "the pleasure to inform you, that we have had the desired Success by having made a Treaty of Perpetual Peace and Alliance with the Chickesaw, Choctaw, upper and lower Creek, Cherokee and Catawba Indians and settled all their Claims and Boundaries with Virginia, North and South Carolina and Georgia to their Satisfaction, which I hope will make the peace with them permanent so that the Inhabitants of these Southern Colonies may be safe from any Indian Depredations for the future." It remained for Governor William Tryon, who succeeded Dobbs in 1765, to mark the line between white and Indian settlement in North Carolina.

In early August 1766 Tryon informed the Board of Trade that he was "of opinion this province is settling faster than any on the continent, last autumn and winter, upwards of one thousand wagons passed thro' Salisbury with families from the northward, to settle in this province chiefly; some few went to Georgia and Florida, but liked it so indifferently, that some of them have since returned." At the end of April he claimed that since the end of the war, settlements in North Carolina had extended more than seventy miles west of the site of abandoned Fort Dobbs. This would have placed colonists beyond the king's Proclamation Line of 1763, yet when Governor Tryon established a line in 1767 between Cherokee and white settlement it was a considerable distance east of the 1763 line. Settlement was prohibited from one mile east of this new line. The *Virginia Gazette* for May 7 commended this move, which was "a matter that seems very interesting to the frontiers of the southern colonies, as many acts of violence have been lately committed by that nation [the Cherokees] for want of proper restrictions as to their hunting grounds." A writer in England noted in 1767 that the war with France over lands beyond the mountains was won, but that the Proclamation of 1763 restricted the colonies to lands east of the "Apalachean" mountains just as the French had done. He said that this new and still forbidden territory was essential if the colonies were to grow and to produce material that could be used in trade with England. The restriction to the seaboard, he concluded as a good "mercantilist," meant that the colonies could produce only enough for themselves with no profit from which to purchase English manufactures. Whatever the reason, North Carolinians were soon risking the "displeasure" of the king by ignoring his proclamation.

The French and Indian War, aside from the obvious benefits of driving out the French and settling the Indian question, also contributed to the breaking down of many local prejudices due to North Carolina's isolation. The colony began to sense that she had much in common with the rest of British America and that her destiny might indeed be related to that of the other colonies. North Carolinians had fought under the command of officers from other colonies as well as those from North Carolina, and this experience under fire was soon to serve them well.

7

THE ECONOMIC ORDER

The abundance of land, the ease of acquiring it, and the relative scarcity of capital and labor were fundamental factors in determining the economy, social order, and political character of colonial North Carolina. Perhaps 95 percent of the people obtained their living from farming and industries closely associated with agriculture, such as the milling of flour and meal and the production of naval stores. Inadequate transportation and communication facilities created an imperative need for self-sufficiency; food, clothing, and shelter had to be obtained on the site. English and colonial leaders encouraged agricultural exports in line with mercantilist principles, demanding "returns" from the American "plantations" of goods that did not compete with British manufactures.

Everything affecting land tenure, such as the size of grants, registration of titles, accuracy of surveys, amount and mode of collection of quitrents, and laws governing forfeitures and escheats, was of vital concern to the people. In North Carolina, as in Virginia and several other colonies, the "headright" system of granting lands prevailed. In the early years of colonization this system provided that 100 acres of land were to be granted to each "undertaker," or head of a family, and 50 acres were to be granted to others. Later, the policy was to grant 50 acres to each individual who paid his way to the colony and settled there, provided he made improvements on his grant of land and fulfilled other conditions. Masters were allotted 50 acres for each servant or slave they brought in. The headright system prevailed throughout the colonial era, but after the royalization of the colony in 1729 the customary method of acquiring land was by purchase. Land was abundant and officials both in England and in the colony were so eager to get North Carolina settled that they often bypassed the headright system, and granted extravagantly large tracts to individuals and companies. During the first three decades of settlement many complaints were made about these huge grants. An Albemarle law of 1669, which prohibited any person from holding more than 660 acres in "one dividend" without special permission of the lords proprietors, was probably designed to keep a few favored individuals from monopolizing the good land. However, dispensation from the proprietors was rather easy to obtain and some tremendous grants were made, notably to governors, members of the council, and other "persons of influence." In the lower Cape Fear Valley "King Roger" Moore had more than 10,000 acres and other members of his family held grants also running into the thousands of acres. In Bertie County Thomas Pollock had one plantation of 40,000 acres. Among others holding extensive grants were Governor George Burrington, Edward Moseley, Cullen Pollock, Governor Gabriel Johnston, Henry McCulloh, and Governor Arthur Dobbs. The Moravian Brethren in Wachovia in 1752 received nineteen deeds for a total of 98,985 acres.

The purchase of land at prices as low as £15 sterling per hundred acres shortly before the Revolution, and the law of primogeniture, by which all the land of those dying intestate descended to the oldest son, helped to build up and perpetuate large estates. The practice of entails, whereby the inheritance of property was restricted to the owner's lineal descendants, made it possible to prevent the division of large estates, and this tended to preserve vast amounts of land within the same family. But the existence of some very large landholdings did not mean that most or even many of the people were large planters. As a matter of fact, the great majority of North Carolinians were small landholders who lived on and cultivated their own soil. At the outbreak of the American Revolution the wealthiest 10 percent of the people in North Carolina owned about 40 percent of the property, whereas in Virginia and South Carolina this figure was between 50 and 60 percent. The middle class of small farmers constituted a majority of the white population. Thus North Carolina was not at all typical of the South, even though the large size of some plantations, the presence of slaves, and the almost exclusively rural character of the population ranked it as decisively Southern.

Land was not held in "fee simple," but a quitrent was due, although frequently it was not paid. The usual rent prior to 1730 was two shillings per hundred acres on "rental land" and one shilling per hundred acres on "purchase land." After 1730 the rates were doubled. These rents were not based on the value of the land or the ability of the owner to pay, and so it is not surprising that they were always odious to the colonists and poorly collected. North Carolina landholders were also handicapped by the inaccuracies of land surveys and the marking of boundaries. Such phrases in deeds as "beginning at a sweet gum on the east side of long pine branch and running to a pine tree on the west side of White Oak Swamp," sometimes led to confusion, controversy, and litigation. But there were other problems of greater magnitude confronting the North Carolina farmer; among the most important of these were the producing and marketing of crops, the prevention of soil exhaustion, the extermination of vermin and pests, and the overproduction of farm products and resultant falling prices.

Agricultural practices in North Carolina were generally backward and unscientific, much as they were in most parts of colonial America. Land was tilled year after year until the soil was exhausted, then new ground was cleared and cultivated. There was little or no crop rotation; barnyard manures were not used, commercial fertilizers were unknown, and leguminous crops, or "green manures," were seldom employed. Land was so abundant and cheap that it was considered easier and more profitable to clear new ground than to increase the productivity of old fields. This was particularly true in the case of tobacco, which was supposed to grow best on "fresh lands." Almost all contemporary writers commented about the slovenly practices of the North Carolina farmers. One declared that the farmers "depend altogether upon the Liberality of Nature; without endeavoring to improve its Gifts by Art or Industry. They sponge upon the Blessings of a Warm Sun and a fruitful Soil and almost grutch the pains of gathering."

There were many handicaps to good farming, not the least of which was an inadequate supply of tools and implements. There was a scarcity of skilled artisans who could make these, and the difficulty and expense of importing them made their acquisition almost prohibitive. Plows were very scarce; Bishop Spangenberg reported that on his trip from Edenton to the Blue Ridge mountains in 1752, he saw "not one plough nor any sign of one." What plows the farmers did have were very crude affairs, "something like a shovel pulled through the earth." Agriculture was also retarded by the failure of the farmers to drain their lands properly, to pay adequate attention to seed selection, to plow correctly, and, as one contemporary wrote, to "keeping the hillocks clean from weeds." Another retarding factor was the "conventional method of cropping," which was passed on from father to son. Prevalent superstitions, which led farmers to plow land and to plant and harvest crops according to the "sign of the moon," also contributed to the perpetuation of primitive agricultural practices.

The farmer suffered from droughts, floods, hailstorms, and other vagaries of nature. One of his greatest problems was that of pests (such as worms, bugs, and weevils) and vermin (particularly crows, wild pigeons, wild turkeys, foxes, and bears). The vermin problem was so critical that Governor Johnston suggested to the 1756 assembly: "For the better preserving your Cattle, Corn, and other grains, I believe you will find it necessary to provide a sufficient reward for the Killing of Vermin which I am informed have done great Mischief in most parts of the Province." The assembly, acting on his advice, passed a law that offered rewards for the "scalps" of various destructive animals.

Agricultural legislation was discussed by practically every assembly, and many laws were passed to promote various aspects of farming. This is not surprising since the vast majority of legislators were farmers or planters. Bounties were offered for the production of flax, hemp, indigo, silk, and several other articles. The production of wheat and tobacco were also encouraged by law. In 1715 sixteen commodities, most of them farm products, were authorized as legal tender; a later law extended this list of "commodity money" to twenty-two products. All of the principal farm crops were included on the list and this tended to stabilize the prices of these articles, though the primary reason for the passage of the law was the dearth of specie in the province. Land grants, the right to use timber from adjacent lands, and exemption from public taxes and militia service, were given in exchange for the operation of mills for grinding grain as well as for sawmills. Scores of laws were passed requiring the inspection and grading of tobacco, pork, naval stores, and other exports. It was also made illegal to ship articles other than those of the best grade. Instead of "stock laws," such as exist today, there was legislation requiring that fields be fenced against livestock and wild animals. Laws were also enacted providing for the branding and marking of horses, cattle, and hogs; for the regulating of the shipment of hides; and for the improving of livestock breeding.

At first North Carolina farmers, like those in other colonies, experimented with a variety of European crops. Olives, silk, French grapes, and a few others failed; wheat, oats, rye, and some others succeeded. The settlers also adopted many Indian crops, notably maize or Indian corn, tobacco, different varieties of beans and peas, white potatoes, and sweet potatoes. The major crops of the colony were tobacco, corn, wheat, peas and beans, and rice.

Tobacco became the leading export or "money crop" of the colony and was grown extensively in the Albemarle Sound area, in the Roanoke River Valley, and later in Granville and other counties bordering Virginia. The culture of tobacco—preparation of the seed beds, transplanting, worming, priming, and suckering—was done in much the same way as it is today. The tobacco was of the burley type, dark in color and heavy in texture, and, in contrast with the present flue-cured methods, it was air-cured or sun-cured—a process taking from five to six weeks; after this the tobacco was taken down, the leaves were stripped off the stalks, and then it was sorted and packed into hogsheads for shipment. The hogsheads were then hauled or rolled to the nearest landing on a navigable stream and put on board ship, usually destined for England. North Carolina legislation required that all tobacco for export be packed in hogsheads containing a minimum of a thousand pounds each and that the tobacco be approved by an official inspector. The growth of tobacco exports was considerable; in 1753, 100,000 pounds were shipped from North Carolina ports and by 1772 this figure had climbed to more than 1,500,000 pounds. These figures do not represent the total export for the colony, since a great deal of North Carolina's tobacco was shipped through Virginia ports. Indeed, one of the most serious economic problems in the colony was that of overproduction of tobacco and resultant falling prices. As early as 1669 "tobacco stinting" negotiations were carried on between the governor of Albemarle County and the governors of Virginia and Maryland. However, these early efforts at intercolonial regulation of tobacco production failed as did the various attempts of the North Carolina assembly to boost tobacco prices by regulating acreages.

Subsistence crops were of first importance to the colonial farmer, and of these corn came nearest to fulfilling the food requirements of both man and beast. The principal crop of North Carolina was corn, a very hardy plant that could be grown in almost any kind of soil and in any kind of climate. Practice in the cultivation of corn varied, but in the main the work was performed by hand. It was not until the close of the colonial era that the use of plows and draft animals, chiefly horses and oxen, became common. Like the Indians, the farmer planted his corn in hills, which were spaced at intervals of about three feet, with little regard to alignment in rows. These hills were dug up with hoes, and, if available, a fish was put in each hill as a fertilizer. From six to ten grains were planted in each hill, and later this was thinned down to two or three stalks. During the growing season, suckers were pulled from the corn, and the hoe was used to draw up dirt around the stalk. The Indian practice of planting beans, peas, squashes, and melons with the corn was also widely followed. What made corn a particularly attractive crop was that, unlike the cultivation of wheat and other cereals, land did not have to be completely cleared or even plowed before planting. In addition, its yield per acre was much greater than that of wheat, and the growing and maturing season was shorter than that of tobacco or cotton. Corn also offered the special advantage that all parts of the plant could be used: the ear for food, fodder and tops for forage for livestock, the husks or shucks for crude mattresses, and the grain for making corn liquor. Despite the fact that corn was not considered a money crop, some farmers, especially the large planters, produced a surplus for market. The exports of corn in the late colonial period, usually to the West Indies, were quite large: 117,389 bushels in 1768 and 176,742 bushels in 1772.

Wheat was cultivated in the colony almost from the beginning. At first it was grown in relatively small quantities in the Albemarle Sound region, but by the middle of the eighteenth century its production had spread northward into the counties along the Virginia border and southward into the Cape Fear Valley. In 1764 Governor Dobbs reported that the Cape Fear region was supplying its own wheat needs and had exported several hundred barrels of flour to the West Indies. By the close of the colonial era wheat production had become quite extensive throughout the Piedmont area. The crop was not grown primarily for bread (corn was used for that); instead, it was raised specifically for its commercial value. In 1772 more than 13,000 bushels of wheat were exported from the colony. Though the yield of wheat was good, it was more difficult to grow than many other crops. First of all, it needed cleared land, and then the soil had to be plowed before the seeds could be planted. In the absence of wheat drills, the seed was sown by hand, and this was always a wasteful method. The growing season was relatively long, and the stalks were subject to many pests, particularly rust and Hessian flies. Harvesting was also a problem because in the absence of reapers and combines, the grain had to be cut with primitive sickles or scythes. A wheat cradle finally came into use shortly before the Revolution. Separating the grain from the chaff (threshing) was done with a wooden flail throughout most of the colonial era. Even in later years the process remained quite primitive with horses or oxen being used to trample out the grain.

Efforts were made by both British and colonial authorities to develop the indigo industry. The culture of this crop was delimited by its peculiar climatic requirement and by its vulnerability to plagues of grasshoppers and caterpillars and to the ravages of drought. Therefore, in spite of the high British bounty for the production of indigo, from which blue dye was made, the colony never became a large producer. Nearly all of North Carolina indigo production was limited to the Brunswick-Wilmington area. The number of pounds of indigo exported from North Carolina increased from a scant 646 in 1768 to a still rather small amount of 1,304 in 1772.

The soil and climate of North Carolina were suitable for the production of hemp (from which rope was made) and of flax (from which linen was made). Although the legislature offered bounties for the production of flax and hemp, the development of these two crops had not passed the experimental stage prior to the American Revolution.

The soils of the coastal area of North Carolina were suited to both the upland and lowland varieties of rice, and some of each was grown in the Lower Cape Fear. In some years the export of this cereal ran as high as two thousand barrels; but rice never became a crop of major importance in the colony. Barley, oats, rye, and buckwheat were the most important of the other cereals grown in the colony. A Moravian diarist noted in 1764 that "rye is more used in the distillery than for bread."

The fine adaptability of the soil and climate of North Carolina for the production of peas and beans was recognized early, and their production attained some commercial importance. They were not in the category of "enumerated articles," which had to be shipped directly to England, but they were listed in the general category of "provisions," which the colony exported principally to the West Indies. Of the vegetables grown for domestic consumption, the sweet potato proved to be of the greatest value to the settlers. It was used as a food for man and beast, and it was relished by both. Among other vegetables grown were carrots, leeks, turnips, squashes, watermelons, cantaloupes, pumpkins, Irish potatoes, artichokes, radishes, beets, onions, shallots, chives, cucumbers, lettuce, cabbage, spinach, parsley, asparagus, rhubarb, cress, and "love apples" or tomatoes (used for ornamentation only). Honey, wine, sorghum, hops, and timothy grass were also produced.

By the close of the colonial era all of the common English fruit trees had been introduced into North Carolina, where they thrived. The anonymous author of *American Husbandry* (London, 1775) said: "Fruit in none of the colonies is in greater plenty [than in North Carolina], or finer in flavour; . . . peaches . . . are so plentiful that the major part of the crop goes to the hogs." Other fruits grown in the colony included apples, pears, plums, figs, cherries, damsons, quinces, nectarines, and grapes of various kinds. Some of these fruits were native to the region, and others, like the fig and peach, were introduced by the settlers. A great variety of berries grew wild in North Carolina and made up an important part of the harvest. Of these, the most significant were blackberries, dewberries, strawberries, raspberries, and huckle-berries.

Most of the North Carolina farmers had an adequate supply of livestock and cattle, though these were not of the best quality. The principal draft animal, the ox, was used for such heavy work as plowing and hauling. The horse, also an indispensable animal, was employed primarily for riding and pulling vehicles, though it is true that some were used for heavier work in the fields and for the transportation of goods to and from market. There were few or no mules in the colony. Sheep were raised in sufficient number to provide considerable quantities of wool for domestic use and mutton for the table. Most of the farmers had milk cows, beef cattle, hogs, chickens, geese and other kinds of fowl. The livestock and cattle, especially the latter, were frequently of the scrub variety and smaller than our present breeds. No selective improvement in the breeds was possible because of the prevalent practice of allowing the animals to run at large in the woods. Horses and cattle were branded by owners and then turned loose to make their own way. This sort of thing worked well enough in the summer, but in winter the stock suffered from the lack of food to such a serious extent that by spring they were "so reduced by hunger and cold that they could hardly recover before fall." With the settlement of the Cape Fear Valley and the Piedmont about the middle of the eighteenth century there was a great increase in the quantity and quality of stock, especially of beef cattle. Extant records reveal that large herds were rare and that only about twenty-five planters owned herds of more than a hundred head and that there were no holdings of more than three hundred head. The average number of cattle owned varied from six to sixteen head. A system of ranching, annual roundups at "cowpens," and branding followed by "long drives" to the coast, to Charles Town, to Virginia markets, and to points as far away as Philadelphia, was the forerunner of the later cattle industry that was to characterize the West. Like the Western cattlemen of the nineteenth century, colonial farmers faced the problem of cattle rustling. All owners were required by law to brand their livestock and cattle, but this did not eliminate thievery. The problem of "trespass of livestock" was also serious in many parts of the colony. For example, in a sixteen-year period in Granville County almost a third of the cases brought before the county court involved this offense.

"Hogs in prodigious numbers," their ears notched with their owner's mark, roamed the unfenced woods. They lived primarily on mast until five or six weeks before slaughter, at which time they were penned and fed on corn in order to "harden their meat." Enormous quantities of pork were consumed by the people, probably to the injury of their health. Large droves of hogs, sometimes as many as five hundred, were driven on foot to markets in Virginia, or even Pennsylvania. In 1733, the governor of Virginia estimated "that 50,000 fat hogs are supposed to be driven into Virginia each year," but this probably was a great exaggeration. Vast quantities of salt pork were exported to the West Indies, and about one-eighth of the total pork and beef shipments from the colonies came from North Carolina.

The colony developed two extensive commercialized industries, or manufactures, for export. These were naval stores (tar, pitch, rosin, and turpentine) and lumber products (chiefly boards, barrels, staves, and shingles). The most valuable of the colony's exports were naval stores, and this was the only industry in which North Carolina held first place among the English colonies. It has been estimated that seven-tenths of the tar, more than one-half of the turpentine, and one-fifth of the pitch exported to England from her colonies was produced in North Carolina. At the beginning of the eighteenth century England was at war, and her navy and merchant marine were at the mercy of the monopolistic Swedish Tar Company in Stockholm. Production in the colonies of essential naval stores would reduce England's dependency on Sweden, and any excess could be reexported to help England gain a favorable balance of trade. In line with the mercantilist philosophy of making England self-sufficient and independent of "enemy nations," Parliament passed the Naval Stores Bounty Act of 1705, authorizing the payment of attractive subsidies on tar, pitch, rosin, and turpentine. In 1706 these articles were placed on the enumerated list to guarantee that they would be shipped only to England.

In response to the enormous demand and the substantial bounties, the production of naval stores grew rapidly. Farmers quickly discovered that the industry complemented ordinary farm work. When the soil was too wet to cultivate, farmers could work in the pine woods; the use of the pines for making tar also aided the farmer in clearing the land for cultivation; and slaves

Engraving depicting a tar kiln.

could be employed in the pine forests during the winter when they were not needed in the fields. Consequently a region that had earlier been considered "hardly fit for human habitation" became the center of an important industry, and the vast forests of pine trees came to be the greatest source of income to the people. In addition, since all these naval stores were shipped in barrels or hogsheads, an extensive cooperage (barrel making) industry developed.

From the very beginning of the exportation of tar from North Carolina to England, members of the Navy Board insisted that it was not as good quality as the tar that was imported from the Baltic area. They complained that it contained sand, chips, and other dross, and that it had a "burning quality" which, according to British experts, was due to improper and hurried methods of manufacture. In 1719 Parliament passed a law insisting on the inspection of all colonial tar, and eventually the adoption of "the Swedish method of production" was demanded. Apparently, however, there was little change in the methods of production throughout the colonial era, though the North Carolina legislature of 1751 did make an effort to improve the quality of naval stores by the passage of its own inspection law. Even in the face of England's complaints about the quality of North Carolina naval stores, the colony shipped vast quantities to the mother country and considerable amounts coastwise to New England. It is noteworthy that the peak year of exports of naval stores to England, both in quantity and monetary value, was 1775–1776, the first year of the American Revolution. More than £94,000 worth of tar, pitch, and turpentine were shipped to England in that year as compared with a scant £8,000 the following year. The importance of these stores to England may afford the chief explanation of the British plans to seize control of North Carolina early in the Revolution.

Almost from the beginning of colonization the lumber industry was encouraged by local and colonial authorities in the form of land grants, exemption from taxes and military service, and various other favors. By the middle of the eighteenth century, perhaps earlier, lumbering had assumed commercial proportions. It was reported in 1766 that the Cape Fear Valley alone had more than fifty sawmills in operation, many of which were producing materials for shipment to England, the British West Indies, and other markets. The lumber industry was more widespread than that of naval stores and it probably outranked it in monetary value. In every community in the colony there was a great demand for wood to build houses, barns, and other buildings, as well as for making furniture, farm implements, and various other items for use in the home and on the farm. Practically all articles, as required by law, were exported in casks, barrels, hogsheads, or some other kind of wooden container. In some years as many as a hundred thousand barrels were used for shipment of naval stores alone; perhaps half again this number were used for the exportation of salt pork, beef, provisions (corn, peas, beans), and other products. The chief lumber exports were barrel staves, headings, and hoops of oak; shingles, largely from cypress; and boards, mainly of pine. The enormous growth in the industry is suggested by this example: in 1753 the colony exported two and a half million shingles, in 1772 the figure had increased to more than seven and a half million. Two-fifths of the shingles, one-seventh of the barrel staves, and one-eleventh of the pine boards exported from England's continental colonies were shipped from North Carolina. In terms of financial value, about one-seventh of the total lumber products from the continental colonies originated in North Carolina.

The records, relating to potash, which is made from the ashes of oak and other hardwoods, are meager, although there are many contemporary references to interest in its production. England was eager to produce potash and pearlash, a refined potash, from the colonies in order to end her dependence upon the Baltic countries. In 1736 Henry McCulloh proposed to send over "a considerable number of Workmen to carry on the Pott Ash trade," but this experiment was not successful and the potash industry never became a large one.

Shipbuilding was not nearly the major industry in North

Carolina that it had become in Massachusetts and some of the other more commercial colonies. Even during one of the colony's most prosperous periods, from 1769 to 1772, only twenty-five small ships were built. Of the 146 clearing Port Roanoke in the year ending April 5, 1772, only 21 were built in North Carolina.

The iron industry was also rather poorly developed in North Carolina. The Board of Trade reported as late as 1764 that "no forges or bloomeries were yet erected, because of sloth or poverty." Four years later two furnaces were in operation and there were prospects for the development of a third.

North Carolina's external trade was probably aided more than it was restricted by the various British navigation acts, especially the Staple Act of 1663 and the Plantation Duty Act of 1673. These laws required that (1) all trade between England and her colonies be carried only in British or British colonial vessels; (2) all European goods exported to the colonies be shipped via England; and (3) all enumerated articles, which included tobacco, be exported from the colony only to British ports. The first of these so-called restrictions actually stimulated shipbuilding and the production of naval stores; the second had very little effect one way or the other; and the third profited the colony by guaranteeing a market for two of its major products, naval stores and tobacco. The colonial legislature actually passed more laws regulating North Carolina trade than did Parliament. There were scores of legislative enactments regulating the duties and fees of pilots, providing for the marking of channels, and requiring the inspection of all exported articles. For revenue purposes tariff duties were levied on such imports as rum and wine. A tariff was also levied on rice in order to protect this developing industry from competition with South Carolina. The lax enforcement of these provincial regulations unquestionably injured North Carolina's trade and was a subject of constant complaint by the governors. Governor Tryon investigated the matter but was finally forced to admit "that the most probable method an Inspector can take to lose his office is being faithful and diligent in the execution of it." The navigation acts and other British trade laws were probably better enforced than the colony's own regulations because of the zeal of British customs officials, who were required to keep a record of exports and imports, to make lists of all ships entering and clearing, and to examine certificates of bonds and ship registration. Their colonial counterparts in no way shared their enthusiasm or determination.

Trade of the backcountry with the outside world was relatively small because of the lack of navigable rivers, slow and expensive land transportation, the paucity of towns, and the scarcity of merchants. Salisbury was not begun until 1755, and then it had only a courthouse and eight "crude dwellings." Charlotte was described as late as 1771 as "an inconsiderable place hardly deserving the name of village." Hillsborough, one of the largest towns in the Piedmont, had only about forty inhabitants as late as 1764. Salem, founded in 1766, was probably the largest town in the area and certainly the chief commercial center. For many years there was very little trade between the Piedmont and Coastal Plain areas. The long and expensive trips to the markets in South Carolina, Virginia, and Pennsylvania led the Moravians and the other shippers of the Piedmont to seek markets closer to home. The merchants of Cross Creek and Wilmington welcomed the effort to divert trade to their communities and heartily supported laws to construct east-west roads. The chief exports of the backcountry were deerskins, hides, cattle, corn, meal, wheat and flour, butter, flax, hemp, and herbs. The major imports of this region were manufactured goods, especially cloth and clothing, kitchen and other household articles, farm implements, rum, and such essentials as salt, sugar, and molasses.

In contrast with the scattered merchants in the backcountry, the towns of the Coastal Plain had a large number of merchants, many of whom were important in the economic, social, religious, and political life of the colony. The colonial merchant was not a specialist; typically he was a general merchant who was usually also engaged in other economic pursuits. Many of them were both wholesalers and retailers; many were planter-merchants; some owned and operated ships; and a number who were money lenders were the main source of credit in their community. The firm of John Hamilton and Company, the largest house operating in North Carolina and perhaps in the whole South, owned many stores and warehouses; held a great variety of local and imported goods, ships, and wagons; operated a cooperage works, a hatter's shop, and a blacksmith shop; and in addition also owned numerous plantations, horses, cattle, and hogs. However, the company probably netted only about £4,000 to £5,000 sterling annually, which was a very small profit considering the nature and extent of the firm's business. Risks incidental to shipping, bad debts, overproduction of goods, unsystematic purchasing by merchants, and other economic factors tended to hold profits to a minimum.

Most of the merchants tried to operate on a cash basis, and some even advertised that they would not give credit: "In God we trust, all others pay cash." However, the scarcity of specie, the use of produce or "country pay" in the purchase of goods, and the frailties of human nature made cash transactions rare. Often the merchants became creditors of the planters and the farmers. At the same time, many merchants were themselves debtors to merchants in Great Britain and "carried on very extensive business without any funds of their own but altogether upon the credit which they had abroad." British merchants sold them goods on credit and thus indirectly were responsible for the financing of various local enterprises. The merchants in North Carolina, as in other colonies, were usually behind in payments to their British creditors.

Specie or hard money was extremely scarce in North Carolina since the settlers brought little of it with them and no coins were minted in the colony. Spanish milled dollars and pieces of eight (one-eighth of a dollar), and other Spanish, French, and Portuguese coins found their way into North Carolina as a result of trade with the West Indies, but the balance of trade was frequently against the colony. Consequently, the meager supply of specie that did exist was constantly being drained. To cope with this problem the colonists resorted to several expedients, such as the legalization of commodity money and the issuance of paper currency. Neither of these alternatives was ever wholly satisfactory. Gresham's law tended to operate, and people paid debts and other obligations with cheap currency and inferior commodities, thus tending to drive the dear money into hiding.

The shortage of specie did not affect the common man in North Carolina. He lived a simple life, producing almost everything he needed for his own family and employing barter as a method of exchange when he had to go beyond his own resources. The wealth of the colony, largely concentrated in the east, took the form of large plantations, town property, ships, and mercantile establishments. Except for clergymen, schoolteachers, an occasional lawyer, and a rare physician, the professions, too, were confined to the seaboard region. The Piedmont and western sections improved economically during the half-century preceding the Revolution, as new lands were cleared and settlement increased; but the income of the western regions never equalled that of the east. The prosperity of both sections improved, but the gap between them remained constant throughout most of the eighteenth century.

Colonial North Carolina had a large number of roads, but, in the language of one traveler, "good roads, like angel's visits, were few and far between." As long as population was confined to the eastern fringe of the colony, as it was during the first half-century of settlement, about the only roads to be built were those that "led to the nearest landing." The proximity of early settlements to watercourses, the sparseness of population, the lack of capital, the general aversion to taxes, the inertia of the people, and other factors delayed the development of an effective highway system. The first roads in the colony were Indian trails or "trading paths," and these were usually well located along the shortest and best routes. As population grew and expanded, these narrow trails were widened and deepened by constant use, and some of them were made into roads by order of the provincial or local authorities. The necessity for road building became increasingly apparent as more and more settlers moved into the backcountry and away from navigable streams. Most of the road legislation and the subsequent road building followed the transfer of the colony to the Crown in 1729. Almost every session of the legislature after that date considered the transportation problem, and scores of road laws were passed. The act of 1764 was the most detailed of these and it empowered county courts "to order the laying out of Public Roads, and establish and settle Ferries, and to appoint where Bridges shall be built, for the Use and Ease of the Inhabitants of this Province; and to clear navigable Rivers and Creeks." The court was authorized to name "Overseers of the Highways or Roads," who were to summon all male taxables, ages sixteen to sixty, to work a certain number of days each year. If this and other road laws had been rigidly enforced, North Carolina would certainly have developed a very good road system. But such was not the case. A visitor from Scotland, Janet Schaw, writing in the 1770s, declared that "the only making they bestow upon the roads in the flat part of the country is cutting out the trees to the necessary breadth, in as even a line as they can, and where the ground is wet, they make a small ditch on either side." The "necessary breadth" was only a few feet, never more than eight. In some cases, tree stumps and roots were left in the road, making travel extremely hazardous. Roads were described by contemporary travelers as "poor," "wretched," "exceeding bad," "miserable," and "very dusty in summer and very muddy in winter." The roads were inadequately marked, and many travelers lost their way because of the lack of signposts.

The last two decades of the colonial era witnessed a great increase in the number of roads and perhaps a slight improvement in their quality. The maps of this period show a network of roads leading from Virginia to South Carolina. There were few east-west roads, chiefly because of the northwest-southeast direction of the rivers, and the natural connection of the backcountry with Virginia and South Carolina. The Great Trading Path, an old Occoneechee trail, from the sound region to the foot of the

mountains was rough and circuitous. The most traveled road in
North Carolina in the late colonial period was the Great Wagon
Road from Philadelphia over which thousands of Scotch-Irish
and Germans moved from Pennsylvania, New Jersey, Maryland,
and Virginia into the Carolina Piedmont.

In some respects the sounds and rivers handicapped land
transportation more than the bad roads themselves. There were
never enough bridges and ferries to develop an effective system.
The ferries, in particular, were inadequate, inconvenient, and
expensive. Travelers were usually at the mercy of the ferry
keepers, especially if they reached a ferry after nightfall. They
would most likely be forced to spend the night in the woods until
the ferry keeper arrived the next morning. The absence of
bridges or ferries over some creeks and rivers made a traveler risk
his life "fording the shallows."

The horse was the indispensable animal for travel and
transport. People rode horseback for long distances, occasionally
as much as fifty miles a day, with the average being nearer thirty.
That the colonial North Carolinians, especially the planters,
were a people on horseback is revealed by the numerous
references to saddles in wills and inventories of the time. Still,
travel on foot remained the surest and safest, though slowest,
form of travel, and the people often walked great distances. It
was reported that a group of Moravians walked from Bethlehem,
Pennsylvania, to the Wachovia settlement in North Carolina, a
distance of over four hundred miles.

Many of the wealthier people had gigs, chairs, chariots,
coaches, phaetons, and post-chaises. These were drawn by horses,
and the speed of travel depended on the nature of the road, the
type of vehicle, the strength of the horse, and the capability of the
driver. There are a few references to coaches traveling as far as
thirty or forty miles a day, but the average distance was probably
not more than twenty miles. Two-wheeled carts and four-
wheeled wagons were used for the transport of some goods,
though the great bulk of tobacco, naval stores, provisions, and
other articles of export reached their point of shipment packed in

a hogshead or other container that was rolled to the nearest landing or warehouse.

It was not only the bad roads and paucity of bridges and ferries that inhibited settlers in North Carolina from traveling about; lodgings and other accommodations along the roads were few and usually of very poor quality. Wagoners often spent the nights "upon dry leaves on the ground with the feet towards a large fire, which they make by the road side wherever night overtakes them, and are covered only with a blanket." Travelers fortunate enough to obtain lodging in the home of a planter or prosperous farmer usually fared well; those who stopped at the homes of the "meaner sort" usually found miserable conditions; and those who stayed at the "ordinaries," also called inns or taverns, faced a thoroughly wretched affair.

North Carolina had many inland waterways that were suitable for small craft and these became important arteries of travel and trade, especially in the Coastal Plain area. Here most of the important towns and plantations were located on or near navigable waters. Various types of craft were used to ply these waters: canoes, usually made of hollowed logs, were propelled by paddles or oars; periaugers, which were made and propelled like canoes, were much larger and heavier; scows and flatboats, which were propelled by poles, were used largely for transporting freight. Shallops, sloops, and yawls were also used on the frequently crooked and uncharted channels. Sand bars, fish dams, logs, and other obstructions in the streams caused many accidents, and this led to the passage of legislation requiring the overseers of roads and their companies of men to clear the streams of obstructions and otherwise improve river channels. Like the numerous laws concerning road maintenance and construction, these provisions were not enforced, and the difficulties of transportation became so serious that inland waterways, with the exception of those in a small portion of the extreme eastern region, had ceased to be of major importance by the close of the colonial era. The leading arteries of trade and travel in the Piedmont and mountain regions were the river valleys rather than the swift and rocky rivers themselves, which were of little or no value for navigation.

The handicap of a dangerous coastline and the lack of good harbors did not prevent the development of foreign and coastwise trade, though North Carolina's commerce was certainly far below that of Virginia, South Carolina, and several other colonies. The most common vessels trading in the coastal waters were the two-masted schooner and the one-masted sloop, ships usually of less than 50 tons capacity. The two-masted brig or brigantine of about 100 tons burden was perhaps the major carrier of naval stores, especially from the ports of Brunswick, Roanoke, and Beaufort. The largest ships operating along the coast were the three-masted "ship," and the two-masted snow, vessels averaging from 150 to 200 tons burden. The speed of these sailing craft was slow. A trip from North Carolina to England took from three to eight weeks; a journey up to New York took from four to five days. Many of the ships carried passengers as well as freight, and the conditions on board were usually crowded, unsanitary, and uncomfortable. In 1762 a group of Moravians sailed from Philadelphia to Wilmington on a twenty-three ton sloop that had "a tiny cabin in which at a pinch six Sisters can sleep, but the rest, including the Captain and two sailors, must do the best they can in the hold, on top of the barrels and boxes."

Means of communication within the colony and between the colony and Europe were slow, uncertain, and expensive. Not until near the end of the colonial era was there anything like an organized postal system. Within the colony, letters and messages were delivered in a variety of ways: by ship captains, merchants, friends, travelers, private messengers, Indians—in fact, by just about anyone who was going somewhere near the addressee. Letters to and from Europe were carried by captains of private vessels, for no government packets had as yet been established. It was common practice in England, for example, for ships sailing to America to hang up a bag in an advertised coffeehouse for letters. By custom, not law, the fee was a penny for a single letter, two pence for a double letter (that is, one containing more than one sheet), and two pence for a package.

Legally the regulation of mail within the colony was a function of the legislature, and as early as 1715 a law was passed ordering that all "public despatches" be carried promptly from plantation to plantation until they reached their ultimate destination, under penalty of £5 sterling for each default. This law made no provision for private letters and was ineffective as to public despatches, which were usually sent by private messengers. In 1755 the legislature, on recommendation of Governor Dobbs, made an agreement with James Davis, the public printer and newspaper publisher in New Bern, by which for a specified sum to be paid annually he "would forward public despatches to all parts of the province" and send messengers every fifteen days from New Bern and Wilmington to Suffolk, Virginia, and bring back official communications. The delivery of private letters seems to have been optional. In 1757 Davis and two other men were appointed for a term of one year to "carry the post" every two weeks between Wilmington and Suffolk. This arrangement was continued in 1758, with Davis having the entire contract.

Governor Tryon was disturbed about the colony's poor postal service and repeatedly urged the legislature to increase appropriations and take other measures to improve the system. In 1764 he succeeded in getting a legislative appropriation of £67, but this sum was thoroughly inadequate to do the job. For years Tryon continued to lodge bitter complaints "that the chain of communication through the Continent should be broke within this provience." His efforts finally met with a modicum of success and, writing in 1771, he informed the legislature that the postmaster general for the colonies had "for some months passed opened a communication by post, between the Southern and Northern Provinces on this Continent, by establishing a regular intercourse between Charles Town and Suffolk, in Virginia." Hugh Finlay, who had spent over three months in North Carolina in 1774 investigating the postal system for British authorities, found that "the only post road in the province was the one which ran through Edenton, Bath, New Bern, and Wilmington and that each of these towns had a postmaster." Finlay arranged for a fortnightly mail service between Wilmington and Cross Creek, and he suggested many improvements in the postal system. None of his recommendations were followed and mail service continued to be irregular, slow, and unsatisfactory.

Poor and inadequate systems of communication and transportation were major factors contributing to the persistent backwardness of North Carolina in the seventeenth and eighteenth centuries. Throughout most of its colonial history, North Carolina remained more isolated than most of the older provinces. The great emphasis placed on farming, the scarcity of capital and skilled labor, the lack of a good domestic market, and high freight rates on both exports and imports, were among the leading causes that helped to retard the development of commercialized industry in colonial North Carolina. These very factors, plus the great bounty of raw materials and the abundance of unskilled laborers, especially women and children, tended to promote many household industries. The colonial farm was an almost self-sufficient unit, supplying itself with essential foodstuffs, clothing, furniture, and other necessities. Almost every household had cards, spinning wheels, and looms to convert wool, flax, and perhaps a small amount of cotton into cloth. Hides of cattle were tanned and made into such useful items as shoes, breeches, and harnesses. Deerskins were made into moccasins, leggings, and caps. Most of the farmer's furniture, farm implements, and household utensils were made from local materials, while wood from the forest provided his fuel and, to a degree, his lighting. Almost every household made its own candles and soap. Surplus fruits and grain were turned into beer, wine, brandy, whiskey, and other alcoholic beverages by people who had no inclination toward prohibition and who believed that such drinks were healthful. The fact that the settlers could develop this self-sufficiency doubtless helped the colony remain insular and somewhat underdeveloped economically during the colonial period.

8

THE PEOPLE AT HOME

Colonial North Carolinians, much like most people elsewhere in the seventeenth and eighteenth centuries, lived in a class-conscious society. The idea that some men were socially superior while others were socially inferior was recognized in the colony just as it was in the British Isles. Everybody knew that some families were wellborn, that others were "middling," and that most were of the "meaner sort." Because of their background and education, the propertied families, who constituted the upper or "Gentleman" class, usually assumed leadership. The pattern of class structure was not, however, absolutely rigid; sometimes a sturdy middle-class family would ascend the scale, and it is certainly true that members of the upper class not infrequently fell from their lofty positions in the social order.

In North Carolina the upper class was sometimes called the "planter class," though planters who owned large estates were by no means the only members of this class. Professional people were also a part of this group: the clergy, doctors, lawyers, merchants, and many of the officers of the government. The wealth of the upper class was based primarily on land and slaves, but indentured servants also enabled them to turn a quick profit on the vast tracts for which they secured grants. Sites along rivers, offering the best means of transportation, were taken up first. Generally the land was easy to clear throughout eastern North Carolina, and many plantations consisted of between five and ten thousand acres while a few planters owned up to fifty thousand acres.

During the colonial period North Carolina was often unjustly berated as the home of an uncouth people. Charles Woodmason, an Anglican minister of South Carolina said in 1765: "The manners of North Carolinians in General, are Vile and Corrupt —The whole Country is a Stage of Debauchery Dissoluteness and Corruption—And how can it be otherwise? The People are compos'd of the Out Casts of all the other Colonies who take Refuge there." But many of the upper class were actually rather well educated. In most cases it is impossible to determine where they received their training, though probably it was accomplished under the watchful eye of parents or private tutors. As early as 1675 there were three officials living in Albemarle who held degrees from Cambridge and one man who had been educated at Oxford. During the colonial period several North Carolinians left for a while to pursue studies at the Inns of Court in London. Frequently these individuals were connected by close ties of marriage or friendship with prominent families in other colonies and in Great Britain. Connections were very helpful to a man who hoped to secure and maintain a position of significance and power in business and government. Only a decided minority of the upper class, however, had titled relatives or were even acquainted with influential people. The majority were simply men who "by shrewdness, thrift, and superior intelligence, had contrived to become rich." As their land holdings increased and their wealth grew, they came to have influence in the affairs of the colony. It was from among these men who demonstrated considerable native ability that the lords proprietors most often chose their deputies, thus making them members of the council and thereby raising them to a level equal to that enjoyed by those who had connections with the important families of England.

The great middle class, whose presence generally gave North Carolina its distinctive character, was dominated by those who owned smaller tracts of land, which they farmed themselves.

Every settler who undertook to clear land on the frontier and build a home for his family did so on an equal footing with his neighbor, although there were a few newcomers who had the advantage of some extra money to spend on livestock or tools. Soon the men with greater incentive, drive, and capability emerged from the masses and laid the foundation for social, economic, and political variety. In most communities signs of ambition and leadership began to appear quite early as certain families built new and more substantial homes and could thus move out of the small simple log houses that they had hastily constructed upon arriving in the colony. Clever and thrifty men found it possible to buy additional land from lazy neighbors and from those who could not resist the temptation of chasing the frontier and moving farther west. Moderate estates, operated with the help of sizable numbers of slaves, were not unknown even in the Piedmont. Before long the need for a center of government and trade gave rise to the development of towns. With this growth came the other members of the middle class, the skilled artisans, traders, clerks, and various assistants to the professional class.

Writing about 1708 John Lawson characterized the mass of people in North Carolina as "very laborious, and [who] make great Improvements in their Way." But he was also quick to note that "the easy Way of living in the Plentiful Country, makes a great many Planters very negligent." He praised the women for their industry and "good Houswifry"; by hard work in weaving and sewing "they have no occasion to run into the Merchant's Debt, or lay their Money out on Stores for Cloathing." Native-born colonists were described as "a straight, clean-limb'd People. . . . The Vicinity of the Sun makes Impression on the Men, who labour out of doors, or use the Water. As for those Women, that do not expose themselves to the Weather, they are often very fair, and generally as well featur'd, as any you shall see any where, and have very brisk charming Eyes, which sets them off to Advantage." Girls were trained in the "Affairs of the House," while children of both sexes were "very docile, and learn any

thing with a great deal of Ease and Method." Many of them
proved to be "good Accountants, which is most coveted, and
indeed most necessary in these Parts."

Nearly seventy-five years after John Lawson wrote these
words, Janet Schaw had similar observations to make about the
settlers in North Carolina. Even though the traveling she did
about the colony was restricted to the areas around Wilmington
and Brunswick, and even though many of her comments were
colored by obvious Tory sympathies, Janet Schaw's general
impression of the vast middle group of people was probably
accurate:

The difference between the men and the women surprised me, but a
sensible man, who has long resided here, in some degrees accounted for
it. In the infancy of this province, said he, many families from Britain
came over, and of these the wives and daughters were people of
education. The mothers took the care of the girls, they were train'd up
under them, and not only instructed in the family duties necessary to
the sex, but in those accomplishments and genteel manners that are still
so visible amongst them, and this descended from Mother to daughter.
As the father found the labours of his boys necessary to him, he led
them therefore to the woods and taught the sturdy lad to glory in the
stroke he could give with his Ax, in the trees he felled, and the deer he
shot; to conjure the wolfe, the bear and the Alligator; and to guard his
habitation from Indian inroads was most justly his pride, and he had
reason to boast of it. But a few generations this way lost every art or
science, which their fathers might have brought out, and tho' necessity
no longer prescribed these severe occupations, custom has established it
as still necessary for the men to spend their time abroad in the fields;
and to be a good marksman is the highest ambition of the youth, while
to those enervated by age or infirmity drinking grog remained a last
consolation.

There was also a lower class of settlers in the colony. This
group has been described by Francis L. Hawks, a mid-nineteenth
century clergyman and author of a history of colonial North
Carolina, as being "composed of the ordinary and uninstructed
emigrants who, in England, would have belonged to the

peasantry or agricultural laborers, some of whom had voluntarily emigrated, and were employed on the farms, where they labored for wages." Lowest on the scale of white citizens of the colony were the subsistence farmers, some of whom only squatted on the land they worked, roaming hunters and trappers, unskilled laborers, and a host of what were called "Christian servants." These included people who had bound themselves out for a period of service in return for their passage to the colonies. Some of the members of this group, however, were present in the colony against their will—they were robbers, debtors, and others who had been convicted of crimes in England and then were transported to America to serve out their sentences under a planter or a professional man. Finally, in this lower class were a great many orphans, who were apprenticed to learn a trade and often also to read and write. The Christian servants were entitled to certain goods at the end of their term of service. Prior to 1715 the so-called "freedom dues" consisted of fifty acres of land; after 1715 this was changed to three barrels of corn and two new suits; and in 1741 this was changed again and became £3 and one sufficient suit. Upon attaining their freedom, of course, Christian servants became eligible for a grant of land, and many of them, through industrious labor, soon advanced up the social scale. Land was so plentiful in the colony that it was not unusual for Christian servants from other colonies to remove to North Carolina at the end of their terms of service.

Janet Schaw echoed the words of Woodmason in her description of the people of the lower class:

Nature holds out to them every thing that can contribute to conveniency, or tempt to luxury, yet the inhabitants resist both, and if they can raise as much corn and pork, as to subsist them in the most slovenly manner, they ask no more; and as a very small proportion of their time serves for that purpose, the rest is spent in sauntering thro' the woods with a gun or sitting under a rustick shade, drinking New England rum made into grog, the most shocking liquor you can imagine.

Although she was no doctor, Miss Schaw diagnosed the ills of North Carolinians:

By this manner of living, their blood is spoil'd and rendered thin beyond all proportion, so that it is constantly on the fret like bad small beer, and hence the constant slow fevers that wear down their constitutions, relax their nerves and infeeble the whole frame. Their appearance is in every respect the reverse of that which gives the idea of strength and vigor, and for which the British peasantry are so remarkable. They are tall and lean, with short waists and long limbs, sallow complexions and languid eyes, when not inflamed by spirits. Their feet are flat, their joints loose and their walk uneven. These I speak of are only the peasantry of this country, as hitherto I have seen nothing else, but I make no doubt when I come to see the better sort, they will be far from this description.

Negroes fell at the very bottom of the social scale in colonial and antebellum North Carolina. While its slave population was smaller than that of any other southern colony—never more than 25 percent of the population, as against South Carolina's 60 percent—North Carolina exhibited the same attitudes on race as did its Southern neighbors. The Revolution did not change this racial composition.

Free Negroes, many of whom were skilled artisans, ranked above the slaves. Professor John Hope Franklin began his study of the free Negro in North Carolina with the year 1790 because information on the subject prior to that date was inadequate. He cited a court order of 1703 requiring Tho. Symons to pay £5 "for yᵉ bringing up a negro boy" as the earliest evidence of a free Negro in North Carolina. Recently published documents, however, suggest that "Maria a negro transport" * belonging to William Symons was present in Albermarle County prior to March 29, 1680.

Aside from fleeting mention of free Negroes in scattered documents, almost nothing is known of this class of people other than the fact that they voted in elections in North Carolina in 1701 and 1703. In other colonies free Negroes gathered in the towns and performed various services, but the absence of towns of

---

* A "transport" was an indentured servant who could expect to be free at the end of a set period of time.

any significant size in North Carolina meant that they had no such opportunity to congregate and be noticed.

It is certainly true, however, that Negro slaves were in the colony long before that date. Some "Gentlemen of Barbadoes" proposed in August 1663, to settle some experienced planters with "Negros and other servants fitt for such labor as wilbe there required," and their settlement at Charles Town on the Cape Fear River undoubtedly did include slaves. Since the number of slaves a master had depended upon his wealth and the amount of land he held, most slave owners in North Carolina actually possessed very few. Slaves were employed in nearly all of the regular activities of a plantation, but their primary use was the clearing and cultivation of the fields. Professional men in the towns often used slaves in connection with their business. They tended livestock in towns, drove vehicles, acted as messengers, and undoutbedly performed an endless number of odd jobs that contributed enormously to an easier life for the members of the middle and upper classes. The activities of slaves were strictly regulated by law, and their rights as individuals were quite limited. The Fundamental Constitutions gave masters complete authority over the bodies of their slaves. A revision made in 1682 shows a softening, though indeed very slight, in the attitude toward slaves:

Since Charity obliges us to wish well to the Souls of all men, and Religion ought to alter nothing in any man's civil estate or right, it shall be Lawful for Slaves, as well as others, to enter themselves and be of what Church and profession any of them shall think best, and thereof be as full members as any freemen; but yet, no slave shall thereby be Exempted from that Civil dominion his master has over him, but be in all things in the Same state and condition he was in before.

This provision did not set a trend of humane legislation concerning the slave. In fact, numerous laws restricting this class of people continued to be enacted throughout the colonial period.*

---

* The bonds of slavery, however, do not appear to have produced any major revolt or large-scale resistance. At least contemporary records of the seventeenth and eighteenth centuries make no mention of any.

An eighteenth-century commentator noted that there were "a great number of Negro slaves born in the country, who prove more industrious and tractable than those brought from the coast of Africa; at least being born in slavery, they have never imbibed that love of liberty which is apt to make men restive and stubborn under the galling yoke of oppression." The same observer noted that children were carefully brought up and provided for by the planters until they were able to work. Houses were then built for them, "and they are allowed to plant a sufficient quantity of tobacco for their own use, a part of which they sell . . . [to] buy hats and necessaries, as linen, bracelets, ribbons, and other toys for their wives and mistresses." He also reported that "several blacks born in the country can read and write; others are bred to trades, and prove good artists; and others are very industrious in improving the plantations, planting rice, corn, and tobacco, and making vast quantities of turpentine, tar, and pitch, they being better able to undergo fatigues, in the sultry heats of the summer, than the Europeans."

Negro slaves became free in North Carolina by several means. Manumission could come by will, by deed, or by legislative enactment. A law passed in 1715 permitted masters to continue the practice of freeing their slaves "as a Reward for his, or their honest and Faithful service," but such freed persons were expected to leave the colony within six months. By a later legislative action, the assembly and county courts were given the power to free slaves, but in such cases their owners were required to post bond so that the slaves would not become public charges. Miscegenation was another source of free Negroes. Children took the status of their mothers; mulatto children born to slave women were slaves, but they were often freed by their white fathers. Mulatto children born to white or Indian women were free. In many cases free Negroes purchased Negro slaves, particularly their own wife, children, or relatives, and then freed them. The population of free Negroes also increased as runaway slaves from other colonies came into North Carolina and passed for free.

In class conscious North Carolina wealth had a great deal to

Mid-eighteenth-century log house from the Piedmont, now restored and maintained by the Moore County Historical Society, Southern Pines. *Courtesy of the Travel and Promotion Division, Department of Natural and Economic Resources, State of North Carolina.*

do with the position a man and his family held. The most obvious signs of wealth were the acres and slaves a man owned, but also important status symbols were the house he and his family lived in and, though to a lesser extent, the clothes they wore and the food they ate. As a man profited he very soon set about improving his home. An ancient log house now used for storage of cotton, tobacco, or fertilizer may still sometimes be seen near a nineteenth-century house or even a twentieth-century structure. In some cases the older log house was simply incorporated into the construction of a larger house. When the colony was first settled, log houses were built as an expedient for providing quick shelter. A few men could construct such a dwelling within a matter of days. As the English became more familiar with the technique of hewing and joining logs, this kind of structure became more durable and thus more permanent. Germans who arrived in the colony had known such houses in their homeland and they were able to bring the construction of these buildings to a very high degree of excellence. Stone houses were also familiar to the Germans, and along with the Scotch-Irish in the Piedmont, where an ample supply of suitable rock could be found, they constructed some stone buildings.

The earliest houses were one or two room buildings with a loft, which was generally reached by a ladder or a narrow stairway. Sometimes a lean-to on the back beside a porch would provide a little additional room. A stick or brick chimney supplied heat for comfort in winter and for cooking year-round. Glass windows were rare for a long time, and if a log cabin had windows, there were solid shutters on wooden or leather hinges to close them. As prosperity followed settlement, houses grew. Rooms and hallways were added, and not infrequently the kitchen and dining room were removed to another building that was set a short distance away. The danger of fire from cooking was always present and this offered some protection for the main house. Sometimes the two buildings would be connected with a covered passageway.

By the middle of the eighteenth century many of the settlers, especially those in the more established communities, showed a vast improvement in the style and structure of their dwellings. Advertisements of houses for sale or rent often included good descriptions and thus give us some idea of the size and style of the buildings. The *Virginia Gazette* for April 7, 1768 advertised a house situated on six lots in Nixonton as "a large dwelling-house, a new large kitchen, a warehouse and wharf, storehouse, garden, and several convenient out-houses, beautifully situated on Little river." On February 23, 1769 the paper described a "pleasantly situated" house on Shocco Creek as being "a good Dwelling-House 40 feet by 24, four rooms below and three above . . . with a kitchen 20 by 16, conveniently done, a dairy, smoke-house, lumber-house, crib and stables, with other necessary out-houses, etc." Although the dwellings were certainly larger and more substantial than the original log houses, most of the homes occupied by North Carolinians in the colonial period offered little more in the way of comforts than had been available in medieval times. Candles, for example, were still considered a very expensive source of light. Janet Schaw recorded in 1775 that "the poorer sort burn pieces of lightwood, which they find without trouble, and the people of fashion use only Spermaceti [whale oil], and if any green wax [candles], it is only for kitchen use."

Few observers commented in elaborate detail on the clothes worn by North Carolinians, but we do know that they wore basically the same styles prevalent in England. Much of their apparel, in fact, was imported from the mother country as were the bolts of cloth from which clothes could be made at home. The inventories of goods shipped from abroad to merchants in the colony include stockings, gloves, hats, and other items of apparel. A contemporary reported: "The cloathing used by the men consists of English cloth, druggets, green linen, etc. The women have silks, calicoes, printed linen, calamancoes, and all kinds of stuffs, some of which are manufactured in the province." If the words of Governor Burrington written in 1732 may be taken at face value, there would seen to have been little difference in the dress worn by men of differing social status. Burrington observed:

"There is no difference to be perceived in Dress and Carriage, between the Justices, Constables and Planters that come to a Court, nor between the Officers and Private men, at a Muster which Parity is in no other Country but this." It was reported once that Colonel John Starkey of Onslow County was trusted by the common people because of "his capacity and diligence, and in some measure from his garb and seeming humility by wearing shoe-strings [instead of silver buckles], a plain coat, and having a bald head [that is, not wearing a wig]."

The *Virginia Gazette* on different occasions described the apparel worn by some men from North Carolina as "a Drab lightish colour'd Coat, with Metal Buttons, a pretty long black Silk Waistcoat"; "a whitish Camblet Coat, lin'd with Red, a blue Cloth Jacket, a blue riding Coat, and a brown Wig"; and "a Grey Duroy Coat half worn, a blue Drugget Waistcoat and Breeches, white Thread Stockings, check'd Cotton Shirts, a brown bob Wig, and a good Castor Hat." A slave was once described as wearing a "Fearnought Jacket and a Pair of Leather Breeches," while another had on a "Bearskin Coat and a Pair of Leather Breeches." Styles changed very little during the whole of the colonial period. People along the frontier, particularly the Moravians and other Germans, wore simpler clothes, just as the people throughout the colony did when working in the fields and the shops.

The personal possessions, especially household goods, of colonial North Carolinians suggest something of the standard of living that they enjoyed. Inventories of estates are the best source for lists of these articles and they give us some interesting insights into the lifestyle of the people. The frequent mention of bed curtains suggests that mosquitoes were a constant threat to a good night's sleep during the warm season. The repeated inclusion of "Tea Kittles," "Tea Pots," and "Tea Cups & sassers" is good evidence that the drinking of tea was greatly enjoyed. Pewter and "puter" occur over and over, frequently with the adjective "old" or "worn" before it; spoons and plates of pewter were used on the everyday table. Cups and saucers, plates, and dishes of green stone, white stone, china, queen's ware, and "Delpha" were commonplace along with castors, silver mugs, silver coffee pots, silver pepper boxes, silver spoons, sweet meat spoons, and a variety of serving pieces and other tableware. Linen napkins and tablecloths were often inventoried. Pillows and bolsters, blankets, and "french Covers," sheets, and quilts also were listed. Other necessary items of bedroom furniture often listed were chamber pots of white stone, earthenware, and pewter. Maple, mahogany, walnut, and pine furniture was included, and among the pieces were chairs, couches, desks, tables, beds, buffets, and chests. Clocks, looking glasses, picture frames, portraits, and jewelry were also mentioned. An almost endless variety of farm equipment was included together with military equipment and such things as compasses, spy glasses, speaking trumpets, and anchors.

Food in season was plentiful if not always varied, but the absence of good means for preserving out-of-season fruits and vegetables often made for an uninteresting table. In 1760 it was said: "Their Food, instead of Bread, is Flour of *Indian* Corn, boiled and seasoned like Hasty-pudding; and this is called Hommony: They also boil Venison, and make Broth of it, and eat all manner of flesh. They make what answers [for] Salt of Wood-Ashes; Long Pepper, which grows in their Gardens, and Bay Leaves, supply their Want of Spice." In all fairness it must be noted that their table was not always this dull. Another observer recited a somewhat more tempting menu:

Their diet, as with us, consists of beef, mutton, pork, venison in abundance, wild and tame fowl, fish of several delicate sorts, fruit, several kinds of sallads, good bread, butter, milk, cheese, rice, and roots. Their liquors are principally rum, brandy, malt liquor, which they import, cyder, persimon-beer, made of the fruit of that tree, and cedar-beer, made of cedar-berries; they also make beer of the green stalks of Indian corn; but the common table-beer is made of molasses. They also drink chocolate, tea, and coffee.

The social customs of the people of North Carolina were not too different from those prevailing in the other colonies. Early and frequent marriages, for example, were common among the colonists. Land and raw materials were plentiful and relatively easy to acquire, but it was lonely for a man on the frontier. A woman was needed for her companionship as well as her ability to perform the chores required by the various household industries. If a farm was to achieve self-sufficiency, a woman and children were vitally needed possessions. Women married young, sometimes at thirteen or fourteen, and, as Lawson noted, "she that stays single 'til 20 is reckoned a stale maid; which is a very indifferent character in that warm country." Large families were the rule, the average number of children being five to seven. Dr. John Brickell, an Edenton physician, said, "women are very fruitful, most houses being full of little ones." Charles Woodmason, with a kind of disparaging alarm, echoed this observation: "But they are so numerous—The Necessaries of Life are so cheap, and so easily acquir'd, and propagation being unrestricted, that the Encrease of People there, is inconceivable, even to themselves." Frequent motherhood combined with the hardships of pioneer life to wear women out early. The inscriptions on tombstones in colonial burying grounds are silent witness to the fact that women, far more so than men, typically died young. It was not often that a woman had a second husband, but there were few men who failed to marry a second time; many, in fact, married a third and some even a fourth time.

Colonial weddings were not social functions. Before 1766 the marriage ceremony could be performed only by a member of the Anglican clergy or, in his absence, by a justice of the peace. To prevent secret marriages, a license and publication of the banns as prescribed by the Book of Common Prayer was required, and to protect the community against the consequences of unlawful unions, a man was required to give bond that there was no lawful impediment to the marriage. Because there were rather few Anglican clergymen and churches, weddings were usually performed in private by justices of the peace. The drabness of such ceremonies stripped them of all their religious solemnity and most of their social appeal. There was no legal provision for divorce in North Carolina, but on occasion a marriage might be declared null and void because of the impotence of the husband. Separations were also sometimes sanctioned by the courts for reasons of desertion or adultery, in which cases provisions were made for the maintenance of a wronged wife and the children.

Although North Carolina did not develop the exciting urban life or large plantation system to the same extent as Virginia and South Carolina, it would be inaccurate to characterize life in the colony as having been entirely dull. One writer reported that their "principal diversions are fishing, fowling, and hunting wild beasts, as deer, bears, racoons, hares, wild turkeys, with several other animals." Horse racing also had a strong appeal for the people, and "they have what is called race-paths, which seldom exceed a quarter of a mile in length, and only two horses start at a time." Several eighteenth-century towns, however, had large oval racetracks located nearby. Another observer noted, "They are also very fond of gaming, especially with cards and dice, at which they play very high." Card tables and backgammon tables appear often in the inventories of estates of deceased eighteenth-century North Carolinians. An advertisement listing a tavern for sale in Halifax mentioned "a Billiard House twenty eight Feet long and eighteen feet wide." Cockfighting also invited "gaming," and cocks were imported from Virginia, England, and Ireland. In an address to the assembly in April 1752, Governor Johnston spoke against the "barbarous and inhuman Manner of Boxing, which so much prevails among the lower Sort of People." It was, he pointed out, "attended with circumstances of Cruelty and Horror, and is really shocking to human Nature." During the past two years, he was told, four violent deaths had been attributed to this custom, and the governor called upon the assembly to pass stringent laws to bring it to an immediate end. There were certainly more gentle forms of entertainment in North Carolina. Dr. John Brickell wrote: "Dancing they are all fond of, especially when they can get a Fiddle, or Bag-pipe; at this they will continue Hours together, nay, so attach'd are they to this darling Amusement, that if they can't procure Musick, they will sing for themselves."

The nineteenth- and twentieth-century idea of taking a vacation purely for pleasure probably never occurred to colonial North Carolinians. Officials traveling in connection with provincial business sometimes took their families along, but more often it was necessity that prompted the colonists' movements. Because sections of eastern North Carolina were unhealthy during the summer, many residents of the Cape Fear region owned summer homes near the ocean. Many eastern planters and merchants also owned such places and their wives, children, and servants spent the summer there. Easterners also frequently paid long visits during this period to relatives in the interior.

The various social classes, national origins, and racial differences present in North Carolina all influenced the course of events in the colony before 1775. Religious differences also marked some of these diverse groups, and the educational opportunities available to them frequently accentuated already existing social problems. The fact that before too long nearly all of the colonists spoke English, however, was a decidedly unifying factor. An English heritage predominated and leaders trained in the ideals of English government were unwilling in this isolated frontier situation to see principles sacrificed. The revolutionary struggle, led in large measure by the upper class, was a leveling influence that began to wipe out class differences, which had become rather deeply entrenched during the colonial period.

9

MIND AND SPIRIT

Thomas Hariot, a member of the Ralph Lane colony at Roanoke Island in 1585–1586, undertook the first Protestant missionary activity in America. He could speak to the Indians in their own tongue, and in his report of the year's activity he related that "manie times and in every towne where I came, according as I was able, I made declaration of the contentes of the Bible." More than three-quarters of a century later King Charles II granted a charter for Carolina that had as its first statement of purpose the declaration that the lords proprietors were men who were "excited with a laudable and pious zeal for the propagation of the Christian Faith . . . in the parts of America not yet cultivated or planted, and only inhabited by some barbarous People who have no knowledge of Almighty God." For all their avowed dedication, the proprietors proved to be very lax indeed when it came to matters of religion. They soon discovered that the people from Virginia who had recently settled within the bounds of the new Carolina had no especial interest in religion either for themselves or for the Indians. The precharter settlers of the Southern Plantation as well as those who arrived after 1663 had come to the colony because of their desire for more land or because they wanted to engage in the fur trade—they were not religious refugees from Virginia.

Instead of pursuing a firm policy that might have led to a Christianizing of the natives as well as the newcomers, the proprietors made no attempts to encourage the introduction of the Anglican faith. For the time being they were unwilling to make religion a barrier to further settlement. The general indifference of the lords proprietors to issues of faith and church accounted to some extent for the generous provisions that were made for religious liberty. In their instructions to Governor Stephens in 1667 the proprietors granted liberty of conscience in matters of religion to all residents in the colony so long as they behaved themselves "peaceably and quietly and not useing this Liberty to Lycentiousness to the Civill Injury or outward disturbances of Others." The Fundamental Constitutions went to considerable length to proclaim the freedom of worship authorized by the lords proprietors. To the natives, who were complete strangers to Christianity, as well as to "those who remove from other parts to Plant there" holding "different opinions concerning matters of Religon," the proprietors agreed to allow all the liberty that might be desired. They did not want to keep such people out of their province, yet it was necessary that "Civil peace may be maintained amidst the diversity of opinions." It was the hope of the proprietors that "heathens, Jews, and other dissenters from the purity of Christian Religion may not be scared and kept at a distance" but by becoming well acquainted with Christians "may, by good usage and persuasion, and all those convincing Methods of Gentleness and meekness Suitable to the Rules and design of the Gospel, be won over to embrace and unfeignedly receive the truth." The proprietors, then, very generously declared that "any Seven or more persons agreeing in any Religion shall constitute a church or profession, to which they shall give Some name to distinguish it from others." Members of such a church were assured that they would not be disturbed in their orderly worship services; but on the other hand, such people were directed not to "speak anything in Religious assembly Irreverently or Seditiously of the Government or Governors or States matters."

An English Quaker, William Edmundson, was the first missionary to visit Albemarle County. After an exhausting walk through the woods and swamps between Virginia and Carolina, he arrived wet and hungry in late March 1672. Purely by chance, when Edmundson emerged from the swamp he approached the house of Henry Phillips on the Perquimans River and discovered that his host was a Quaker from New England who had not seen a member of the faith in seven years. The following day, Sunday, March 23, Edmundson conducted the first recorded religious service in Carolina. In his journal he noted that the people there had "little or no religion, for they came and sat down in the meeting smoking their pipes." Yet they listened carefully and in "a little time the Lord's testimony arose in the authority of his power, and their hearts being reached by it, several of them were tendered and received the testimony." Crossing the river on Monday, Edmundson held another meeting at which "several were tendered with a sense of the power of God, received the truth and abode in it." After three days the missionary left, having laid the foundations for the growth of the Friends' faith in the new colony.

Edmundson returned to Albemarle County in 1676 and found the settlers in the midst of serious Indian troubles. Nevertheless he held services at several places and noted that the "People were tender and loving, and there was no room for the priests, for Friends were finely settled, and I left things well among them." This observation by Edmundson has been taken to mean that by that time the Quakers had established at least one regular meeting, but the record of a Quaker married in 1680 is the first firm evidence of an organized Quaker meeting. The following year two more monthly meetings were mentioned, and before the end of the century the Perquimans Monthly Meeting was holding regular services on the Perquimans, Pasquotank, Yeopim, and Little rivers, all on the north side of Albemarle Sound.

Quakers tried to remain aloof from the various commotions that rocked Albemarle in the late 1670s, but they were not always successful. They were accused of involvement, and several of them were seized by some of the rebels. The peaceful Friends also faced imprisonment after 1680 for their failure to comply with a law requiring service in the militia by all males over sixteen years of age.

When John Archdale, the Quaker proprietor, reached Albemarle County in 1683, his presence spurred considerable interest in the faith. In 1698, two years after his departure, the North Carolina Yearly Meeting was founded. Quakers composed the only religious organization in the colony during the seventeenth century. Most of the colonists, however, were probably Anglican by early training, but the absence of churches and clergy gave them little or no opportunity to engage in formal worship. They lacked the necessary means of opposing and suppressing the dissenting Quakers, who continued to spread their influence. With the settlement of the Piedmont, Quakers began to move into that part of North Carolina. By about 1750 there were some living at New Garden near modern Greensboro, and within a few years many more began to arrive from Pennsylvania, New Jersey, and Virginia. Between 1771 and 1775 several large families from Nantucket Island, Massachusetts, arrived to escape the approaching war in that region. From the New Garden center numerous Quakers moved out to establish settlements in the adjacent counties and eventually even into areas beyond the boundaries of North Carolina.

By the early years of the eighteenth century Quakers were only one of several groups of dissenters that were active in the colony. An Anglican missionary, the Reverend John Blair, said in 1704 that the people might be grouped into four categories.

[First were the Quakers] who are the most powerful enemies to Church government, but a people very ignorant of what they profess. The second sort are a great many who have no religion, but would be Quakers, if by that they were not obliged to lead a more moral life than they are willing to comply to. A third sort are something like Presbyterians, which sort is upheld by some idle fellows who have left their lawful employment, and preach and baptize through the country, without any manner of orders from any sect or pretended Church. A fourth sort, who are really zealous for the interest of the Church, are the fewest in number, but the better sort of people, and would do very much for the settlement of the Church government there, if not opposed by these three precedent sects.

While granting broad religious liberties, the Fundamental Constitutions at the same time anticipated the establishment of

the Church of England. In 1701 the assembly passed an act
creating five parishes and naming vestries for each. A special tax
was approved to support ministers, build churches, and provide
glebes, but the act was disallowed by Crown officials, who
considered the salaries inadequate. Vestries were appointed,
nevertheless, and a church was erected at what was soon to
become Edenton.

A second vestry act was passed and it declared that the
ecclesiastical laws of England were also in effect in North
Carolina. This meant that dissenters could now hold office only
after taking a qualifying oath by which they affirmed belief in
the Trinity and subscribed to the Anglican Church's Thirty-nine
Articles of Faith. This was a sharp break with tradition in the
colony and it resulted in an armed uprising. Heretofore the
religious scruples of the Quakers against taking oaths had been
respected and their affirmation accepted. When Robert Daniel
became governor in 1704 he insisted that Quakers take an oath
of allegiance in accordance with the law before undertaking any
official duty or sitting as members of the assembly. They refused,
of course, and demanded that the old custom of affirmation be
continued. The Quakers' seats in the assembly were declared
vacant and another act was then passed requiring an even
stricter oath of office. The Quakers complained to Governor
Johnson in Charles Town and secured Daniel's removal.

Thomas Cary, a Charles Town merchant, succeeded Daniel,
but he, too, insisted on the enforcement of the law. To make
matters worse, the assembly outraged the Quakers by passing an
act "that whoever should promote his own election, or sit and
act, not qualifying himself first by taking the oaths, should forfeit
five pounds." This so upset the Quakers that they sent John
Porter to London to appeal directly to the proprietors for relief.
Through the influence of John Archdale, Porter's mission
succeeded. He returned in 1707 with orders that recognized the
affirmation of Quakers, removed Cary from office, appointed
new proprietary deputies, authorized the council to elect a
president to act as governor, and directed that a free assembly be
elected. When Porter arrived, Cary happened to be in South

Carolina and William Glover, as president of the council, was acting governor. This arrangement seemed satisfactory to everybody, and Porter and the Quakers accepted it. But when new appointees offered to qualify as councillors, Glover would not admit them until they took the prescribed oath. Porter and the Quakers formed a strange alliance with Cary, who had just returned from Charles Town, to try to turn Glover out of office. Glover refused to yield and the two factions prepared for civil war. Reason prevailed for a brief time, however, and an agreement was reached to submit the rival claims of Glover and Cary to an assembly. But new complications arose. Both Glover and Cary issued writs of election, and when the assembly met in October 1708 there were two rival sets of delegates from several precincts. Glover refused to recognize the legality of any action taken by delegates who would not take the oath. But the Cary faction, which was in the majority, brushed aside Glover's claims and decided everything in Cary's favor. Glover, still claiming to be the lawful governor, withdrew into Virginia, leaving the Cary party in possession of the government.

The Cary party remained in power for nearly two years and declared all the laws passed during the Glover regime to be void. They also appointed a number of Quakers to office. The proprietors were slow to act, but they finally sent Edward Hyde, who was said to be a cousin of Queen Anne, to become deputy governor of the northern part of Carolina. They expected him to receive his commission from the governor at Charles Town, who, unfortunately, died before Hyde arrived, leaving the man without a commission and with no real authority. Hyde reported to North Carolina anyway, and it was claimed that the "awfull respect" of the people for the queen's kinsman induced both sides to put aside their quarrels. They joined in an invitation to Hyde to assume the government as president of the council pending further instructions from the proprietors. Hyde accepted, but showed such a lack of tact in dealing with the situation that Cary soon withdrew his support. Graffenried, a member of the council at the time, wrote that Cary "became an open and declared rebel and brought together a gang of tramps and rioters by means of promises, and . . . by means of good liquor, rum, and brandy, to which he treated the rabble, he secured many adherents, and they finally came to an open rebellion against Mr. Hyde." Cary held Hyde's forces at bay until Governor Spotswood of Virginia came to Hyde's assistance. Cary was captured and sent back to England to face a charge of treason. He was never tried, however, probabably because of a lack of evidence. Nonetheless, his defeat put an end to the rebellion in the colony.

In 1715, after the temporary silencing of Quaker opposition, four new Church of England parishes were created, rectors' salaries were increased, and a tax was authorized to provide funds for purchasing glebes for the parishes. In 1751 the law was altered to make vestrymen subject to election by the freeholders of each parish every two years rather than appointed by the assembly. Elected vestrymen were required to take an oath that they would not "oppose the Liturgy of the Church of England, as it is by law established." It was hoped that this requirement would ease the friction in cases where dissenters were elected to the vestry. Provision was also made for a fine of twenty shillings to be levied on any freeholder who refused to vote for a vestry. The number of parishes had grown to twenty-four by 1754, and some years later it was directed that every clergyman should be licensed by the Bishop of London (in whose jurisdiction the American colonies lay), but that vestries might select and install their own clergymen. If they failed to do this, at the end of a year the governor might appoint a rector to fill the vacancy. The governor might also suspend offending ministers. Ecclesiastical officials in London objected to the delegation of so much power to the vestry and secured the disallowance of this act, yet they refused to authorize a bishop for the colonies. Under the various acts passed after 1715 new parishes were established, churches built, and tax support provided. Unitarians and Roman Catholics were effectively excluded from the enjoyment of their religions in North Carolina, but other dissenters were, by comparison, relatively free. An act of Parliament recognized the Moravian Church as a Protestant episcopal church and permitted Moravians the same rights and privileges as those enjoyed by members of the Anglican Church. By 1760 Presbyterian ministers were exempt, as Anglican clergymen had been previously, from attending militia muster, and after 1766 they were allowed to conduct marriage ceremonies. All the marriages that they had previously performed were retroactively legalized.

Enforcement of the establishment of the Anglican Church was difficult. It is highly doubtful if anyone "conformed" because of the law, yet missionaries sent by the Society for the Propagation of the Gospel in Foreign Parts, an English missionary organization, reported that they baptized many adults and children. These conversions represented people of Anglican persuasion who had had no previous opportunity to accept the sacraments. Except for Cary's rebellion and a few local incidents associated with the election and qualification of vestrymen, there was no widespread opposition to the attempts to establish the church. The people, by and large, were indifferent to these efforts.

A total of forty-six Anglican clergymen served in North Carolina from 1701 until 1783. The Society for the Propagation of the Gospel provided thirty-three of these men who were to serve in twenty-two different stations in the colony. The society paid them a modest salary and also provided a library, appraised at £10, for each man with an additional £5 for the purchase of books that were to be distributed among his parishioners. Numerous letters survive in the society's files in London attesting to the gratitude of the churchmen in the colony for the work of the society. Some of the Anglican ministers, however, gave people cause to complain of their bad behavior. One had such a dishonorable reputation that he "brought great grief and shame to the friends of the Church." Another was called "quarrelsome, selfish, and covetous." One was accused of making public houses "his places of Rendezvous." Some of these complaints undoubtedly were justified; others may have been nothing more than a means of expressing resentment over the necessity of paying taxes to support the Established Church.

Half a dozen North Carolinians made the long and expensive trip to London so that they could be ordained. Their subsequent reports to the society indicate that they travelled regularly through a large area of the colony, calling routinely at many preaching stations. The Reverend Clement Hall, one of the most diligent of the group, summed up his thirteen years of work by estimating that he had traveled over fourteen thousand miles and baptized more than ten thousand people. On occasion during his tours, when services were held outdoors, he preached to congregations of up to six hundred people.

Governor Dobbs and his successor, William Tryon, were more active than any of the other governors in attempting to set the church on a firm road to establishment, yet when Dobbs died in 1765 his funeral had to be conducted by a magistrate because a Church of England priest could not be found within a hundred miles. The failure of England to authorize bishops for the colonies, the lack of clergymen, the failure to collect the taxes levied to support the church, the fact that parishioners were scattered, and the opposition from dissenters, particularly the Quakers, all combined to prevent the church from gaining enough strength to survive the shock of the Revolution.

There were a few Baptists in North Carolina as early as 1695, but they experienced no significant growth in numbers for well over half a century. By 1775, however, there were sixteen churches in the colony and several thousand Baptists. Each congregation of Baptists was independent of all the others, and this was a feature of the denomination that had great appeal to the colonists. The growth of the denomination dates from the arrival of Shubal Stearns of Boston in the Sandy Creek community in November 1755. Stearns, a former Congregationalist, was accompanied by Daniel Marshall, a native of Connecticut and a former Presbyterian. Both men had fallen under the influence of George Whitefield. They promptly organized Sandy Creek Baptist Church with sixteen members, most of whom had come from Connecticut. Their neighbors were Quakers, Moravians, Lutherans, and Presbyterians. The doctrines and practices of the Baptists were different from anything North Carolinians had encountered heretofore. "Strong gestures and a single tone of voice" were employed by Baptist preachers; and tears, tremblings, screams, shouts, and acclamations were said to mark the reactions of their congregations. Many people made light of the highly charged emotional meetings, but nevertheless the effects of the Baptists were widely felt. In less than fifteen years the membership of Sandy Creek Baptist Church grew to over six hundred, and within seventeen years, forty-two churches and one hundred and twenty-five ministers had "sprung from the parent church." Little or no formal training was required to be a minister, and farmer-preachers were not uncommon. From Sandy Creek Church many missionaries went out to establish new congregations among the farmers on the frontier. In a very short time churches were organized in what is now Randolph, Chatham, Orange, Guilford, Davidson, Surry, Montgomery, Anson, and Granville counties. In 1758 the Sandy Creek Association was organized, and for the next twelve years all the separate Baptist churches in Virginia and the Carolinas were affiliated with this association.

Baptists were among the most active opponents of the Established Church, and royal governors on many occasions found opportunity to condemn the whole denomination for the opposition expressed by some individual members. Not a single adherent to the Baptist faith is known to have held an office of importance either at the local or the provincial level before the Revolution, but it was from among the members of this church that much of the leadership of the early revolutionary movement was to emerge.

Unlike the Baptists, the German-speaking people that settled in the colony did not resist the tax levied to support the Established Church, and they took no part in the occasional attempts to prevent the installation of an Anglican minister in a local parish. In many cases the Germans as well as the Swiss at New Bern actually joined the Anglican Church. In the Piedmont, however, these people established the churches that they had known at home. There were three different churches represented: Lutheran, German Reformed, and Moravian. The government found all of these to be far more acceptable than the Baptist Church, and they certainly enjoyed the fact that the

Germans succeeded in living so peacefully with their Swiss neighbors.

About 1747 the first of many German families reached North Carolina. They were Lutherans or German Reformed in affiliation and very devout, but many years passed before they had any pastors. A union church in what is now Cabarrus County was formed in the late 1740s; in 1771 the Lutherans withdrew peaceably and formed their own church. The Lutherans' first minister, the Reverend Adolph Nussman, arrived from Germany in 1773, by which time other congregations had been formed. Prior to the Reverend Nussman's arrival, services had been conducted by laymen who frequently were also teachers, or by ministers who happened to be passing through the community.

The German Reformed Church was known by various names: German Presbyterian Church, Reformed Evangelical Church, Dutch Presbyterian, and Calvinist Congregation. Almost as soon as the members of this church completed their houses in North Carolina, they erected a schoolhouse which also served for Sunday services until a more substantial church could be built. Like their neighbors, the Lutherans, these people were dependent upon laymen and passing ministers for service for a number of years. The Reverend Samuel Suther, however, began to hold regular services in Mecklenburg County in 1762, and because there were so few ministers available, he sometimes even conducted services as far away as Orange County.

The Moravians, occupying an isolated tract of land, kept themselves apart from other Germans in the colony. The first congregation was formed in Bethabara in November 1753 when the initial group of settlers arrived. Their church was an integral part of their community and an important factor in their removal to this isolated part of the colony. Since an act of Parliament recognized the Moravian Church as an episcopal church and not as a dissenting body, provincial officials authorized Dobbs Parish to be laid out for them. The Moravian Church was the only independent, fully organized church in the colony. When outsiders visited the northern Piedmont in the Wachovia tract to trade in Moravian stores, to seek medical or dental care, or to find safe refuge from Indians, sermons were preached in English for their benefit. Non-Moravians of whatever faith were offered, and many often accepted, baptism and other sacraments at the hands of Moravian ministers. In addition, attempts were made to establish mission stations among the Indians. Music played an important role in the religious services of the Moravians, and this attracted many people who wanted to see and hear their stringed and wind instruments.

With rare exceptions the Presbyterians in colonial North Carolina were either Scotch-Irish or Highland Scots. The Scotch-Irish greatly exceeded the Highland Scots in number and they certainly made a more lasting impression on the colony. They first arrived in the early 1730s and settled Henry McCulloh's land along the upper Cape Fear River. Before long the Scotch-Irish organized what they called a society for worship. As Presbyterians they were dissenters, of course, and as such they were careful to avoid the more formal word *church*. They used such terms as *society* and *meeting* to escape the scrutiny of royal officials. This early Presbyterian organization was formed on Goshen Swamp, a tributary of the Northeast Cape Fear River, and about 1755 Grove Church was established at the nearby site of Kenansville. In the middle of the eighteenth century Scotch-Irish Presbyterians in large numbers began to move into the Piedmont. The earliest took up land in Orange County and soon thereafter others were moving down the Great Wagon Road from Pennsylvania into newly-formed Rowan County. John Anderson was the pioneer settler in the Hawfields, which became one of the centers of the Presbyterian Church in the Piedmont. A number of congregations were organized in this area from which Alamance, Guilford, Rockingham, and other counties were formed. Between 1752 and 1762 over a hundred Scotch-Irish families took out grants for land within the bounds of Thyatira (or Cathey's Meeting House, as it was also known), and elders of the congregation conducted regular services. A meetinghouse stood on the banks of the Yadkin River east of Salisbury by 1755, and ten congregations had been formed in Mecklenburg County by 1770.

The Highland Scots who settled in the Cape Fear River Valley beginning about 1732 had no established minister for many years. This was due not to a lack of religious fervor and conviction, but to the extreme poverty of the people and the shortage of Gaelic-speaking ministers in Scotland. On several occasions the settlers sent petitions back to Scotland seeking the appointment of a minister, but their requests went unheeded.

Missionaries from Pennsylvania, Virginia, New York, and New Jersey visited Presbyterian communities on a more or less regular basis beginning in 1742. The Reverend Hugh McAden preached among the Highland Scots in 1756, and by the next year they apparently had a church. Late in 1758 the Reverend James Campbell arrived, and within a few weeks he accepted an offer from the Highland Scots to serve them regularly. Campbell conducted services in Gaelic at three churches on a regular schedule and visited others at widely scattered points. At least three congregations were organized by about 1770. There were at this time approximately sixty-five thousand Highland Scots and Scotch-Irish in North Carolina of whom about two thousand were members of thirty-five churches. For organizational purposes the Presbyterian churches of Virginia and North Carolina had formed the Hanover Presbytery in 1755, but in 1770 all the member churches from the two Carolinas withdrew to form the Orange Presbytery.

Methodists existed in North Carolina, but as elsewhere they did not establish an independent church. Instead, they formed a society within the Anglican Church until 1784 when they finally broke away as a separate denomination. Their beginnings may be traced to a small religious club that was formed by John and Charles Wesley and others at Oxford University in 1729. The Reverend George Whitefield, an Anglican priest and follower of the Wesleys, visited Virginia in 1740. On June 24 of that year James Murray from Wilmington wrote Whitefield: "As the great aim of your life is to do good by propagating the Gospel, it is the opinion of many People of good sense that there is Not a Province in America where your preaching is So Much wanted as in this." However, it was not until 1772 that the first Methodist sermon was preached in the colony. The service was conducted by Joseph Pilmore, a layman who had been working with John Wesley and the Methodist society. Then in 1773 or 1774 Robert Williams of Virginia extended his preaching circuit to include North Carolina and formed the first society in the colony. The growth of this denomination was slow; at the beginning of the Revolution Methodists in North Carolina numbered only 683.

Governor Dobbs, addressing the assembly on September 22, 1736, deplored the "almost total Want of Divine Worship throughout the Province." Except for North Carolina he knew of no "Colony belonging to a Christian Nation, where some effectual Provison has not been made, for paying Public, and at stated Times, that Adoration, and Homage to Almighty GOD, so highly becoming all Rational Creatures, and for instructing the People in their Duty to the Supreme Author of their Being, to one another, and to themselves." Considering the neglect of this aspect of the life of North Carolinians, he concluded, "no Body will be surpriz'd at the many Disorders which have always prevailed among us; especially when it is considered how little Care there is taken of the Education of Youth."

Dobbs probably was unaware of the first rumblings of the Great Awakening, which were being heard at the very time he spoke. Wesley and Whitefield soon stirred a new interest in religion that manifested itself in a variety of ways. Great revivals and preaching missions swept England and the colonies. The cold formalism and dispassionate ritual of the old church services gave way to an unbridled enthusiasm and personal participation in religious affairs that had been unknown heretofore. A proper sense of inner conviction and a feeling of personal relationship with God marked those who experienced the Great Awakening.

Revivals were characterized by shouting and weeping and various other signs of physical reaction, and this had enormous appeal to many of the settlers. Their new religious experiences suggested that they did not have to depend any longer upon traditionally ordained ministers or on any kind of ecclesiastical hierarchy. Laymen assumed real importance in the affairs of the church, and with their new role they demanded more authority. This sense of personal and religious freedom marking the church soon was transferred to the political realm and it acted to stimulate the growing democracy. Equality of all men before God was one of the important beliefs of the new donominations, and this emphasis began to break down many of the barriers erected by the old social, political, and economic orders. From its beginning in the late 1730s, through its peak in the middle of the century, to its decline on the eve of the American Revolution, the Great Awakening was a powerful influence in North Carolina as it was in other colonies. Conversions were numerous and church membership grew, but it must be noted that not all conversions represented good intentions. Some people simply could not adhere to the strict discipline of any of the established churches, and their dismissal from church membership for drunkenness, adultery, and bastardy was far from rare.

Whitefield was the single most influential leader and he visited the colony a number of times between 1739 and 1765. Because of the sparse population, however, he seldom had congregations numbering more than a hundred, but people did come from many miles away to hear him. An Anglican minister complained during this period that "Methodists of late have given me a great deal of trouble . . . by preaching up the inexpediency of Human Learning & the practice of moral virtue & the great expediency of Dreams Visions & immediate Revelation." He was convinced that "the poor ignorant people were being deluded" by the popular preachers who moved about through the colony. The Great Awakening prepared the way for the Baptist, Presbyterian, and a little later the Methodist churches which were established throughout the colony.

The church in North Carolina performed many important secular functions. The vestry had custody of the official set of weights and measures in many of the counties. This church body was responsible for seeing to the welfare of poor widows and orphans, and it often attended to the apprenticing of children to learn a trade. The history of education in the colony also was closely related to the church since among all the religious sects, especially Anglicans, Quakers, Presbyterians, and Moravians, education was regarded as one of the prime responsibilities of the church. Most of the teachers were either preachers, lay readers, or candidates for the ministry.

Although there must have been schoolteachers in North Carolina before 1700, the earliest one about whom we have any records is Charles Griffin, a lay reader in the Established Church who arrived from the West Indies in 1705. Almost immediately he opened a school in Pasquotank precinct, which tradition locates on Symons Creek, an arm of Little River, near the old town of Nixonton. Griffin was about twenty-five when he arrived in the colony and although an ardent Anglican, he settled in Pasquotank precinct, the center of Quaker influence, which was noted for its prosperous character and comparatively dense population. Griffin's school was successful and held in high esteem. William Gordon, the Anglican misionary, reported in 1709 that "the Quakers themselves send their children to his school, though he had prayers twice a day at least, and obliged them to their responses, and all the decencies of behaviour as well as others." Griffin was paid by private subscription, and both boys and girls attended the school.

Griffin's work as a lay reader was also highly successful. Within a short time after his arrival in the colony he established what was described as an orderly Anglican congregation in this predominantly Quaker parish. William Glover, president of the council and acting governor, wrote the Bishop of London that Griffin, through his decent behavior, his industry and unblemished life, and "by apt discourses from house to house, according to the capacities of an ignorant people [had] not only kept those he found, but gained many to the Church in the midst of its enemies." Missionary Gordon also informed the Society for the Propagation of the Gospel that he was surprised to see the order, decency, and seriousness with which public worship was carried on in Pasquotank in comparison with the other precincts. "This they owe," he said, "to the care of one Mr. Griffin . . . whose diligent and devout example has improved them so far beyond their neighbors." Gordon urged Griffin to give up his school in Pasquotank, where the Reverend James Adams, a missionary from the Society for the Propagation of the Gospel, had recently settled, and move to Chowan precinct. Despite the efforts of the Pasquotank people to retain him, Griffin moved and soon organized a school in Chowan. By April 1709, Griffin was doing so well that Adams, who had taken charge of Griffin's old school, wrote the society praising Griffin's character and work. By October of that year, however, Adams had a different story to tell. "I wrote you formerly of one Mr. Griffin, who behaved himself very remarkably in the office of a reader and schoolmaster. He has fallen into the sin of fornication, and joined with the Quaker's interest, which has proven [a] great stumbling-block to many of our persuasion." On this unexplainable note Charles Griffin's career as a schoolmaster in North Carolina came to an abrupt end. He moved to Virginia, and in 1715 Governor Spotswood employed him to instruct Saponi Indian children. Three years later Griffin became master of the Indian school at the College of William and Mary.

Of all the Anglican missionaries in the colony it was James Reed who was perhaps the most deeply interested in education. In 1762 he preached a sermon to the assembly recommending that public schools be established. Favorably impressed by Reed's dedication and zeal, the assembly ordered the sermon printed and distributed in all of the counties of the province. In 1764 Reed and Thomas Thomlinson, a teacher from England, began construction of a school in New Bern that was to be attended by both boys and girls. After it opened, the school was maintained by a tax on imported spirituous liquors, legislative appropriations, and ground rent from certain church lands. Thomlinson operated the school effectively, but in 1772 when he "corrected and turned out of school . . . for very disobedient and stubborn Behaviour" the children of two of the trustees, his immediate dismissal was demanded. The trustees accomplished this without giving him notice and without paying his salary. His dismissal was strongly opposed by Governor Josiah Martin, who wrote the Bishop of London urging him to recommend repeal of the law empowering the trustees to dismiss a schoolmaster without the governor's consent, but no action was taken on his recommendation.

The massive influx of Scotch-Irish and Germans into the Piedmont gave a marked impetus to education. Governor Dobbs wrote the Board of Trade in 1755 that the Scotch-Irish desired "A Teacher of their own opinion and choice." As early as 1756, three years after their first settlement in Wachovia, the Moravians had schoolteachers, a "day school," and a "school for the older boys." In 1760 the Reverend James Tate, a Presbyterian, opened the first classical school in the colony in Wilmington. During the same year Crowfield Academy was founded in Mecklenburg County. The most noted of the classical schools was the Reverend David Caldwell's "log college" established in 1767 in what is now Greensboro. This school had an enrollment of about fifty students each year and survived until well into the nineteenth century. It served as an academy, a college, and a theological seminary; from it were graduated many of the men who were later to become leaders in North Carolina and other colonies.

Education in North Carolina as elsewhere in America has always been one of the primary concerns of the family as well as of the government and the church. Early in North Carolina's history, when there were few towns and schools and the population was widely dispersed, the job of educating children was left largely to the parents. They taught their own children or, in the case of the more affluent, they either employed tutors or sent the youngsters to a subscription school. For their higher education the children of wealthier parents were sent to Virginia, Pennsylvania, New Jersey, New England, and even to the universities of England and Scotland. Wills and inventories of

Armorial bookplates of colonial
North Carolinians.

estates of the time reveal this deep concern for education, especially of boys. In 1697 Alexander Lillington directed that "my executors carry on my son John, in his learnings as I have begun and that All my Children be brought up in Learning, as conveniently as can bee." John Hecklefield in 1721 wanted his son to be educated "after the best manner the country will permit." In 1730 George Durant hoped that his son "should have as good Learning as can be had in this Government." Thomas Bell in 1733 bequeathed the profits from his estate to the education of a niece and nephew "in as handsome and good a manner as may be." Edward Salter in 1734 desired that his son should "have a thorough education to make him a compleat merchant, let the expense be what it will." And, in the same year, John Baptista Ashe requested in his will that one son be trained in law, one in merchandise, and a daughter "be taught to write and read and some feminine accomplishments which may render her agreeable; and that she be not kept ignorant in what appertains to a good house wife in the management of household affairs." Edward Moseley in 1745 provided for the higher education of his children when the time came for them to have "other Education than is to be had from the Common Masters in this Province . . . for I would have my children well educated." John Pfifer of Mecklenburg County provided funds so that his children might "have a reasonable Education and in particular my son Paul to be put through a liberal Education and Colleged." When Governor Johnston died in 1752 he left a legacy to a nephew "now at school in Newhaven [Yale] in the Colony of Connecticut." In 1757 James Murray wrote his sister: "It is my settled Intention if I live and let my Family Increase as it will, to carry on Tom's Education at the Expence of £200 or £300 Ster. and to make a Lawyer of him, if he has not an aversion to it."

The children of the poor, and particularly orphans and illegitimate children, received some education through the agencies of indentured servitude and the apprenticeship system. Masters and guardians were required by law to give their wards the "rudiments of learning" and to teach them a useful trade. In addition, there were numerous legacies for the education of the poor. In 1710 John Bennett of Currituck County provided in his will "that forty shillings be taken out of my whole Estate before any decision be made to pay for ye schooling of two poor children for one whole year"; and that if he died without heirs, his whole estate was "to remain and bee for ye use and benefit of poor Children to pay for their Schooling and to remain unto ye world's End." It has been suggested that the coming of public education was forehsadowed in such wills as those of James Winwright in 1744 and James Innes in 1760. Winwright willed that the "yearly Rents and profits of all the Town land and Houses in Beaufort Town [be used] for the encouragement of a Sober discreet Quallifyed Man to teach a School at least Reading Writing Vulgar and Decimal Arithmetick." He set aside £50 sterling "to be apply'd for the Building and finishing of a Creditable House for a School and Dwelling house for the Master." So far as the records reveal no school was ever established from the Winwright legacy. Colonel Innes's bequest included his plantation at Pleasant Point, "Two negro Young Woomen, One Negro Young Man and there Increase," a large number of horses, cattle, and hogs, his books, and £100 sterling "For the Use of a Free School for the benefits of the Youth of North Carolina." It was not until after the Revolution that this legacy became available for educational purposes.

Governor Johnston, who had been a university professor in Scotland, was concerned about the availability of education throughout the province. In an address to the assembly in 1736 he said: "In all civilized Societys of men, it has always been looked upon as a matter of the greatest consequence to their Peace and happiness, to polish the minds of young Persons with some degree of learning, and early to instill into them the principles of virtue and religion, and that the Legislature has never yet taken the least care to erect one school, which deserves the name in this wide extended country, must in the judgment of all thinking men, be reckoned one of our greatest misfortunes."

The assembly replied: "We lament very much . . . the general neglect in point of education, the main sources of all Disorders and Corruptions, which we should rejoice to see removed and remedyed, and are ready to do our parts, towards the reformation of such flagrant and prolifick Evils." The legislature, however, was in no hurry to act in this regard, even though Johnston and his successor, Dobbs, repeatedly urged "provisions for the education of youth." The assembly did pass a law in 1745 "to erect and build a School-house" at Edenton, but the provisions of the act were never carried out. Bills for the establishment of "free schools" were defeated in the legislatures of 1749 and 1752. Finally, in 1754 an act was passed appropriating £6,000 "for founding and endowing a Public School," but shortly afterward the money was "borrowed and employed" for military purposes. Subsequent attempts to secure this money for its original purpose were unsuccessful. The only legislation relating to public education that made its way past the legislative barrier were bills incorporating the academy at New Bern in 1766 and one at Edenton in 1776.

Queen's College in Charlotte (not to be confused with the present college of that name which was established in 1857) was the first and only college to be founded in colonial North Carolina by the government. Governor Tryon favored the establishment of a "publick Seminary, in some Part of the back Country of this Colony for the Education of Youth" in the belief that "such an institution . . . would be very beneficial, by instructing the rising Generation of the Principles of Religion and Virtue." The council endorsed this idea: "The object is important. Morals and good government depend greatly on early Instruction and Virtuous Example." On January 15, 1771, the assembly passed "An Act for the Founding and Establishing and Endowing of Queen's College in the Town of Charlotte in Mecklenburg County." It was designed as a "publick seminary" to enable such of the youth of the province who had "acquired at a Grammar School a competent knowledge of the Greek, Hebrew, and Latin Languages to imbibe the principles of

Science and Virtue, and to obtain under learned pious, and exemplary teachers a collegiate or academic mode of instruction a regular or finished education in order to qualify them for the service of their friends and Country." The college was authorized to grant "the degree of Batchelor and Master of Arts." The rules and ordinances of the college were "to correspond and be as near as may be agreeable to the Laws and Customs of the Universities of Oxford and Cambridge or those of the Colleges in America." The college was to be financed by "a duty of six pence per gallon on all rum or other spirituous liquors brought into and disposed of in Mecklenburg County" for ten years following the passage of the act. It has been said that Queen's was founded under Presbyterian auspices, and so to "forestall anticipated opposition in England," it was required that the president be a member of the Church of England. Despite Governor Tryon's strong endorsement, the charter for the college was disallowed by the king and the privy council in April 1772 on recommendation of the Board of Trade. The board had raised the question of whether the Crown should encourage "toleration by giving Royal Assent to an Establishment, which in all its consequences, promises great and permanent Advantage to a sect of dissenters from the Established Church who have already extended themselves over the Province in very considerable numbers." Princeton College in New Jersey, also founded under Presbyterian auspices, had been chartered twenty-five years earlier, but a new king and changed conditions doomed Queen's College. A year elapsed before official word was received of the disallowance of the college's charter, and in the meantime the school had opened its doors to students with the Reverend James Alexander as president. It continued to operate as a private school and without a charter until 1777 when the assembly of the independent state of North Carolina chartered the institution as Liberty Hall.

The long agitation for public schools finally bore fruit in the state constitution of 1776. Section 41 provided: "That a School or Schools shall be established by the Legislature for the convenient Instruction of Youth, with such Salaries to the

Masters paid by the Public, as may enable them to instruct at low prices; and all useful Learning shall be duly encouraged and promoted in one or more Universities." This provision was considered by many people to be a mandate for public schools and state-supported higher education, but decades were to pass before the constitutional directive became effective.

In addition to their serious concern over education, another revealing indication of the cultural interests of the people of colonial North Carolina was the extent and character of their libraries. The earliest libraries to exist in the colony were those sent by the Society for the Propagation of the Gospel. The largest and the most important of these was the "free public library" of 176 volumes sent to Bath by the Reverend Thomas Bray, founder of the society. The assembly of 1715 passed a law "for the more effectual preservation" of this library, but it was eventually scattered. Some of the volumes have survived and are now in various public and private libraries in the state. Personal libraries were often listed in the wills and inventories of North Carolinians. Most of the private collections were small, usually from 20 to 50 volumes, but there were some rather large collections. James Milner's library inventoried 621 volumes; Dr. John Eustace had 282, while the Reverend James Reed owned 266. The library begun by Governor Gabriel Johnston and continued by his nephew, Samuel Johnston, at Hayes plantation, contained more than a thousand volumes—a library which is still there. Most of the books in the colonial libraries were works on theology, moral philosophy, law, literature, history, and medicine and they were in English as well as Greek, Latin, Hebrew, German, and French. Among the authors represented were Homer, Ovid, Virgil, Caesar, Grotius, Coke, Blackstone, and Montesquieu; the favorites seem to have been Shakespeare, Bacon, Milton, Locke, Voltaire, Addison, Steele, and Swift. Some of the libraries also had issues of *The Spectator*, *The Tatler*, and the *Annual Register*, among other journals, all testifying to a degree of culture not generally attributed to North Carolinians in the eighteenth century.

The printing press came late to North Carolina; nine other continental English colonies already had printers by the middle of the eighteenth century. The absence of towns of any significant size, the diffusion of population over an extensive area, the lack of regular postal service, and the limited demand for books and periodicals among the people generally made the maintenance of a press a risky financial venture. There seemed to be no popular demand for newspapers and except for public printing there was not enough business in the colony to support a printing establishment. As in several other colonies, the press was brought to North Carolina only because it was necessary to print and circulate the laws of the legislature. For well over half a century before the first press arrived the laws were copied in longhand and sent in this form to the proper officials at all levels of government. This was never a satisfactory arrangement, and the revisal and printing of the laws had been sought for a long time. In 1746 the legislature was told that "for want of the Laws of this Province being revised and printed, the Magistrates are often at a loss how to discharge their Duty, and the People transgress many of them for want of knowing the same." Accordingly a law was passed to appoint commissioners to revise and print the laws. Aware of the approaching need for the services of a printer, the assembly appointed James Davis to the post of public printer. He set up his press at New Bern in June 1749, and before the end of the year he had printed the fourteen page journal of the legislature that sat from September 26 through October 18, 1749. In 1751 he published the revisal of the laws, *A Collection of all the Public Acts of Assembly, of the Province of North Carolina: Now in Force and Use*. During his career as public printer, which extended over a period of thirty-three years, Davis issued several other revisions of the laws. In 1753 he published the Reverend Clement Hall's *A Collection of Many Christian Experiences, Sentences, and Several Places of Scripture Improved*, which was the first nonlegal book written by a North Carolinian to be published in the colony. Davis was also the father of journalism in North Carolina. In 1751 he began publication of *The North Carolina Gazette*, a weekly that continued to appear for six years. In 1764 he began to issue the *North Carolina Magazine, or Universal Intelligencer*, but soon discontinued it. In 1768, however, he revived the *Gazette*, which continued for a decade.

In 1764 Governor Dobbs brought charges of neglect of duty against Davis and a committee appointed by the assembly induced Andrew Steuart of Philadelphia to come to North Carolina. The bill to install Steuart as the new public printer was defeated in the council, whereupon Governor Dobbs went ahead and appointed the Philadelphian "his Majesty's printer." The assembly denounced the appointment as an act "of a new and unusual nature unknown to our laws" and "a violent stretch of power" and then they reinstated Davis public printer. Steuart settled in Wilmington where, in September 1764, he began publication of a newspaper, *The North Carolina Gazette*, which continued for three years. In 1769 Steuart was drowned in the Cape Fear River and his press was purchased by Adam Boyd, the third and last of the pre-Revolutionary printers in the colony. In 1769 he began publication of the *Cape Fear Mercury*, which continued publication until late in 1775.

Although North Carolinians, largely because of their scattered settlements, the lack of adequate centers of trade, and the diversity of their population, often appeared to suffer when compared to eastern Virginians or to South Carolinians around Charles Town, they were neither so heathen nor so uneducated as their detractors sometimes pictured them as being. Churches and schools of varying degrees of respectability existed, far apart though they were. Touring missionaries and itinerant teachers made their way around the colony just as did the strolling players of the day with their dramatic performances. North Carolinians were neither wholly unlettered nor unread; their powers to reason, to petition (as well as to sign their petitions), and to argue logically for their rights based on religion, law, and the rights of man, were often demonstrated—in the east in resistance to the Stamp Act, for example, and in the west in the work of the Regulators.

10

EAST VERSUS WEST

East-west sectionalism has been one of the most important and enduring factors in the history of North Carolina. From the very beginning there were fundamental differences between these two regions in physiography, national stocks, religion, social life, and economy. The east, which was settled largely by Englishmen and Highland Scots established an economy that was based on the plantation system with its unfree labor and aristocratic ideals. The west, on the other hand, was settled largely by Scotch-Irish and Germans, with an economic order of small farmers, free labor, and democratic ideals. The Anglican Church was relatively strong in the eastern counties, but it was almost nonexistent in the backcountry, which by the late colonial era was largely Presbyterian and Baptist, though there were many other sects in this area, notably Quaker, Lutheran, Moravian, and Reformed. The commerce of the east was largely an oceangoing trade with England, the West Indies, and the commercial colonies of the Atlantic seaboard, particularly Virginia and South Carolina. The backcountry had great difficulty making trade contacts and was thus restricted largely to overland trade with South Carolina, Virginia, and Pennsylvania.

During the proprietary period there was little commercial intercourse between the east and west and, because of the sparseness of back country population and inadequate east-west transportation facilities, little conflict arose between the sections. However, the growth and expansion of the Piedmont population after 1750 created problems of new counties, raised the old question of representation in the legislature, and brought forth complaints about eastern domination. By far the most serious causes of sectional rivalry and conflict were political in origin. They centered around the key issue of control of the provincial government by the planter aristocracy of the east. All the other problems that were to emerge, involving land, religion, money, trade and local government, were related to this question and could not be solved until the western counties had more equitable representation in the legislative, executive, and judicial branches of the government.

The undemocratic character of government at all levels was a source of irritation to most of the people in the back country. The unit of representation in the assembly was the county, and there were more counties in the east than in the rapidly growing west. Since counties could be created only by legislative enactment, this situation was likely to continue. As population increased in the Piedmont, the eastern-dominated legislature did, of course, create more counties in the west, but at the same time it also created additional counties in the east in order to guarantee that control would not be lost to the newly settled region. Of the nine borough towns, each of which had one representative in the assembly, only Salisbury and Hillsborough were in the Piedmont. (The other boroughs were Bath, Brunswick, Edenton, New Bern, Campbellton, Halifax, and Wilmington.) In the fifteen years after 1740, seven new western counties and six eastern counties were created, though nearly all the population increase was in the west. In 1754 the six westernmost counties—Anson, Granville, Johnston, Orange, Cumberland, and Rowan—had twenty-two thousand people and only twelve representatives. The remaining counties in the colony had forty-three thousand people and forty-five representatives. In 1766 Orange County alone had more white male taxables than Chowan, Pasquotank, Perquimans, Currituck, and Tyrrell combined; yet it had only two representatives, while these five northern counties had twenty-five. By 1771 about one-half of the colony's estimated quarter of a million people lived in the six western counties plus Mecklenburg, which was created from Anson and Rowan in 1762, yet these seven counties had only seventeen members (including three borough members) as compared with sixty-one for the other counties. The ratio for eastern representation was one representative for each seventeen hundred people; in the west it was one representative for each seventy-three hundred people. Not only did the east dominate the assembly, it also had control of the other branches of provincial government. From 1765 to 1771, the so-called Regulator period, the governor, all members of his council, all the judges, the treasurers, and the speakers of the house lived in the east.

As inequitable as representation was in the assembly, the undemocratic character of local government and the conduct of local officials were even greater grievances to the farmer of the back country. The common people resented the fact that not a single local official was chosen by popular vote. Justices of the peace, who also constituted the county court, were appointed by the governor, and it was this court that controlled almost every phase of local government and administration. It appointed, or nominated to the governor for appointment, the sheriff (who had an extremely important and powerful role in government as the major executive official of the court and the chief election official), constables, overseers of roads, patrollers, inspectors, town commissioners, and almost all local officials.

It is noteworthy that as a rule about two-thirds of the members of the assembly were justices of the peace; thus there was an alliance between the political leaders of the colony and the appointed local officials. The inevitable result of this undemocratic system was the centralization of political power and the evolution of what came to be called the "courthouse ring"—the "sheriff and his Bums," as one Regulator phrased it. As bad as this system was, it had its ardent defenders among the planter aristocracy of the east. These men stoutly resisted the idea of a popularly elected court. The distinguished James Iredell, attorney and pamphleteer, commenting on the proposed state constitution of 1776, expressed the view held by many conservatives when he wrote: ". . . a draft of the Constitution was presented to the house yesterday, and lies over for consideration . . . there is one thing in it which I cannot bear, and yet I am inclined to think it will stand. The inhabitants are empowered to elect the Justices in their respective counties, who are to be judges in the County Courts. . . . Numberless inconveniences must arise from so absurd an institution."

Multiple office holding, one of the most deplorable features of the colonial government, was a constant source of irritation and complaint. This practice existed in other colonies and was permitted by North Carolina law, but the people found it an odious system, especially when the officeholders were outsiders who seemed to hold the people in contempt. It is true that many, perhaps most, of the local officials were natives of the county which they served, but some, especially the most hated ones, such as Edmund Fanning and Henry Eustace McCulloh, were "foreigners." As one contemporary wrote: "to it [the county] come the merchant, the lawyer, the tavernkeeper, the artisans, and court officials, adventurers in the perenial pursuit of gain." A later writer made the exaggerated statement that "they [the officials] were, all of them or nearly all, of Northern or European birth, who came to the Southern provinces to make their fortunes, in what place, or by what means, they cared not." At a later period these political opportunists would have been called carpetbaggers. Edmund Fanning, a native of New York and a close friend of Governor Tryon, was the recognized leader of the courthouse ring in Orange County. He was a lawyer, register, superior court judge, colonel in the militia, assemblyman from Orange, and later borough representative from Hillsborough. Fanning hated the common people and they in turn detested him. Francis Nash, perhaps considered a "native" of Orange County, though he was born in Virginia, was a member of the assembly, clerk of court, justice of the peace, member of the county court, and captain of the local militia. John Frohock of Rowan County was a member of the assembly, clerk, justice of

Judge James Iredell.
Courtesy of the Library of Congress.

Edmund Fanning.

the peace, member of the county court, and colonel in the militia. There were many other instances of multiple office holding and alliances between local courthouse rings and eastern politicians.

In defense of these officials and of this system, it should be noted that the eighteenth-century concept of public office was quite different from what it is today. An office was then considered a gift of either the king or his agent, the governor, and the property right of the office holder. Hence one could buy and sell an office and military commissions. Instead of salaries, all of the local officials in colonial North Carolina received fees that were fixed by law. Most of the people, however, were ignorant of the law, which was changed frequently, and so they were always suspicious that excessive fees were being taken and illegal distraints being made of property for nonpayment of fees and other dues. Sheriffs, "sub-sheriffs," and clerks were constantly being accused of charging higher fees than the law allowed, and there are on record many sworn charges to illegal distraint of property. In 1768 ninety-nine people signed a formal complaint against Clerk Samuel Spencer, which read: "As to the Clerk his extortions are burthernsome to all that fall in his power as he takes double and sometimes treble his due. And tho it is true he purchased his office from Colonel Frohock and gave to the amount of one hundred and fifty pounds for it yet it's unreasonable we should bear the expense by way of extortion."

County and provincial officers, especially Fanning and Frohock, were satirized in "ambling epics and jingling ballads" by Rednap Howell, "poet of the Regulation," in a broadside entitled *When Fanning First to Orange Came.* Some of the best known verses follow.*

> Says Frohawk to Fanning, to tell the plain truth,
> When I came to this country I was but a youth:

---

* This was a true ballad and was handed down orally for many years. The earliest printed version dates from 1826 while another is only a portion of the ballad and dates from 1842. The excerpt is a new composite of several traditional versions.

My father sent for me, I wa'nt worth a cross,
And then my first study was to cheat for a horse.
I quickly got credit and strait ran away,
And haven't paid for him to this very day.

Says Fanning to Frohawk, 'tis a folly to lie,
I rode on an old mare that was blind in one eye,
Five shillings in money I had in my purse,
My coat it was patch'd but not much the worse.
But now we've got rich, and 'tis very well known,
That we'll do well enough if they'll let us alone.

When Fanning first to Orange came,
He look'd both pale and wan:
An old patch'd coat upon his back,
An old mare he rode on.
Both man and mare wa'nt worth five pounds,
As I've been often told;
But by his civil robberies,
He's laced his coat with gold.

Some historians have accepted the charges of Howell, Herman Husband, and other Regulator leaders without critical examination of contemporary records. Others have had little good to say about these so-called leaders of the rabble. Perhaps the truth about the Regulator movement lies somewhere between the two extreme views. Carl Bridenbaugh, one of the leading authorities on colonial history, wrote: "By pamphlet, ballad, and stump speech they [Howell and his fellow propagandists] made Colonel Fanning the symbol of misgovernment and extortion, although his crime seems to have been only that he was Tryon's friend." Bridenbaugh goes on to say that Howell's broadside "has probably blackened a name forever. The Regulators may have lost the war, but they certainly won the history."

By 1765 an atmosphere of general unrest persisted throughout most of the western counties, though no organized movement of protest had been established. There were charges of extortion, illegal fees, excessive taxes, and various other evils of local government. Little or nothing was said about representation in the legislature; paper currency and its depreciation received no mention, and the views of some popular writers to the contrary notwithstanding, little was said about arbitrary rule of the mother country. These poor farmers were concerned about problems closer home.

The growing tension between the east and west was heightened in 1766 by the passage of an act of the legislature that was aimed at establishing a permanent capital for the colony. For many years the royal governors and various colonial leaders had realized the need for a fixed seat of government. The assembly had been an itinerant body meeting at Edenton, New Bern, Wilmington, Bath, or at any place where the governor called it to sit. The governor, the councillors, and the treasurers all lived in different areas, and there existed no suitable buildings for housing their scattered records, which had to be carried from session to session in a common cart. As early as 1747 Governor Johnston said: "It is impossible to finish any matter as it ought to be while we go on in this itinerant way. We have now tried every town in the Colony and it is high time to settle somewhere." In 1758 Governor Dobbs succeeded in getting the legislature to pass a law locating the capital at Tower Hill on the Neuse River, but when the Privy Council learned that the capital was to be located on lands belonging to the governor himself, the law was disallowed. During his term of office, Governor Tryon repeatedly pressed the legislature to take some action on establishing a capital. People in the east were apprehensive that it might be located at Hillsborough, which had become something of the unofficial capital of the whole backcountry, and this led the representatives from the Albemarle and Pamlico Sound regions and the Cape Fear to unite in favor of New Bern. Governor Tryon recommended that town as a central location, and the assembly, in November 1766, passed "An Act for erecting a Convenient Building within the town of New Bern for the residence of the Governor." For this purpose the assembly voted £5,000, a sum that was increased by an additional £10,000 the next year. Owing to the inadequacy of funds in the treasury, the legislature ordered that the original £5,000 be paid "out of the money appropriated by Act of Assembly for erecting of Public Schools, and purchasing glebes," but provided that this sum must be repaid from a tax on alcoholic beverages and from a poll tax.

Work on the "Palace" for the governor was begun in 1767 under the supervision of John Hawks, whom Tryon had brought from Lincolnshire, England, "to superintend the work in all its branches." Hawks's plan included a brick two-story house, eighty-seven feet wide and fifty-nine feet deep, connected by curved colonnades with two outlying wings. The Palace, which served as both the governor's residence and the capitol, was completed in 1770 and was considered to be the finest government house in the English colonies. Here was the seat of government under the province's last two royal governors, Tryon and Martin. North Carolina's First Provincial Congress (1774) in defiance of royal authority and the independent state's first General Assembly (1777) also met here. The inauguration of the first constitutional governor, Richard Caswell, took place here, and it was frequently the seat of government until 1792 when Raleigh became the state capital. William Attmore, viewing the Palace in 1787 when it had already been turned to uses other than those of the royal governor and assembly, wrote: "The King of G. Britain's Arms, are still suffered to appear in a pediment at the front of the Building; which considering the independent spirit of the people averse to every vestige of Royalty appears Something strange." He commented upon the "very elegant" interior features including "the grand Staircase lighted from the Sky by a low Dome, which being glazed kept out the Weather." In 1791, when President Washington was tendered a "magnificent ball" at New Bern, his horses were stabled in the executive offices, and he described the Palace as "now hastening to ruin." In 1798 a fire destroyed all but the west wing, which for the next century and a half, "served as a warehouse, dwelling, stable and carriage house, parochial school, and chapel," before it was converted into an apartment house in 1931. During the 1950s a complete and authentic restoration, based upon extensive physi-

Tryon Palace, New Bern, built between 1767 and 1770. Ravaged by a fire in 1798, the building was restored from 1952 to 1959 and is now handsomely decorated with eighteenth-century furniture. *Courtesy of the Travel and Promotion Division, Department of Natural and Economic Resources, State of North Carolina.*

Chowan County Courthouse in Edenton, built about 1767 and used as a courthouse ever since. It has been called "perhaps the finest Georgian courthouse in the South." *Courtesy of the Travel and Promotion Division, Department of Natural and Economic Resources, State of North Carolina.*

cal and documentary research, was made and Tryon Palace is now one of the outstanding showplaces of North Carolina.

When the Palace was first completed, the assembly referred to it as "truly elegant and noble." Its construction apparently met with general approval in the east, but in the backcountry there was a great deal of bitter opposition. In 1768 one irate westerner wrote: "Not one man in twenty of the four most populous counties [Orange, Rowan, Mecklenburg, and Anson] will ever see this famous house when built, (as their connections and trade do, and ever will more naturally center in South Carolina)." The poll tax levied for the construction of this "unnecessary building" was particularly odious to the west, which had more people, but less wealth, than the east. One farmer in Mecklenburg County declared that "a man that is worth £10,000 pays no more than a poor back settler that has nothing but the labour of his hands to depend upon for his daily support."

The opposition to the building of the Palace was only one manifestation of unrest among the settlers of the backcountry. In the 1759 "Petition of Reuben Searcy and Others," expressing the views of "Sundry of the Inhabitants" of Granville County, the attorney general of the province was accused of exacting extortionate fees, of preventing the appointment of justices of the peace for the northern part of the county, and "through his wiles and false insinuations to which art and chicanerie he owes his great success and high preferment in this province" of imposing both "on the inferior class of mankind," and on Governor Dobbs. In his *Impartial Relation* (1770), Herman Husband implied that Searcy was prosecuted for libel, but the court records reveal no such action. One of the best written protests against the malpractices of local officials was "An Address to the People of Granville County," prepared by George Sims, schoolmaster of the Nutbush community, and dated June 6, 1765. This "Nutbush Address" described the "notorious and intolerable abuses" that the people were suffering, and specified such grievances as excessive taxes, high quitrents, extortionate fees, and fraudulent accounting of public monies. It declared that it was "not our mode, or form of Government, nor yet the body of our laws, that we are quarreling with, but with the malpractice of the Offices of our County Court, and the abuses which we suffer by those empowered to manage public affairs."

A dramatic illustration of the tension and unrest in the western counties was the so-called War of Sugar Creek. In May 1765 John Frohock and six other surveyors on the lands of Henry Eustace McCulloh and George Selwyn were soundly whipped by a group of more than one hundred angry farmers, "many of whom were Armed with Guns," led by Thomas Polk. McCulloh, writing to Fanning a few days after this incident, declared that "had I been present—I most assuredly and without ceremony had been murdered," and that the irate farmers had "declared solemnly—publicly, they will put me to death." Governor Tryon, hearing about this "Great Breach and Disturbance of His Majesty's Peace and Government," issued a proclamation on May 18, 1765, offering pardon to "any persons concerned in the said Riot" who would give the names of "the several Rioters" to him or to his attorney general. He never received any names.

The first effort of the western farmers to obtain relief from injustice through peaceful means was made by some citizens of Orange County in August 1766. A paper, later called "Regulator Advertisement, Number One," was circulated at the meeting of the county court at Hillsborough calling on all residents of the province to resist local oppression and to put an end to the extortion of county officers. It asked the people of Orange to elect delegates to "attend a general meeting on the Monday before the next November court at a suitable place where their is no Liquor . . . at which meeting let it be judiciously enquired whether the free men of this County labor under abuses of power or not." Herman Husband, an outstanding leader of the Regulators, said that this document was publicly read at court and that Thomas Lloyd, one of the assemblymen from Orange, "declared his approval of it, and the rest acknowledged it was reasonable." Other Orange officials, however, took the attitude that they were not responsible to the people; Fanning declined to refer his conduct to "the shallow understanding of the mob." The people of the county then appealed to the assembly, but this body failed to take satisfactory action to redress their grievances and the agitation continued.

Though the Regulators were unhappy about the "waste of Public funds," they were more concerned about the dishonesty of the sheriffs and other local officials. And Governor Tryon was inclined to agree with their complaints. Writing to the Earl of Shelburne in 1767, he declared that "the sheriffs have embezzled more than one half of the public money ordered to be raised and collected by them . . . about 40,000 pounds . . . not five thousand of which will possibly ever come into the treasury as in many instances the sheriffs and their securities are either insolvent or retreated out of the province." Tryon realized the need for reform in county government, and at this point the assembly agreed, declaring that: "The abuses in the department of the Sheriff's Office cry aloud for and shall receive the strictest attention and correction; . . . nor shall the imbezzlement and irregularities committed by other Collectors of the Public revenues escape the most exact inquiry nor anything be wanting on our part to prevent such abuses for the future." Accordingly laws were enacted to regulate the fees of inferior court clerks and to correct other evils in the administration of justice. Tryon thought that these laws should stop the "temptations that led to fraud, embezzlement, and other irregular practices," and he asked the people to petition the assembly whenever they became aware of specific instances of abuse.

Among the petitions presented to the assembly of 1768 was one signed by thirty citizens of Orange and Rowan. It read:

Your poor petitioners having been continually Squeez'd and oppressed by our Publick Officers both with Regard to their fees as also in the Laying on of Taxes as well as in Collecting together with Iniquitous appropriations, and wrong applications. . . . We humbly supplicate your Worships to take under your serious consideration, we labor under Extreme hardships about our levies, Money is very scarce and hardly . . . to be had would we Purchase it at ten times its value and we exceeding Poor and lie at a great distance from Trade . . . for Gods sake Gentlemen be not negligent or unconcerned in an affair of such importance. On your breath depends the Ruin or Prosperity of thousands of poor Families, and tho' to Gentlemen Rowling in affluence, a few shillings per man, may seem triffling yet to Poor people who must have their Bed and Bed Clothes yea their Wives Petticoats taken and sold to defray these charges, how Tremendous judge ye must be the consequences, an only Horse, to raise Bread or an only cow to give milk to an Helpless family by which in a great measure are other wise supported, seized and sold and kept for a single levy. . . . Good God Gentlemen, what will come of us when these demands come against us Paper Money we have none Gold and Silver we can purchase none. . . . To be concluded, it now depends on you whether we shall be made happy or miserable. Save us Save us from Inevitable Destruction for the Lords sake Gentlemen Exert yourselves this once in our favour and your Petitioners as in duty bound shall every pray.

The year 1768 also marked the formal organization of the Regulators, a name adopted because their primary goal was to gain the right to regulate their own local government. "Regulator Advertisement, Number Four," drawn up about January of that year, is perhaps the clearest statement of the evils of government that these people proposed to regulate.*

1. That we will pay no Taxes until we are satisfied they are agreeable to Law and Applied to the purposes therein mentioned unless we cannot help and are forced.
2. That we will pay no Officer any more fees than the Law allows unless we are obliged to it and then to shew a dislike to it & bear open testimony against it.
3. That we will attend our Meetings of Conference as often as we conveniently can . . .
4. That we will contribute to Collections for defraying necessary expenses attending the work according to our abilities.
5. That in Cases of differences in Judgment we will submit to the Majority of our Body.

---

* The word "Regulator" did not appear in this document; it was first used in "Regulator Advertisement, Number Six," of March 22, 1768.

Soon after "Regulator Advertisement, Number Six" appeared near the end of March 1768, a Regulator had his horse, saddle, and bridle distrained for nonpayment of taxes. On April 8, about seventy Regulators rode into Hillsborough and fired "a few guns into the Roof of Colonel Fanning's House, to signify they blamed him for all this abuse." On April 23, the indignant Fanning wrote Governor Tryon that

the late orderly and well-regulated County of Orange, is now (O my favourite County and people how art thou fallen) the very nest and bosom of rioting and rebellion—The people are now in every part and Corner of the County, meeting, conspiring, and confederating by solemn oath and open violence to refuse the payment of Taxes and prevent the execution of Law, threatening death and immediate destruction to myself and others, requiring settlements of the Public, Parish, and County Taxes, to be made before their leaders—Clerks, Sheriffs, Registers, Attornies and all Officers of every degree and station to be arraigned at the Bar of their Shallow Understanding and to be punished and regulated at their Will, and in a word, for them to become the sovereign arbiters of right and wrong.

Fanning went on to say that he expected "an attack from the whole united force of the regulators or rebels" at which time he intended "to bravely repulse them or nobly die." In Tryon's reply to Fanning four days later, the governor referred to the disaffection in Orange as "an infatuation, instigated by a few Persons, whose characters are as desperate as their Fortunes, and who having nothing themselves to lose, scruple not to involve men of a far different character and stamp, into all the Calamities and Miseries of civil discord, and who out of the general confusion, assuredly hope that the increase of their fortunes, may keep pace, with the weight, and measure of their Crimes." Tryon also issued two proclamations: one ordered the Regulators to disperse to their homes, the other called out the militia of Bute, Halifax, Granville, Rowan, Mecklenburg, Cumberland, and Johnston counties to be "held in readiness" to march to the aid of Fanning.

"Regulator Advertisement, Number Eleven," dated May 21, 1768, the best written and calmest of the Regulator documents, and signed by approximately five hundred residents of Orange County, was the climax of the Regulator attempts to obtain justice by peaceful and legal means. It began with an apology to the governor for anything that might be construed as derogatory to the king or the law, and it assured Tryon that neither disloyalty nor disaffection was the cause of their troubles, but "the corrupt and arbitrary Practices of nefarious and designing men who being put into Posts of Profit and Credit among us . . . use every artifice, every Fraud, and where these failed threats and menaces were not spared whereby to squeeze and extort from the wretched Poor." It also rebuked the "heated, unruly spirits" who had fired into Fanning's house. James Hunter and Rednap Howell carried this petition to Brunswick and presented it to the governor on June 20. After a meeting with the council, Tryon replied to the petition, declaring that the Regulator grievances did not justify their course of action. He ordered them to give up the name of "Regulators," to pay their taxes, and to be sure not to molest officers. Herman Husband later wrote that Tryon was "inclined to the other side, multiplying all our faults to the highest pitch he was capable of." Yet the governor, realizing the truth of some of the Regulator charges, also issued a warning to all officers and lawyers against taking excessive fees. He ordered that a list of legal fees be published, and then he directed the attorney general to prosecute all officers and lawyers charged with extortion. He also promised to go to Hillsborough in person at the next court session, in July, where he hoped to "find everyone at peace."

When Tryon arrived at Hillsborough in August, rumors were rife that he was raising the militia to suppress the Regulators and that he was calling on Indians to attack from the rear. Meantime Fanning had been indicted for taking excessive fees, and his trial had been set for the September session of court. On the other side of the controversy, Husband and Butler had also been arrested for "inciting the populace to rebellion" and were to be tried at the same court. Two other Regulators were also in prison awaiting trial. Threats that the imprisoned Regulators were to be rescued and reports of a general uprising prompted Tryon to call out the militia. A force of 1,461 men marched to Hillsborough for the meeting of the court. Tryon's action further irritated the Regulators and measurably increased the debt of the already impoverished colony by more than £4,500. A large number of Regulators—3,700 according to Husband—were present in Hillsborough when the court convened, with Maurice Moore as the presiding judge. Husband was tried and acquitted; Butler was fined £50 and sentenced to six months' imprisonment; the other two Regulators were fined £25 each and given sentences of three months. But the governor, eager to "quell the disturbances," released the prisoners and suspended the payment of their fines for three months. Fanning was found guilty of taking a six shilling fee when the legal charge was only two shillings and eight pence. He was fined the nominal sum of "one penny and costs" and he resigned his office, which was some consolation to the Regulators.

The Regulators continued to press their demands for reform in local government. Again they decided to carry their case to the assembly, and this time they hoped for some action because in the 1769 elections Orange, Granville, Anson, and Halifax counties had elected solid Regulator delegations. Ironically enough, Edmund Fanning was chosen to the assembly from Hillsborough, which had recently been made a borough through the influence of Governor Tryon. Meanwhile the Regulator organization was gaining new recruits and spreading into new areas. There were disorders in Rowan and Edgecombe counties and attacks on court officials in Anson and Johnston. But the most dramatic incident was the Hillsborough Riot. The court docket was filled with cases both for and against the Regulators, who had been coming into town for days "until the place was filled with a great number of these people called Regulators shouting, halooing and making a considerable tumult in the streets." When the court assembled, a group of about one

Governor Tryon and the Regulators.

hundred and fifty Regulators, led by Herman Husband, James Hunter, Rednap Howell, and William Butler, armed with sticks and switches, marched in and occupied all the available seats. Then Jeremiah Fields, acting as the Regulator spokesman, informed the presiding judge, Richard Henderson, that the Regulators had reason to believe that they could not obtain justice in his court, and hence they were determined to obtain it by their own means. According to Henderson's account all went well for about half an hour as most of the Regulators withdrew from the courthouse. Within a short time, however, bedlam broke loose. The Regulators attempted to strike the judge and compelled him to leave the bench. They next assaulted and severely whipped John Williams, a local attorney. William Hooper was "dragged and paraded through the streets," and treated with every mark of contempt and insult. Turning next to Edmund Fanning, who was hiding behind the judge's bench, the mob pulled him out of the courthouse by his heels, dragged him through the streets, and gave him a brutal whipping. They then broke into his house and burned his papers, destroyed his furniture, and finally demolished the building. Alexander Martin, Michael Holt, Thomas Hart, and many others were whipped. The mob rioted through the streets, smashing the windows of private residences and terrorizing the inhabitants. Unable to enforce order and fearing for his own safety, Judge Henderson adjourned court and left for his home in Granville County, leaving "poor Col. Fanning and the little Borough in a wretched situation." The next day, the Regulators took over the deserted courtroom and tried their own cases in a mock court. The entries made on the court docket were bitter, sarcastic, and sometimes vulgar. In *McMund* v. *Courtney* the comment was "Damned Rogues"; in *Wilson* v. *Harris,* "All Harrises are Rogues"; in *Brown* v. *Lewis,* "The Man was sick. It tis damned roguery"; in *Fanning* v. *Smith,* "Fanning pays cost but loses nothing"; in *Hogan* v. *Husbands,* "Hogan pays and be damned."

When the assembly convened at New Bern on December 5, 1770, an atmosphere of panic was running through the province.

Tryon summoned the council, which advised him to use the militia to quiet the disturbances. In his address to the assembly, he denounced the "seditious mob" at Hillsborough and urged the enactment of laws to meet the emergency. The result was the passage of the Johnston Riot Act on January 15, 1771. This "Bloody Act," as the Regulators called it, provided that prosecutions for riots might be tried in any county regardless of where the incidents took place. It also outlawed any person resisting or avoiding arrest and authorized the governor to suppress the Regulators by military force.* Husband was expelled from this session of the assembly on charges of libel and as "not being a credit to the Assembly." He was jailed at New Bern but the Craven County grand jury failed to find a true bill against him and he was released. Reaction to the "Bloody Act" was swift and defiant. The Regulator organization increased in numbers, and resolutions were drawn up in several counties against the "riotous act." In at least two counties the Regulators pledged themselves to pay no more taxes, declared Fanning an outlaw to be killed on sight, forbade any sessions of court, and threatened to kill all lawyers and judges.

Tryon, who had already accepted a royal appointment to become governor of New York, acted with drastic and dramatic swiftness. He called for a special session of court to be held at Hillsborough, and, acting on the advice of the council, he summoned the militia "with all expedition" to protect the court and to quell the Regulators. Tryon marched from New Bern to Hillsborough with an estimated fourteen hundred militiamen and camped on Great Alamance Creek, near present Burlington. On May 16 he was met by a force of about two thousand Regulators who asked for an audience with the governor. Tryon refused to communicate with them "as long as they were in arms against the government," and gave them one hour to lay down

---

* It is noteworthy that some years after the Regulator War had ended Governor Martin was notified by the Privy Council that portions of this law were "irreconcilable with the principles of that constitution, full of danger in its operation, and unfit for any part of the British empire."

their arms and disperse. At the end of the hour, he gave the order to fire; two hours later the ill-equipped and poorly led Regulators were defeated and scattered. Tryon's losses were nine killed and sixty-one wounded; the Regulators suffered nine dead and an undertermined number of wounded. Tryon's terse report about the Battle of Alamance claimed: "a signal victory was obtained over the obstinate and infatuated rebels."

Twelve Regulators were tried for treason and all were convicted. Six were hanged, but the others were pardoned by the governor. Tryon offered clemency to all Regulators who would lay down their arms and submit to authority, and within six weeks more than six thousand capitulated. Husband, Howell, Hunter, and several other Regulator leaders had left the province before the Battle of Alamance. Many Regulators, perhaps numbering in the thousands, moved to the Tennessee country. Morgan Edwards, writing in 1772, declared that these people "despaired of seeing better times and therefore quitted the province. It is said that 1,500 families have departed since the battle of Alamance and to my knowledge a great many more are only waiting to dispose of their plantations in order to follow them." Tryon and Fanning, the two officials most hated by the Regulators, had also left North Carolina for good.

In evaluating the role and importance of the Regulators in colonial history some writers have made the statement, unsupported by documentary evidence, that most of these people were Loyalists in the Revolution, which occurred only a few years after Alamance. Professor R. O. DeMond wrote that "an examination of the records reveals that of 883 of the known Regulators, 289 were Whigs, 34 Tories, and 560 Revolutionary status unknown." Some writers have also boasted of Alamance as "the first battle of the American Revolution." Concerning this claim, what Professor R. D. W. Connor wrote some years ago remains valid:

The Regulators made no such claims for themselves. . . . The Regulators were not contending for a great constitutional principle lying at the very foundation of human government such as inspired the men who fought the Revolution. Every grievance of which the former complained could have been removed by their own representatives in an assembly chosen by the people; the American people sent no representative to the British Parliament. . . . The one was an insurrection, the other a revolution. . . . The Regulators did not dispute the constitutional right of the Assembly to enact the laws of which they complained: they merely objected to the improper execution of these laws. Then too, there is no continuity between the Regulation and the Revolution. The principles of the revolt against the Stamp Act did not die with the repeal of the act, but became the living issue in the great Revolution. The movement of the Regulators expended itself at Alamance and died out with the removal of the causes and persons which gave rise to it.

The movement to insure justice for the inhabitants of the back-country was interrupted by the American Revolution and its aftermath, but the later renewal of the east-west conflict reached its grand climax and victory for the west in the Constitutional Convention of 1835.

11

PRELUDE TO REVOLUTION

With the acquisition of Canada and the other territorial gains at the end of the French and Indian War in 1763, the area of the British Empire in America was more than doubled, and the problems of governing it were made all the more complex. At home the war had increased Britain's national debt by at least £60 million at a time when the English taxpayers were already groaning loudly under extremely heavy financial burdens. Across the Atlantic in the colonies the enlarged empire brought many complications. Practically all the newly won territory was a wilderness, sparsely inhabited by Indians who had been allied with the French during the series of wars that had just ended. British statesmen feared that France, defeated but by no means crushed, might soon launch an attack somewhere in America to regain her lost empire and prestige. In addition, some of the older and more established English colonies were growing increasingly lax in their loyalty toward the mother country.

The immediate task of finding a solution to the financial and imperial problems was in the hands of George Grenville, chancellor of the exchequer, whom George III made prime minister in 1763. Grenville, a brother-in-law of William Pitt, did not share Pitt's sympathy with the colonial point of view. Like many other British leaders, for example, Grenville thought that the colonists ought to pay part of the cost of their own defense and colonial administration. To provide for this the Grenville ministry, in cooperation with Parliament and with the approval of the king, instituted a series of measures known as the New Colonial Policy. Parts of this policy were new, while other aspects of it were merely modifications of old laws. One of the new features was the decision to station permanently some ten thousand British soldiers at critical places in the colonies. By the Mutiny Act of 1765 (also called the Quartering Act), the colonists were required to assist in provisioning and maintaining these troops.

Grenville was a staunch mercantilist, and as such he believed that the future strength of the empire depended on the total elimination of all forms of illicit trade. In order to enforce the trade laws and to check smuggling, ships of the royal navy were assigned to American waters. The customs service was reorganized and enlarged, and provision was made for all cases of smuggling to be tried in Vice-Admiralty courts without the benefit of sympathetic juries. The Sugar Act of 1764, a modified continuation of the Molasses Act of 1733, was designed to eliminate illegal trade between the continental colonies and the foreign West Indies. The provisions of this act cut the duty on foreign molasses in half, but increased duties on various kinds of sugar, put a tax on a number of new items, such as coffee and indigo, and described procedures for more effective collection of duties. The Sugar Act was a minor irritant to North Carolina importers of sugar, molasses, and other dutiable articles listed in the law, and the act met with little organized opposition. This was in sharp contrast to the violent reaction of Massachusetts, Rhode Island, and some of the other commercial provinces. To prevent the colonies from paying their debts to British creditors in depreciated currency, the Currency Act of 1764 forbade the issuance of any more paper money and required the colonies to "retire on schedule" all paper currency that had been issued in the war just ended.

Because the Sugar Act was calculated to produce but a small percentage—one-third at best—of what Grenville believed the colonies should contribute toward their administration and defense, he proposed to raise most of the remainder through "certain stamp duties." Grenville originally proposed a stamp tax for the colonies in March 1764, but because it was the first attempt at *direct* taxation of America, he gave a year's respite so that the colonies might have an opportunity to suggest a more satisfactory method of raising the desired revenues. The alternative, also proposed by Grenville, was that each colony be asked to raise its quota through its own legislature. Most American answers to this were protests and clearly revealed the mounting colonial resentment of Parliamentary taxation. Six colonies— North Carolina was not one of them—forwarded vigorous objections through their assemblies.

In December 1764 the Board of Trade considered these protests and denounced them as showing "a most indecent respect" for Parliament. Early in February 1765 the colonial agents, headed by Benjamin Franklin, gained an audience with Grenville. The prime minister reiterated his position that the colonies "can and ought to pay something to the cause" and there was "no better way than to lay such a tax." He agreed, however, that if the colonies had a better plan he would adopt it. Franklin suggested the old requisition method, which Grenville rejected because he believed that an individual colony would never accept or meet its own quota.

On February 13, 1765 the Stamp Bill was introduced into Parliament. There could be no more delay because increasingly vehement protests were coming from the English people themselves, who feared that their own taxes might become even higher unless additional revenue was raised in America. The debates on the bill in Parliament were not exciting. In fact, Edmund Burke said that he had never heard more languid ones, and Robert Walpole wrote that there was "nothing of note in Parliament" the day the bill was passed. Only four members of the House of Commons spoke against the measure, of whom the most prominent was Colonel Isaac Barré. He, "with Eyes darting Fire," proclaimed that Americans were "Sons of Liberty" fighting the cause of all Englishmen. Yet he also went on to admit that "the more sensible people" in the colonies would not deny Parliament's right to tax them. On March 22, 1765 the Stamp Bill, which had passed both the House of Commons and the House of Lords, became law.

The Stamp Act was to become effective on November 1, 1765, and its proceeds were to be used "toward further defraying the expenses of defending, protecting, and securing" the American colonies. The law required that stamps or stamped paper, costing from a half penny to £10 and payable only in specie, be used for a great variety of items: newspapers, pamphlets, legal papers, mortgages, bills of lading, skins, parchments, college diplomas, almanacs, playing cards, dice, tavern licenses, and advertisements. On some of these items the tax was graduated, for example, the costlier or larger the almanac, the heavier the stamp tax. Certain items were tax-exempt, such as Bibles and other religious publications, school books, assembly proceedings, marriage certificates, and bills of exchange. Administration of the law was placed in the hands of commissioners of stamp duties in Great Britain, who were to operate through special stamp distributors in each colony. As under the Sugar Act, heavy fines and forfeitures were provided for infringement, and penalties were to be equally divided among the informant, the governor, and the British treasury. Cases might be tried "in any court of record or in any court of admiralty."

In spite of the protests raised against the Stamp Act prior to its passage, Grenville and many other Englishmen actually anticipated no serious colonial opposition; nor for that matter did some colonial leaders, including Franklin, Richard Henry Lee, and James Otis, expect the colonists to persist in their protests once the law became effective. After all, stamp taxes had been used in England for a long time and their rates at home were generally higher than those imposed on the colonies. When William Tryon took office as governor of North Carolina on April 3, 1765, the Stamp Act was the leading topic of discussion in the political circles of all the English colonies in America. Even before his arrival the people had already made up their minds as to what course they would pursue. As early as 1760 the assembly had declared that "it was the indubitable right of the Assembly to frame and model every bill whereby an aid was granted to the King, and that every attempt to deprive them of the enjoyment thereof was an infringement of the rights and privileges of the Assembly." Then, in October 1764 the assembly announced very directly its opposition to the right of Parliament to impose internal taxes on the colonies as being "against what we esteem our inherent right and Exclusive privilege of imposing our own Taxes."

North Carolina, like other colonies, resisted the Stamp Act from the first on the ground that it was a violation of the traditional principle of English liberty that there must be no taxation without representation. In 1765 in a pamphlet entitled *The Justice and Policy of Taxing the American Colonies in Great Britain, Considered,* Judge Maurice Moore, a native son of the Lower Cape Fear, denounced the Stamp Act and denied the right of Parliament to impose it on the colonies. He also rejected the prevalent English idea of "virtual representation" insofar as the colonies were concerned. At the same time he contended that direct representation of the American colonies in Parliament was impractical, if not impossible. Therefore, he concluded, they could not "with the least degree of justice be taxed by the British Parliament." When Governor Tryon asked John Ashe, speaker of the assembly, what the attitude of the colony would be toward the Stamp Act, Ashe replied: "We will resist it to the death."

It was at about this time that Ashe, Cornelius Harnett, Hugh Waddell, Abner Nash, Robert Howe, and other radical leaders began organizing the Sons of Liberty, particularly in the Wilmington area. The title of this organization was derived from Barré's reference in his speech against the Stamp Act. North Carolina was primarily a colony of rural residents and many of her most influential leaders lived on plantations and farms rather than in towns. Unlike the prevailing pattern in other colonies, the Sons of Liberty in North Carolina lived in rural areas. In the towns membership in the organization generally consisted of small tradesmen, mechanics, common seamen, and the unemployed; in the rural districts, small farmers filled the ranks. Although the Sons of Liberty were denounced by Governor Martin as "mobs," they were not a disorderly, riotous group.

Opposition to the Stamp Act was a popular movement in North Carolina, especially in the Lower Cape Fear, "though directed and controlled by a few trusted leaders," such as the men who were instrumental in forming the Sons of Liberty. On June 8 the Massachusetts legislature urged all of the colonies to send delegates to a congress that was to be held in New York City in October for the purpose of considering the Stamp Act and other British laws relating to America. North Carolina, along with three other colonies—New Hampshire, Virginia, and Georgia—was not represented at the Stamp Act Congress. The reason for North Carolina's absence was that Governor Tryon refused to call the assembly in time to choose delegates, an action for which he was strongly reprimanded when that body met the next year. But the governor could not prevent public demonstrations within the province, a number of which occurred during the summer at Edenton, New Bern, Cross Creek, and other places. For obvious reasons the Cape Fear, as the center of North Carolina's trade, as the residence of Governor Tryon, and as the home of the newly appointed stamp master for the colony, Dr. William Houston, became "the chief scene of the resistance and its course determined the course of the province."

The first significant demonstration in the colony against the Stamp Act took place in Wilmington on October 19, 1765. It was Saturday and many people from the vicinity had come into town. By seven o'clock in the evening about five hundred people had assembled at the courthouse, where they burned in effigy the Earl of Bute, whom they mistakenly blamed for the passage of the hated act. The crowd then proceeded to every house in town, routed out the men and escorted them to the bonfire. They concluded their evening's celebration by drinking toasts to "Liberty, Property, and No Stamp Duty," and "otherwise disporting themselves until midnight, without doing any Mischief." This demonstration was so exciting that it invited repetition. On the evening of October 31, which was Halloween and also the day before the Stamp Act was to take effect,

a great Number of People again assembled, and produced an Effigy of Liberty, which they put into a Coffin, and marched in solemn Procession with it to the Church-Yard. . . . But before they committed the Body to the Ground, they thought it adviseable to feel its Pulse; and when finding some Remains of Life, they returned back to a Bonfire ready prepared, placed the Effigy before it in a large Two-arm'd Chair, and concluded the Evening with great Rejoicings, on finding that LIBERTY had still an Existence in the COLONIES.—Not the least Injury was offered to any Person.

The following morning, November 1, the Stamp Act went into effect under very peculiar circumstances. Almost everyone in the colony had heard about it, but not even Governor Tryon had received official notice of the law or a copy of it, nor had any stamps arrived. Consequently, the law could not be enforced. Without stamps, clearance papers for ships could not be issued, and without these, ships could not enter or leave. The port was closed and shipping was paralyzed. Likewise, the courts could not operate for lack of stamps to authenticate necessary legal documents. Because of the lack of stamps the local newspaper had stopped appearing. When publication was resumed, the newspaper was published on unstamped paper and with a skull and crossbones at the place where the stamp was to have been affixed.

The people of the area were inactive until mid-November. By that time Dr. Houston had received formal notice from England of his appointment as stamp distributor for North Carolina. When Houston visited Wilmington on November 16, "three or four Hundred People immediately gathered together, with Drums beating and Colours flying, and repaired to the House, the said STAMP OFFICER put up at, and insisted upon knowing, 'Whether he intended to execute his said Office, or not?' He told them, 'He should be very sorry to execute any Office disagreeable to the People of the Province.' But they, not content with such a Declaration, carried him into the Court-

House, where he signed a Resignation satisfactory to the Whole."
According to an account of this episode in the *North Carolina
Gazette*, there was "not the least Insult offered to any Person."
Governor Tryon and Dr. Houston probably felt otherwise. But
Tryon, who was ill at the time, was eager to placate the populace
before any stamps arrived. Accordingly, he sent a special
invitation to the leading citizens of the area to dine with him at
his house on November 18. About fifty merchants and other
gentlemen of New Hanover, Brunswick, Duplin, and Bladen
counties accepted. The governor "urged to them the expediency
of permitting the circulation of stamps," though he did not wish
to discuss the question of Parliament's right to tax. He even
offered to pay the tax personally on any legal documents on
which he, as governor, received a fee. He also promised to pay for
a specified number of wine licenses for the various towns of the
colony. Tryon's guests replied to him in writing the next day,
saying that they thought it was "securer conduct" to prevent to
the utmost of their powers the operation of the Stamp Act in any
of its features.

The situation was becoming critical. No ships had cleared the
port of Brunswick since November 1, and unless stamps were
used no ships could leave port, no cargoes could be landed, no
courts of law could be open, and no newspapers, books, or
pamphlets could be printed. Tryon wrote: "No business is
transacted in the Courts of Judicature. . . . and all Civil
Government is now at a stand." The situation was deteriorating
in other parts of the province as well. The Reverend James Reed,
writing from New Bern said: "Tho' the people here are
peaceable and quiet yet they seem very uneasy, discontented,
and dejected. The Courts of Justice are in a great measure shut
up and it is expected that in a few weeks there will be a total
stagnation of trade."

The struggle reached a climax early in 1766. In January two
merchant ships anchored at Brunswick, the *Dobbs* and the
Patience, were seized by Captain Jacob Lobb of the British *Viper*
because their clearance papers were not stamped. Later a third

vessel, the *Ruby,* shared a similar fate. Captain Lobb delivered the ships' papers to Collector William Dry so that proceedings might be instituted against them in the Vice-Admiralty Court. Dry consulted the attorney general and submitted three queries to him. First, did failure to obtain clearances on stamped paper justify the seizures? Second, should judgment be given against the vessels "upon proof being made that it was impossible to obtain clearances" on stamped paper? Third, should the proceedings be instituted in the Vice-Admiralty Court at Halifax, Nova Scotia, rather than in North Carolina? The attorney general's decision in February that Lobb's seizures were legal and that the two ships that had been detained should be sent to Nova Scotia for legal proceedings, was the signal for armed resistance. On February 18 a meeting in Wilmington of "the principal gentlemen, freeholders, and inhabitants" of several counties elected leaders and signed an "Association Against the Stamp Act." The next day several hundred armed patriots marched to Brunswick and posted a guard around Governor Tryon's residence. After an argument with the governor they broke open the collector's desk and took the papers of the seized vessels. On February 20, after reinforcements had augmented their number to an estimated one thousand men, a group of "insurgents" boarded the *Viper* and compelled the captain to release the seized merchant vessels. The next morning a "detachment of sixty men came down the avenue, and the main body drew up in front in sight and within three hundred yards" of Tryon's residence. Cornelius Harnett, at "the head of the detachment," asked to speak with Mr. Pennington, "his Majesty's Comptroller," who had taken refuge in Tryon's house. At first the governor declined to send forth his guest, but Harnett, "standing face to face and eye to eye with the Governor," declared that the people would take Pennington by force if he were longer detained. Tryon was firm, but Pennington resigned his office and went with Harnett and the "inhabitants in arms" into the main part of town. Here "in a circle of cheering patriots" he took oath, along with all the other officials who were gathered there, except the governor, "that they would not, directly or indirectly, by themselves, or any other person employed under them, sign or execute in their several Offices, any stampt Papers, until the Stamp Act should be accepted by the province."

The *North Carolina Gazette,* commenting on the Brunswick demonstration, said: "It is well worthy of observation that few instances can be produced of such a number of men being together so long and behaving so well; not the least noise or disturbance, nor any person seen disguised with liquor, during the whole of their stay in Brunswick; neither was any injury offered to any person, but the whole affair was conducted with decency and spirit, worthy the imitation of all Sons of Liberty throughout the continent." In no other colony was the resistance by force so well organized and executed. Governor Tryon knew each of his opponents in this struggle; not one of them made any attempt to disguise himself or to conceal his identity in any way. Acting in a forthright manner, without fear, these men succeeded in preventing the operation of the Stamp Act in North Carolina. In so doing they gave clear evidence of their support of the belief that Parliament had no right to levy such a tax in America.

American opposition, particularly the nonimportation agreements, soon made itself felt in England. Thousands of workers lost their jobs as their employers were faced with countermanded orders from the colonies. Merchants could not collect their debts from colonials and bills of exchange were returned from America protested. Newspapers printed more and more letters and articles blaming the current economic recession on the Stamp Act, and Parliament was flooded with petitions from British merchants and manufacturers urging repeal. Even George III, in the face of turmoil in America and growing opposition at home, favored modification of the law. Grenville was not in office when the storm broke, so it became the responsibility of the newly formed ministry, headed by Lord Rockingham, to end the crisis. Repeal seemed the only solution. With William Pitt, "friend of America," leading the fight, the House of Commons and the House of Lords voted favorably, and on March 18, 1766 the king signed the repeal measure. Throughout England there was rejoicing. Celebrations, bonfires, and the ringing of bells followed the good news. Members of Parliament who had voted for repeal had "saved England from ruin." "The Joyous News" was received throughout the colonies with jubilation, but in their excitement the colonies seemed to have overlooked the Declaratory Resolution of March 18, 1766. In this statement Parliament asserted that it "had, hath, and of right ought to have, full power and authority to make laws and statutes of sufficient force and validity to bind the colonies and people of America . . . in all cases whatsoever." Parliament still retained the right to tax the colonies.

When the Rockingham ministry failed to find a substitute for the repealed Stamp Act, and when the Sugar Act did not produce the expected revenue from America, there were severe political repercussions in England. George III, highly displeased with Rockingham, succeeded in having a new ministry formed in August 1766. Its nominal head was Lord Grafton, but the king actually looked to William Pitt, who was soon to be elevated to the peerage as the Earl of Chatham, for the real help in building the new government. Another prominent member of the ministry was Lord Shelburne, secretary of state for the Southern Department, who was considered a friend of the colonies. The other outstanding figure was Charles Townshend, chancellor of the exchequer, popularly known as "Champagne Charlie." This "mosaic ministry" was formed primarily to deal with domestic affairs since it was believed by many Englishmen that the repeal of the Stamp Act marked the end of troubles in America. This might indeed have been the case had Pitt retained his health, but he soon suffered a recurrence of the gout that incapacitated him. Consequently, Townshend was able to assume the practical leadership of the ministry. Unfortunately for England and the empire, his views concerning America were closer to those of Grenville than to those of Chatham. His attempts to use coercion rather than conciliation reopened the whole question of the relationship of the colonies to Parliament and to the empire.

As chancellor of the exchequer, Townshend was responsible for the delicate task of preparing the annual budget. One of the first items to come under consideration was the cost of maintaining the army. While these estimates were being debated in the House of Commons, George Grenville insisted that the colonies pay at least part of the £400,000 allocated in the proposed budget for colonial defense. On his own responsibility and without even consulting the rest of the cabinet, Townshend assured Grenville and his supporters that he could raise the money in the colonies without antagonizing the Americans. Because the colonies had objected so strenuously to a direct tax (the Stamp Act), he decided to revert to indirect taxation as the best means of making the colonies nearly self-supporting. By May 1767 Townshend had three major proposals ready for parliamentary action. The first was designed to raise additional revenues in America through new customs duties. Under the second proposal, the revenues so derived would be used to pay the salaries of colonial governors, judges, and other royal officials. The third proposal suggested rigid enforcement of the new duties by a board of customs commissioners in America. All three proposals passed Parliament without strong opposition.

The most controversial Townshend measure was the Duty or Revenue Act, passed on June 29, 1767, to become effective the following November 20. Duties, expected to produce some £40,000 annually, were levied on wine, glass, lead, painters' colors, and tea. As the proceeds were to be used primarily to pay the salaries of governors, judges, and other royal officials, this meant an innovation for America, a civil list. To help the reorganized customs service enforce the law, writs of assistance (general search warrants) were specifically legalized. All violators of the act were to be tried in Vice-Admiralty courts. This law and the energetic efforts to enforce it gave a new impetus to union sentiment in the colonies, which was highlighted by the Massachusetts Circular Letter of 1768. The letter, written by Samuel Adams, was sent to all the continental colonies, inviting the cooperation of all the provinces in concerted measures of resistance in order that their remonstrances and petitions to the king "should harmonize with each other." Hoping to check the mounting opposition to British policies, Lord Hillsborough, secretary of state for the colonies, demanded that the Massachusetts legislature rescind the letter and that the assemblies of the other colonies treat it with contempt on pains of "an immediate prorogation or dissolution." Massachusetts refused to rescind, and the other colonies "applauded her spirit."

When the assembly convened in North Carolina, Speaker John Harvey laid the Massachusetts Circular Letter before it. The assembly took no formal action, but instead it voted to send "an humble, dutiful and loyal address" to the king, asking for a repeal of the "several acts of Parliament imposing duties on goods imported into America." Samuel Johnston and Joseph Hewes, two of the leading members of the assembly, were so disgusted with the "pusillanimity" of that body that they refused to serve on the committee to prepare the address, but the other members, under Harvey's leadership, agreed to participate. The committee's address to the king reminded him that in the past whenever it had been "found necessary to levy supplies within this Colony requisitions have been made by your Majesty or your Royal Predecessors and conformable to the rights of this people, and by them chearfully and liberally complied with. . . ." The address, however, firmly denied the right of Parliament to tax the colonies: "This is a Taxation which we are fully persuaded the acknowledged Principles of the British Constitution ought to protect us from. Free men cannot be legally taxed but by themselves or their Representatives, and that your Majesty's Subjects within this Province are represented in Parliament we cannot allow, and are convinced that from our situation we never can be. . . ."

Speaker Harvey sent a letter to the Massachusetts legislature in which he declared that the North Carolina assembly will "ever be ready, firmly to unite with their sister colonies, in pursuing every constitutional measure for redress of grievances so justly complained of." Other colonies also rallied to the support of Massachusetts. The Virginia legislature denounced recent British actions in a series of resolutions, which were sent to the other assemblies "requesting their concurrence therein." The governor of Virginia responded by dissolving the legislature, but the "burgesses promptly met as a convention." They agreed on a Non-importation Association and circulated its provisions throughout the colonies. When the North Carolina assembly met in October 1769, nonimportation agreements had already been generally adopted by the other colonies. On November 2 Speaker Harvey presented the Virginia resolutions, and without a dissenting vote they were adopted almost verbatim. The assembly agreed on sending a second protest to the king in which once again the right of Parliament to tax the colonies was denied. The assembly's protest also denounced the carrying of any American to England for trial as "highly derogatory to the rights of British Subjects . . . as thereby the inestimable privilege of being tried by a jury of the Vicinage will be taken away from the party accused." Governor Tryon censured the assembly for its action, declared that it "sapped the foundations of confidence and gratitude," and made it his "indispensable duty to put an end to this Session." Whereupon Speaker Harvey called for a meeting of the members of the assembly "independent of the governor." A "convention" met in the courthouse at New Bern with Harvey as "Moderator"; sixty-four of the sixty-seven assemblymen attended. In a two-day session this extralegal body drew up a nonimportation association, which pledged the signers—all those in attendance—to a course of economy, industry, and thrift. The following was unanimously agreed upon: to "encourage and promote the use of North American manufactures in general, and those of this province in particular"; to neither import themselves nor purchase from others any goods, except paper, "which are or shall hereafter be taxed by act of Parliament for the purpose of raising a revenue in America"; and to consider "every subscriber who shall not strictly adhere to his agreement, according to the true intent and meaning thereof . . . with the utmost contempt." The association agreement was circulated throughout the province and led to the formation of several local associations.

The adoption of nonimportation associations was one thing; enforcement of the agreements was something else. There were constant reports of merchants selling at exorbitant prices "old moth-eaten clothes" that had been on their shelves for years. Some merchants also defied the rules by importing goods, much to the chagrin of those who abided by the agreements.

In North Carolina the merchants of the Cape Fear were the largest importers of British goods, and their reaction to nonimportation was of prime importance. Fortunately, Cornelius Harnett, the "Pride of the Cape Fear" and one of the leading merchants in the province, was also chairman of the Sons of Liberty, and his influence had great effect on other merchants. As soon as news of Parliament's partial repeal of the Townshend taxes reached Wilmington, Harnett called a meeting of the Sons of Liberty in the Wilmington District. A large number of "the principal inhabitants" attended (June 2, 1770) and they "meaningfully agreed to keep strictly to the nonimportation agreement" and to cooperate with the other colonies "in every legal measure for obtaining ample redress of the grievances so justly complained of."

The Townshend taxes did not yield the revenues that had been anticipated, and the mounting opposition in the colonies surprised many British leaders. Parliament, once again yielding to pressure from the colonies, modified its policy. In early 1770 it repealed all of the taxes, except the three pence per pound tax on tea, which was kept at the insistence of George III, in order to "retain the principle." News of repeal reached North Carolina in late spring 1770 and met with general approval. Those who had suffered most during the days of nonimportation, merchants and shippers, had seen their profits decline and their ships tied up in port. Yet, most of them had gone along with nonimportation to help win the struggle over taxation. Now that Britain had relented on everything but the tax on tea, these conservatives looked forward to better times, and they were not disappointed.

Harnett's House (top) and Lillington Hall (bottom), homes of two of
North Carolina's prominent colonial and Revolutionary leaders in the
Lower Cape Fear section.

Conditions quickly returned to normal, and colonial trade with England jumped from £4.5 million in 1770 to over £7 million in 1771.

During the interval of calm that followed repeal of the Townshend taxes, however, Governor Josiah Martin and the assembly were engaged in a bitter quarrel over the "foreign attachments clause." A number of British merchants trading with North Carolina had become extensive landowners in the colony. Under the Tryon Court Law of 1768, the court had power to attach this property for debts owed by nonresidents to North Carolinians. The British merchants strenuously objected to this provision, and Governor Martin received royal instruction not to approve any law having the foreign attachments clause. On the one side of the controversy that developed over the provision was the governor of North Carolina and the authorities, merchants, and others in England who wished to do business and own property in the colony without being subject to the colony's laws. On the other side was the North Carolina assembly, representing the creditors of the British merchants. After prolonged controversy between the council, which opposed the foreign attachments provision, and the house, which favored it, a compromise was reached by the passage of a court law containing the attachments clause, but with a provision suspending its operation "until the King's pleasure could be learned." The king rejected this law and instructed Governor Martin to set up courts of oyer and terminer by the "ever ready prerogative," that is, without legislative sanction.

In March 1773 Martin appointed Maurice Moore and Richard Caswell judges to sit with Chief Justice Martin Howard to hold these courts. When the assembly met in December, the governor informed it of the "royal disallowance," but at the same time he was forced to ask for legislative appropriations for the expense of his "prerogative courts." Not surprisingly the assembly flatly refused to vote such an appropriation, declaring that "we cannot consistent with the Justice due to our Constituents make provisions for defraying the expense attending a measure which we do not approve." Martin prorogued the assembly, asking the members to present fairly the facts at issue to their constituents before taking any further action. When the assembly reconvened in March 1774, its members told Martin that they had consulted the people, who "have expressed their warmest approbation of our past proceedings, and have given us positive instructions to persist in our endeavor to obtain the process of Foreign Attachments upon the most liberal and ample footing." Martin appealed to the assembly for a compromise, but it stood its ground. The usual bill with the usual clause was passed, and, as expected, Governor Martin rejected it. This was the end of the struggle over the foreign attachment clause, for the only other assembly that met in North Carolina under royal rule remained in session only four days and never had time to enact a court law. The colony, therefore, remained without courts for the trial of civil cases until after independence was declared.

Throughout the colonies, the leaders of the Whigs, as the opponents of British policies were now called, held many conferences to work out a plan for united action. Up to this time the radical cause throughout the colonies had apparently been slowly dying even though the Whig leaders had been desperately striving to keep it alive. The first answer in late 1772 seemed to be the committees of correspondence. Such committees, chiefly on a local basis, had been in vogue for some time, especially during the Stamp Act crisis. The Sons of Liberty had also made effective use of such committees in communicating among themselves.

During the summer of 1773 the Virginia House of Burgesses created a standing Committee of Correspondence and Inquiry "to obtain the most early and authentic intelligence of all British Colonial Acts or proceedings of the Administration which might relate to or affect the British Colonies in America and to keep up and maintain a Correspondence with the sister colonies respecting these considerations." In December of that year, the North Carolina assembly created its first Committee of Correspondence, consisting of John Harvey, Robert Howe, Richard Caswell,

Edward Vail, John Ashe, Joseph Hewes, and Samuel Johnston. This committee was authorized: "To obtain early information of any acts of the British government in regard to the colonies, and to correspond with committees of other colonies as to their plans of resistance." Its first action was the issuance of a statement that the inhabitants of all the colonies "ought to consider themselves interested in the cause of the town of Boston as the cause of America in general"; that they would "concur and cooperate in such measures as may be concerted and agreed on by their sister colonies . . ."; and that in order to promote "conformity and unanimity in the Councils of America . . . a continental congress was absolutely necessary." The committees of correspondence in all the colonies spread radical propaganda, fought conservative control, and revealed the value of cooperation. John Fiske wrote that this system "was nothing less than the beginning of the American Union. . . . It only remained for the various intercolonial committees to assemble together, and there would be a congress speaking in the name of the Continent."

Despite the efforts of the radicals, the committees of correspondence might have died of inertia had not Parliament come to their assistance in the spring of 1773 by passing the Tea Act. The measure was not intended to be either regulatory or revenue-producing; it was designed solely to prevent the failure of the British East India Company, which was facing certain financial ruin. Early in 1773 bankruptcy of the long-established firm seemed imminent as a combination of events brought a deficit of over a million pounds. The company's main assets were some seventeen million pounds of tea stored in far-flung warehouses. Under the provisions of the Tea Act the company could ship its tea directly to the colonies and sell it to colonial consumers through its own agents. Hitherto, the tea first had to be sent to England, where it was sold at auction to English tea merchants, who in turn reexported it to the colonies. The Tea Act changed all this and gave the company a monopoly of the American market. It could sell the tea more cheaply than before because no English tax was added and no middlemen's or retailers' profits increased the final cost. The only unusual burden would be the three pence per pound tax that remained from the Townshend duties.

The Tea Act gave American radicals the very opportunity they had been seeking to stir up the colonists again. The most dramatic and perhaps the most important colonial opposition was expressed in various "tea parties" in Boston, New York, Philadelphia, and Charleston. By far the most significant of these was the Boston Tea Party, where on the night of December 16, 1773, some £15,000 worth of tea belonging to the British East India Company was dumped into the sea by citizens of Boston disguised as Indians. This "wilful destruction of private property" was soon followed by the four Coercive or Intolerable Acts of Parliament. These closed the port of Boston temporarily, virtually annulled the charter of Massachusetts, authorized the transportation to England for trial of persons accused of crimes, and legalized the quartering of troops even in private homes. These acts were deeply resented by colonial leaders and all of the colonies quickly rallied to the support of Massachusetts. North Carolinians, for example, sent shiploads of provisions "for the relief of the distressed inhabitants of Boston."

Meanwhile North Carolina was having a tea party of its own. Edenton was one of three North Carolina ports to which the relief supplies for Boston were sent in the summer of 1774. On October 25, fifty-one ladies from at least five counties gathered under the leadership of Mrs. Penelope Barker and declared that they could not "be indifferent to whatever affected the peace and happiness of the country." The ladies, anxious to give proof of their patriotism, signed an agreement to do everything they could to demonstrate their support of the American cause. The Edenton Tea Party has been called the "earliest known instance of political activity on the part of women in the American colonies."

The most significant reaction to the Intolerable Acts of 1774 was the call for a "general congress of the colonies to bring about united action in the emergency." The Virginia House of

Contemporary English caricature of the Edenton Tea Party. *Courtesy of the Museum of History, Raleigh, North Carolina.*

Burgesses, meeting informally and unofficially on May 27, 1774, sent a letter to all the colonies asking for a congress "to deliberate on those general measures which the united interests of America may from time to time require." Then, on June 17 the Massachusetts legislature issued a formal call for a congress. It resolved "that a meeting of Committees from the several Colonies on this Continent is highly expedient and necessary," and suggested Philadelphia as the place and September 1 as the time. When North Carolina's Governor Martin heard of the proposed meeting, he indignantly refused to summon the assembly in time to elect delegates to the congress. In response, Speaker Harvey declared that the people would hold a convention without the governor. Some of the leaders of the assembly held conferences to discuss the proper means of calling such an extralegal meeting, and at a great mass meeting in Wilmington on July 21, a statement was issued declaring it "highly expedient that a provincial Congress independent of the governor" be called on August 25. New Bern was the site finally chosen for the meeting.

Governor Martin, alarmed by these proceedings, hastily called his council into session. He represented the situation to them as extremely critical and sought advice as to "the measures most proper to be taken, to discourage or prevent these Assemblies of the People." The council, after taking a whole day "maturely to consider the Subject," could think of nothing better than a proclamation, which the governor issued on August 13, directing the people to hold no more county meetings, but "more particularly that they forbear to attend, and do prevent as far as in them lies, the meeting of certain Deputies. . . ." On August 25 Martin again called his council together, and this time he notified them that many delegates had already come to New Bern for the congress. He asked their advice as to whether he could reasonably take "any further measures" to prevent their meeting. The council was of the "unanimous opinion that no further steps could be properly taken at this juncture."

When the First Provincial Congress met on August 25, thirty of thirty-six counties sent a total of seventy-one delegates to form the most revolutionary body ever to assemble in North Carolina. John Harvey was unanimously chosen to preside over the congress as moderator. For more than a decade, this man had been the undisputed leader of the so-called popular party in the colony. For many years a member of the assembly from Perquimans County and its speaker since 1766, he had constantly opposed the concept of prerogative government. He maintained steadfastly that the Carolina charter was a compact between sovereign and people which neither could rightfully violate. He had also insisted that no number less than a majority could legally be considered a quorum of the assembly because it had been so stated in the charter. Harvey repeatedly emphasized that no power on earth could constitutionally levy taxes on the people of North Carolina except their own elected representatives in the assembly, and he rejected the theory that the colonies were "virtually" represented in Parliament.

The congress remained in session for only three days, but during that time "it fully launched North Carolina into the revolutionary movement." It adopted a resolution that denounced the acts and policies of the British ministry and Parliament, though professing loyalty to George III. It declared that "any act of Parliament imposing a tax is illegal and unconstitutional. That our Provincial Assemblies . . . solely and exclusively possess that right." The resolution expressed sympathy for the people of Massachusetts who had "distinguished themselves in a manly support of the rights of America in general," and it affirmed that the cause for which they suffered "is the Cause of every honest American." It was in this spirit that a nonimportation and nonexportaton agreement was adopted. The idea of convening a general congress was endorsed, and the colony pledged to support its action. It elected William Hooper, Richard Caswell, and Joseph Hewes to be the delegates to such a congress. The First Provincial Congress of North Carolina was an event of enormous significance. It offered a practical demonstration of self-government, originating in the people; it tended to give cohesion and unity to the Whigs; and it was an example of intercolonial cooperation in defiance of royal authority.

The work of the First Continental Congress, which met in Philadelphia, September 8–October 26, 1774, is well known and need only be summarized briefly here. Its purpose was to formulate a clear statement of colonial rights, to put economic pressure on Parliament and on England in general, and to promote a stronger feeling of unity among the twelve colonies represented (Georgia had no official representation). It rejected by a close vote the Plan of Union that was proposed by Joseph Galloway of Pennsylvania, and it adopted a Declaration of Rights and Grievances, a Petition to the King, and Addresses to the People of Great Britain and also to those of British America. Its most important action was the adoption of the Continental Association, a complete nonimportation, nonexportation, non-consumption agreement, which would be enforced by committees of safety in the various colonies. In a sense, this was a declaration of economic warfare on the mother country, and the effects of this boycott were soon to become apparent. Trade between England and the colonies dropped about 97 percent within a year, and the imports from Britain to North Carolina fell from £378,116 in 1774 to £6,245 in 1775. The First Continental Congress completed the union of the colonies, established that union on an institutional basis, and used the significant term "The United Colonies." It launched something of a political and economic revolution that soon led to the overthrow of royal governments in most provinces. North Carolina was one of these.

Governor Martin, understandably disturbed by recent developments, tried to stem the tide of revolution in North Carolina. He summoned the assembly to meet at New Bern on April 4, 1775. Meanwhile John Harvey had called the Second Provincial Congress to meet at the same place on April 3, in order "to act in union with our neighboring colonies" and to elect delegates to the Second Continental Congress, soon to convene at Philadelphia. Interestingly enough, the composition of the two groups that came to New Bern was almost identical. Harvey was elected speaker of the assembly and moderator of the congress. Governor Martin denounced both bodies; both denounced him. The congress adopted resolutions stating the right of the people to hold meetings and to petition the king for redress of grievances; it approved the Continental Association and urged everybody to support it; it reelected Hooper, Caswell, and Hewes, as delegates to the next continental congress; and it endorsed the idea of committees of safety. The assembly accomplished somewhat less than the congress. It approved the Continental Association, endorsed the actions of the First Continental Congress, and approved the reelection of the three North Carolina delegates. On April 8 an enraged Governor Martin dissolved the last royal assembly that ever met in North Carolina.

As early as January 30, 1772 Governor Martin wrote Lord Hillsborough, secretary of state for the colonies, complaining about "the propensity of this people to democracy." Writing on June 30, 1775 to Hillsborough's successor, the Earl of Dartmouth, Martin declared that the authority of royal government "is here as absolutely prostrate as impotent, and nothing but the shadow of it is left." Unless "effectual measures" were speedily taken, he wrote, "there will not long remain a trace of Britain's dominions over these colonies." His own personal situation had become "most despicable and mortifying. . . . I daily see indignantly the Sacred Majesty of my Royal Master insulted, the Rights of His Crown denied and violated, His Government set at naught, and trampled upon, his servants of highest dignity reviled, traduced, abused, the Rights of His Subjects destroyed by the most arbitrary usurpations, and the whole Constitution unhinged and prostrate, and I live alas ingloriously only to deplore it."

By the spring of 1775 the opponents of reconciliation between the Crown and the colonies were in control both in England and in America. Radicals dominated public opinion as well as the committees of correspondence and the committees of safety in all the colonies. The tension had grown so severe that only a slight incident was needed to turn rebellious opposition into open warfare. That incident took place in Massachusetts on April 19, 1775, when General Gage attempted to seize military stores that the Whigs had gathered. The action taken there led to the battles of Lexington and Concord—to the "shot heard round the world." War had come; royal government had collapsed, and there was a desperate need for agencies that could enforce the measures and resolutions of the Provincial Congress and the Continental Congress. North Carolina had come to this point almost by accident. She had benefited from England's mercantile policy, and bounties offered by Parliament had certainly been responsible for the development of the extensive naval stores industry in the colony. There were no reasons based on social grounds to seek separation, and the Anglican Church had been so feebly supported from abroad and was so weak at home that few could complain of religious oppression. The whole question of independence turned on the colony's insistence that her political rights be recognized. Most of the men who insisted so relentlessly on this point had been trained in the principles of English government. It was only when the rights of colonials as Englishmen were, in their opinion, violated that these men became active. And even then they joined only reluctantly in the Revolutionary movement.

12

INDEPENDENCE AND STATEHOOD

The First Provincial Congress of August 1774 recommended that "a committee of five persons be chosen in each county" to enforce its measures. Soon thereafter the First Continental Congress recommended the establishment of a similar system of committees of safety throughout the thirteen colonies. In North Carolina the plan as finally worked out proposed setting up one committee in each town, one in each county, one in each of the six military districts, and one for the province at large. In the latter part of 1774 and the early months of 1775 eighteen counties and four towns in the colony set up safety committees, members of which were usually chosen by mass meetings. The most active and effective of these bodies were those of New Hanover, Pitt, Craven, Rowan, Mecklenburg, Tryon, and Surry counties. Governor Martin denounced these "extraordinary tribunals" as "motley mobs" and "promoters of sedition." There is no question but that they were extraordinary, and from Martin's viewpoint they certainly did promote sedition; but they were definitely not "motley mobs." Many of the men who served on them were persons of considerable wealth, intelligence, character, and culture. One of the primary tasks of the safety committees was the enforcement of the nonimportation and nonexportation agreements. This was a difficult and disagreeable task, and one which, at times, provoked criticism—even from the Whigs. Large quantities of goods were imported in violation either of the spirit or the letter of the prohibition—some goods were ordered by honest merchants before the nonimportation agreements became effective; some were brought in only in technical violation of the resolves; and some were imported by disloyal merchants who purposely set out to test the determination of the patriots. All shipments, regardless of who ordered them or why or when they were ordered, were seized and sold at public auction for the benefit of the public fund.

The Wilmington-New Hanover Committee of Safety regulated trade to the extent of seizing British cargoes, fixing the price of imported goods, urging all merchants not to sell or export gunpowder, and calling on all householders in Wilmington to "sign the association." The committee required the merchants to sell their gunpowder for public use and also imported it from other colonies. Agents were employed to manufacture gunpowder and men were hired to mold bullets. The committee seized the public arms and compelled every person who owned more than one gun to surrender all but one for the public service. Arms and ammuniton were smuggled in from other colonies and the West Indies in such quantities that Governor Martin "lamented that effectual steps have not been taken to intercept the supplies of warlike stores that . . . are frequently brought into this colony, and asked for three or four cruisers to guard the coast, for the sloop stationed at Fort Johnston is not sufficient to attend to the smugglers in the [Cape Fear] river alone." The committee of safety also undertook to reorganize the militia.

The Wilmington-New Hanover Committee of Safety was not alone in its efforts to unite the people behind the cause of the Continental Association and to ready the colonists for armed conflict. Committees of safety in other counties also assumed bold initiatives in punishing those who failed to abide by the resolves of the nonimportation agreements and in preparing the counties for possible battle.

The Halifax County Committee of Safety resolved to have "no commerce or dealing" with a prominent merchant of Halifax who had refused to sign the Continental Association. Three merchants of Edenton, who had imported goods contrary to the prohibition of the association, were summoned before the Chowan County Committee of Safety and required publicly to acknowledge their error and to promise obedience in the future. The property of at least one Loyalist in this county was seized. The Chowan Committee of Safety undertook to raise a fund "for the encouragement of Manufactures" and offered premiums for wool and cotton cards and for the production of steel "fit for edged tools." The Craven County Committee of Safety ordered that all persons who refused to sign the association be disarmed. In Pitt County the price of salt was set by the Committee of Safety, while in Rowan County all prices were regulated. A Baptist preacher in Rowan who had signed a "Protest against the cause of Liberty" was compelled to appear and express his regret "in the most explicit and humiliating Terms." This Committee of Safety in Rowan also called for one thousand volunteers to be "ready at the shortest Notice to march out to Action."

On May 31, 1775 the Mecklenburg County Committee of Safety adopted a set of resolves declaring "That all commissions civil and military heretofore granted by the Crown to be exercised in these colonies are null and void and the constitution of each particular colony wholly suspended." The document called upon the people of the county to meet and elect military officers "who shall hold and exercise their several powers by virtue of this choice and independent of the Crown of Great Britain and former constitution of this Province." Any person accepting office from the Crown was declared to be "an enemy to his country." The *South Carolina Gazette* of June 13, 1775 printed the text of these resolves and a copy was forwarded to Lord Dartmouth in England by Governor James Wright of Georgia. Governor Martin also sent a newspaper account of the resolves to England and wrote that they "surpass all the horrid and treasonable publications that the inflammatory spirits of this Continent have yet produced." The day after the adoption of the resolves, the Committee of Safety of Rowan County, which had declared only a year before that they were "ready to die in defense of the King's title to his American dominions," resolved "that by the Constitution of our Government we are a free People, not subject to be taxed by any power but that of that happy Constitution which limits both Sovereignty and Allegiance," and "that it is our Duty to Surrender our lives, before our Constitutional privileges to any set of Men upon earth."

Governor Martin, greatly agitated by recent events, issued a bitter proclamation against the "depredations" of the safety committees, but to no avail. A few months earlier, on March 16, 1775 he had written to General Thomas Gage, commander of all British forces in North America, asking for arms and ammunition, but his letter had been intercepted by the Whigs. Meanwhile he planted the half dozen cannon that he had before the Palace in New Bern only to have some of them carried off by what he called a "motley mob stimulated with liquor." Rumors were rife of plans for local Whigs to seize the Palace. The distraught governor fled on May 24 to Fort Johnston near the mouth of the Cape Fear River.

On June 19 the North Carolina delegation in the Continental Congress sent an address to the county and town committees of safety, urging them to support the revolutionary movement and declaring that "the fate of Boston," which was then occupied by British troops, "was the common fate of all." Among other things, the address also expressed the apprehension and indignation of the colony over the Restraining Act that Parliament had passed in April to punish the colonies for the "disorders that prevailed" in them. The act cut off colonial trade with Great Britain and the West Indies. The fact that North Carolina (along with New York and Georgia) was excluded from the provisions of the Restraining Act prompted the North Carolina delegation to include the following remarks in their address:

North Carolina alone remains an inactive Spectator of this general defensive Armament. Supine and careless, she seems to forget even the Duty she owes to her own local Circumstances and Situation. . . . Do you ask why then you are exempted from the Penalties of the Bill restraining Trade? The Reason is obvious. Britain cannot keep up its Naval Force without you; you supply the very sinews of her strength.

Restrain your Naval Stores and all the Powers of Europe can scarce supply her; restrain them and you strengthen the hands of America in the glorious contention for her liberty. . . . We conjure you by the Ties of Religion Virtue and Love of your Country to follow the Example of your sister Colonies and to form yourselves into a Militia. . . .

From his refuge at Fort Johnston, Governor Martin wrote the Earl of Dartmouth on June 30 warning that the people "freely talk of Hostility toward Britain in the language of Aliens and avowed Enemies." In another letter written shortly thereafter he attributed this attitude to "the influence of Committees," which he said "hath been so extended over the Inhabitants of the Lower part [Cape Fear area] of this country . . . and they are at this day to the distance of an hundred miles from the Sea Coast, so generally possessed with the spirit of revolt" that the "spirits of the loyal and well effected to the Government droop and decline daily." He went on to say that "the authority, the edicts and ordinances of Congresses, Conventions, and Committees are established supreme and omnipotent by general acquiescence or forced submission, and lawful Government is completely annihilated."

On July 5 Lord Dartmouth wrote Martin saying, "Almost every other Colony has catched the flame, and a spirit of Rebellion has gone forth, that menaces the subversion of the Constitution." He strongly urged the governor to make "vigorous efforts both by land and sea to reduce his Rebellious Subjects to obedience." But the governor, hearing that committee members of the Wilmington area were planning to attack Fort Johnston and seize his person, fled to safety aboard the British *Cruizer*, lying offshore. Apparently he left the fort just in the nick of time because on July 18, according to his own report, militiamen of the area, led by Robert Howe, John Ashe, and Cornelius Harnett, "wantonly in the dead hour of night set on fire and reduced to ashes the houses and buildings within the Fort." Two days later, on July 20, the day the Restraining Act was to take effect, the Wilmington Committee of Safety denounced the law as "a base and mean artifice to seduce them into a desertion of

the common cause of America," and declared that North
Carolina would not accept "advantages invidiously thrown out"
by the law, but would continue to adhere strictly to the plans of
the Continental Congress.

Governor Martin attributed the rapid growth of revolutionary
sentiment in North Carolina to the propaganda of the safety
committees. His "fiery proclamation" of August 8, 1775 denounced these committees, especially the one at Wilmington, for
circulating "the basest and most scandalous Seditious and
inflammatory falsehoods," calculated to "impose upon and
mislead the People of this Province and to alienate their
affections from His Majesty." He deplored the "malice and
falsehood of these unprincipled censors" and their "evil, perni-
cious and traiterous Councils and influence. . . ." He insisted
that the majority of the people in the province were still loyal to
the mother country, but he feared that "the assembling Convention at Hillsborough will bring the Affairs of this Country to a
Crisis which will make it necessary for every man to assert his
principles."

The convention mentioned by Martin met at Hillsborough on
August 20, 1775, with 184 delegates present out of the 207 who
were elected, representing every county and borough town.
Earlier in the summer, about the middle of July, the Wilmington
Committee of Safety had written to Samuel Johnston urging him
to call another congress.* "Our situation here is truly alarming,
the Governor collecting men, provisions, warlike stores of every
kind, spiriting up the back counties, and perhaps the Slaves,
finally strengthening the fort with new works, in such a manner
as may make the Capture of it extremely difficult. In this
Situation Sir, our people are Continually clamouring for a
provincial Convention. They hope everything from its Immediate Session, fear every thing from its delay." Finally, in August
Johnston issued the call for the Third Provincial Congress. Before

---

* John Harvey had died in May, and so the task of convening another
congress fell to Johnston.

proceeding to business, every member signed a "test oath," professing allegiance to the Crown while at the same time unequivocally declaring that "neither Parliament, nor any Member or Constituent Branch thereof," had a right to impose taxes on the colonies. A Committee of Secrecy was appointed to procure arms and ammunition. A committee was appointed to confer with Highland Scots, who had recently settled in North Carolina, "to explain to them the Nature of our Unhappy Controversy with Great Britain and to advise and urge them to unite with the other Inhabitants of America in defense of those rights which they derive from God and the Constitution." Another committee was authorized to try to win the support of the Regulators for the Whig cause.

On August 25 the Provincial Congress replied to Governor Martin's proclamation, declaring "that the said Paper is a false, Scandalous, Scurrilous, malicious and sedicious Libel, tending to disunite the good people of this province, and to stir up Tumults and Insurrections, dangerous to the peace of His Majesty's Government and the safety of the Inhabitants, and highly injurious to the Characters of several Gentlemen of acknowledged Virtue and Loyalty; and further, that the said paper be burnt by the common Hangman." The congress resolved that, since Governor Martin had "deserted" the colony, it was necessary to establish a temporary government. Accordingly a committee of forty-five members was chosen for the "regulation of the Internal Peace, Order and Safety of this Province." A resolution was adopted saying that all people in the colony "are bound by the Acts and Resolutions of the Continental and Provincial Congresses, because in both they are freely represented by persons chosen by themselves." The Provincial Congress also

Resolved that hostilities being actually commenced in the Massachusetts Bay by the British troops under the Command of General Gage . . . and whereas His Excellency Governor Martin, hath taken a very active and instrumental share in opposition to the means which have been adopted by this and the other United Colonies for their common safety as well as to disunite them from the rest as to weaken the Efforts of the Inhabitants of North Carolina to protect their Lives, Liberties and Properties against any force which may be exerted to injure them . . . defending this Colony, preserving it in safety against all attempts to carry the said Acts into Execution by Force of Arms, this Colony be immediately put into a state of defence.

The congress then worked out plans for what has been called "the most elaborate provisional government on the continent." The legislative body was to be the Provincial Congress, with five members from each county and one from each of the six borough towns, elected by the freeholders of their respective units. The central executive and administrative authority was to be the Provincial Council consisting of thirteen members, two from each of the six military districts, who would be chosen by the qualified voters, and one at large, who would be elected by the Provincial Congress. There were to be safety committees in each county, town, and military district, the members of which were to be chosen annually by popular vote.

The most critical problem confronting the Hillsborough Congress of 1775 was that of raising men, money, and supplies for war. The Continental Congress had called on the "United Colonies" for troops, and the Hillsborough Congress of 1775 responded by authorizing two regiments of five hundred men each for the "Continental Line," and six battalions of five hundred minutemen each. It was recommended that all inhabitants procure bayonets for their guns "as soon as possible, and be otherwise provided to turn out at a minute's warning." A bounty of twenty-five shillings was allowed each private soldier and noncommissioned officer to purchase "a hunting Shirt, Leggins, or Splater dashes and Black Garters, which shall be the Uniform; and that the Manual exercise for the said Minute Men be that recommended by His Majesty in 1764." An allowance was made of ten shillings per annum "for a good smooth bore or Musket, and twenty shillings for a Rifle, to the owners for the use of their Guns." To procure the funds desperately needed for the prosecution of the war, the Provincial Congress ordered the immediate collection of all back taxes. It also authorized the issuance of 125,000 dollars in "bills of credit," ranging in denominations from one-fourth of a dollar to 10 dollars. To redeem these bills a poll tax was levied on each taxable, and social ostracism was threatened and severe penalties were imposed for refusal to accept the bills or for counterfeiting them.

North Carolina was not prepared for war, and there were sharp divisions of opinion within the colony about the war and the way it should be conducted. The very idea of waging war upon the mother country was abhorrent to many, even to some of those who had a thorough distaste for British laws and policies. There were three elements or parties in the province. First there were the Whigs, or Patriots, who were willing to fight England for a "redress of grievances" and even for independence, if necessary. Most of the small farmers and artisans belonged to this group, but the Whigs also included among their ranks many large landowners, some wealthy merchants, and even a few Anglican clergymen. Second, there were the Loyalists, commonly called Tories, but also known as King's Men, Royalists, and occasionally referred to by Whigs as "these damn rascals." Most members of this group supported the idea of peaceful opposition to British policies or redress of grievances within the empire, not separation from it, and they opposed war at all cost. This element included many—perhaps most—of the old class of officials, many of the wealthy merchants, some of the large planters and professional men, some Anglican clergymen, and those conservatives who dreaded despotism on the one hand and feared anarchy on the other. The chief sources of loyalism in North Carolina were to be found in the merchant class and among the Scottish Highlanders. The loyalty of the merchants was compelled by virtue of the fact that British imperial policy had protected their trade and safeguarded their markets. The Highlanders had taken an oath of allegiance to the Crown before migrating to America. Furthermore, they held their lands direct from the Crown, and their leading industry—naval stores—was subsidized by Parliament. Not to be ignored is the fact that the Highlanders thoroughly disliked the group in control of the North Carolina assembly. Loyalists also included in their camp some former Regulators (not as many as is commonly supposed), who were aggrieved over their defeat at Alamance in 1771 by the eastern militia. The third group in the colony was much smaller than the other two and included people who might be classified as neutrals. These were Moravians, Quakers, and a large number of the German settlers in the Piedmont counties.

In the first year of the war the Whigs and Loyalists seem to have been about evenly divided, with the Whigs enjoying a slight majority in both the government and in the total population. The Whigs, in complete control of the Provincial Council, Provincial Congress, and safety committees, had a decided advantage, which they used to win converts to the patriot cause. Not to be overwhelmed by their adversaries, Governor Martin and the Loyalist leaders made desperate attempts to win converts to their side by offering rewards and by threatening reprisals. During 1775 and early 1776 the Whig policy of conciliation which the provisional government followed proved hopelessly ineffective. Consequently, in 1777 the Whig-dominated legislature adopted a strict policy of coercion, which became increasingly harsh as the war continued. This policy eventually led to the confiscation of many large estates owned by Loyalists and to a large migration from the state, especially of the Scottish Highlanders and, to a lesser extent, the Regulators. Although no armed conflict occurred in the South until six months after the shooting war had begun in Massachusetts, the North Carolina Provincial Congress continued to make military preparations. It was also keeping a keen eye on the Cherokee Indians, who were becoming restless and thus giving the Whigs a sure cause for worry.

Meantime Governor Martin had worked out a grandiose scheme for the British conquest of North Carolina. In a letter to Lord Dartmouth on June 30, 1775, he outlined his plan and requested its immediate approval. According to his plan, Martin was to raise at least nine thousand Loyalists, of whom he estimated one-third would be Highlanders and one-third would be Regulators. Lord Charles Cornwallis was to sail from Cork, Ireland, with seven regiments of British regulars, escorted by a fleet of fifty-four ships. Sir Henry Clinton was to sail from Boston with two thousand British regulars and take command of the combined forces, which were to be concentrated in the Wilmington-Brunswick area by the middle of February 1776. Governor Martin sent Alexander Schaw to London to present the scheme to Dartmouth.

Before Schaw even reached his destination, activities were already taking place in the colonies that were designed to assure the success of Martin's plan. In July General Gage ordered Lieutenant Colonel Donald MacDonald and Captain Donald McLeod to North Carolina to recruit men for a battalion of the Royal Highland Emigrant Regiment. Governor Martin appointed MacDonald brigadier general of the militia and then named McLeod lieutenant colonel. He also issued commissions to twenty-five others in various counties of the colony, empowering them "to raise and organize troops and ordering them to press down on Brunswick by February 15th." The British government promised to all Highlanders who joined the service of the Crown two hundred acres of land, remission of arrears in quitrents, and twenty years of tax exemption. These attractive offers and Martin's untiring labors resulted in a large number of recruits. He received reports that the Loyalists were "in high spirits, were fast collecting, and were well equipped with wagons and horses." They planned to leave one thousand men at Cross Creek; the remainder of the troops were to march upon Wilmington. North Carolina Whig leaders, aware of Martin's plan for a British invasion and disturbed by the recruiting of troops and by reports of Loyalist activity in various places, began to mobilize their forces.

The first military activity of North Carolina troops in the American Revolution actually took the form of aid to Virginia and South Carolina rather than battle on home soil. In

November 1775 the provisional government of Virginia asked North Carolina for military assistance against the British in the Norfolk area, where Governor Lord Dunmore was reported to be "burning houses, ravaging plantations, and carrying off slaves." Dunmore seized Norfolk and issued a proclamation emancipating slaves if they would join the British forces. This proclamation, as well as the governor's construction of a fort on the road leading from Norfolk southward, alarmed North Carolina Whigs, and three regiments were ordered to Virginia. About the same time, the provisional government of South Carolina called on North Carolina for troops to aid in the suppression of the "Scovellites," a group of people from the backcountry who had become "ardent Tories." Some seven hundred North Carolina men from Rowan and Mecklenburg counties joined the forces of General Richard Richardson of South Carolina. On December 22 they crushed the Scovellities in what has been called the Snow Campaign, because the battle was fought in a raging snow storm.

On January 3, 1776 Martin received official word from Lord Dartmouth that the British ministry had approved his plan. He was notified that Clinton and Cornwallis had received their orders to sail, and that he might proceed at once with his part of the program. Accordingly, on January 10 Martin issued a proclamation calling upon all loyal subjects to "unite and suppress the rebellion" in North Carolina. By about the middle of February, an estimated sixteen hundred Highlanders led by Donald MacDonald had assembled at their rendezvous at Cross Creek, and on the eighteenth of that month, they began their march toward Wilmington. Colonel James Moore, who directed the strategy of all the Whig forces, was determined to keep the enemy from reaching Wilmington. A secondary objective was to take possession of Cross Creek. To achieve these goals, Moore marched his own forces to Elizabeth Town; Colonel Richard Caswell was sent to take possession of Corbett's Ferry on Black River; and Colonel Alexander Martin and Colonel James Thackston were sent to occupy Cross Creek. Colonel Alexander Lillington and Colonel James Ashe were ordered to reinforce

Caswell, and, if a junction could be effected, they were to secure Moore's Creek Bridge, some eighteen miles above Wilmington. It was over this bridge that the Loyalists would have to march if they were to reach Wilmington.

By a series of skillful maneuvers, directed by Moore and executed by his subordinates, the bulk of the Whig forces, numbering about eleven hundred men, reached Moore's Creek Bridge on the evening of February 26. The Highlanders, now numbering about fourteen hundred men, marched all night through swamps and dense underbrush and finally reached the bridge about sunrise the following day. They immediately launched an attack. The Whigs had removed much of the flooring of the bridge and had greased the log sleepers with soft soap and tallow. This made the crossing extremely difficult and added considerably to the confusion in the Loyalist ranks. Falling into the neatly set trap, the Highlanders were met by a whining storm of swan-shot and bullets. For three minutes they faced the devastating fire and persisted in their attempts to cross the bridge; then, leaving their commander, McLeod, dead, the survivors hastily fled. The Whigs suffered only one killed, one wounded; the Loyalists had about fifty killed and wounded. Moore reached the scene soon after the battle was over and pursued the Loyalists. He captured 350 guns, 1,500 rifles, 150 swords and dirks, 13 wagons, £15,000 in gold, 850 soldiers, and several officers, including General MacDonald.

This overwhelming Whig victory, which has been called the "Lexington and Concord of the South," was applauded throughout the colonies. Most of the British press, in sharp contrast, either ignored or minimized the significance of the battle. *The Gentleman's Magazine* of London said the battle was of little consequence as "they only reduced a body of their own, supported by no one company of regular troops." But the *Annual Register* declared that the Whigs "had encountered Europeans (who were supposed to hold them in the most sovereign contempt, both as men and soldiers) and had defeated them with an inferior force." Unquestionably, the victory at Moore's Creek

Diorama showing the Loyalists crossing Moore's Creek Bridge in the face of patriots' fire. *Courtesy of Moore's Creek National Park.*

Bridge saved North Carolina from conquest, and it probably postponed the defeat of South Carolina and Georgia for three more years. After the battle, the tide of war turned away from North Carolina, and during the next four years the state was free from both invasion from without and insurrection from within.

It has been said that the Battle of Moore's Creek Bridge was "the Rubicon over which North Carolina passed to independence and constitutional self-government." Before that event most Whig leaders had dreaded rather than sought independence; there was much talk about reconciliation before the battle, little thereafter. William Hooper, writing from the Continental Congress at Philadelphia, said that "it would be Toryism to hint the possibility of future reconciliation." John Penn, arriving in North Carolina after the congress, wrote: "The recent events in the colony have wholly changed the temper and disposition of the inhabitants that are friends of liberty; all regard or fondness for the king and nation of Britain is gone. A total separation is what they want. Independence is the word most used. They ask if it is possible that any colony after what has passed can wish for reconciliation. The convention have tried to get the opinion of the people at large. I am told that in many counties there was not one dissenting voice."

The Fourth Provincial Congress met at Halifax on April 4, 1776. On the following day Samuel Johnston, its presiding officer, summed up the general feeling of those in attendance: "All our people here are up for independence." Robert Howe echoed this when he declared, "Independence seems to be the word. I know not one of the dissenting voice." On April 8 a committee of seven, headed by Cornelius Harnett, was appointed "to take into consideration the usurpations and violences attempted and committed by the King and Parliament of Great Britain against America, and the further measures to be taken for frustrating the same, and for the better defence of this Province." On April 12 the committee's report was adopted unanimously by the 83 delegates present of the 148 who had been elected from thirty-four counties and eight towns. The last paragraph of the famous Halifax Resolves reads: "Resolved, That the delegates for this Colony in the Continental Congress be impowered to concur with the delegates of the other Colonies in declaring Independency, and forming foreign alliances, reserving to this Colony the sole and exclusive right of forming a Constitution and laws for this Colony, and of appointing delegates from time to time (under the direction of a general representation thereof), to meet the delegates of the other Colonies for such purposes as shall be hereafter pointed out." This was the first official state action for independence, and it should be noted that it was not a declaration for North Carolina alone, but a recommendation to the Continental Congress that independence be declared by all the colonies.

The day after the adoption of the Halifax Resolves, the Provincial Congress selected a committee to draft "a temporary Civil Constitution." After considerable debate on the "outline" presented by the committee, the congress voted, on April 30, not to adopt a state constitution at that time. A committee was then chosen "to form a temporary form of government until the end of the next congress," and it was decided that the Council of Safety should have "full power and authority to do and execute all acts and things necessary for the defence and protection of the people of this colony." Thus the council of safety, a permanent body continuously in session, became the governing body of the state. Cornelius Harnett, its president, was for all practical purposes the governor of North Carolina.

A copy of the Halifax Resolves was sent to Joseph Hewes in the Continental Congress. Newspapers in other colonies printed the document, and some urged their congresses to "follow this laudable example." Elbridge Gerry of Massachusetts, for example, said that it was a "noble and decisive measure." Then, on May 15 Virginia's congress instructed its delegates in the Continental Congress to "move for independence." And on June 7, 1776 Richard Henry Lee urged "that these United Colonies are and of right ought to be free and independent States. . . ." The Continental Congress adopted this resolution on July 2, and two days later it approved the final draft of the Declaration of Independence,* written largely by Thomas Jefferson. The North Carolina Council of Safety was meeting at Halifax when it received news of the national Declaration of Independence on July 22. It immediately adopted a resolution declaring that the "good people" of the colonies "were absolved from all Allegiance to the British Crown," and ordered all safety committees in the state to have "the same proclaimed in the most public Manner." With the adoption of the national Declaration of Independence and the authorization by the Continental Congress that states draw up constitutions, the Council of Safety ordered that an election be held October 15 to choose delegates to the Fifth Provincial Congress, which was to meet at Halifax. The voters were asked to pay the greatest attention to the election of delegates who were "not only to make Laws for the Good Government of, but also to form a Constitution for this State, that this last as it is the Corner Stone of all Law, so it ought to be fixed and Permanent, and that according as it is well or ill Ordered it must tend in the first Degree to promote the happiness or Misery of the State."

An exciting and bitter campaign ensued. The Whigs, who had appeared unified in their prosecution of the war, were sharply divided on the question of what the nature of the new government should be. The conservative Whigs, led by Samuel Johnston, James Iredell, William Hooper, and Archibald Maclaine, wanted few structural changes from the old government. They favored a strong executive, an independent judiciary with life tenure, adequate protection of property rights, and property qualifications for voting and officeholding. The radical Whigs, led by Willie Jones, Thomas Person, and Griffith Rutherford, advocated what they called a "simple democracy" in which there would be a strong legislature, a weak executive subordinate to the legislature, and religious freedom with no established church. After a bitter contest for delegates that was accompanied by

---

* William Hooper, Joseph Hewes, and John Penn signed this "immortal document" for North Carolina.

"Tumult and disorderly Behaviour" and even "fraud and debauchery" at the polls in several counties, 169 delegates were finally elected. The conservatives and radicals won about an even number of seats with the so-called moderates holding the balance of power. Samuel Johnston, who was burned in effigy and defeated at the polls, wrote shortly thereafter: "Everyone who has the least pretensions to be a gentleman is borne down *per ignobile vulgus*—a set of men without reading, experience, or principles to govern them."

The Fifth Provincial Congress met at Halifax on November 12, 1776, and Richard Caswell, a moderate, was chosen president unanimously. On November 13 a committee of eighteen members was appointed to draw up a "Bill of Rights and Form of a Constitution." Thomas Jones of Edenton, spokesman for the committee, reported the state constitution on December 6 and the bill of rights on December 15. The Declaration of Rights was adopted on December 17 and the North Carolina Constitution the next day. Both were ordered printed and distributed throughout the state. Following the practice of other states, these documents were not submitted to popular vote. The war was the paramount problem, and there was no time for another bitter political campaign.

The bill of rights, consisting of twenty-five articles enumerating the rights of the people against any government, was "declared to be part of the Constitution of this State and ought never to be violated on any pretense whatsoever." It contained statements of rights that the colonists had asserted under English laws but which they had been denied by the king and Parliament; it reaffirmed ideas enunciated in the English bill of rights of 1689; and it contained statements, some verbatim, from the Maryland, Pennsylvania, and Virginia bills of rights. Popular sovereignty and separation of powers were strongly emphasized, as was the notion that there should be three separate branches of government. The bill of rights guaranteed freedom of elections, freedom from arbitrary taxation, supremacy of civil power over the military, right of assembly, and frequent elec-

Constitution House, Halifax, meeting place of the Provincial Congress which drew up the state constitution in 1776. *Courtesy of the Travel and Promotion Division, Department of Natural and Economic Resources, State of North Carolina.*

tions. It stressed the individual's rights in criminal trials; trials only upon indictment, presentment, or impeachment; trial by jury; immunity from excessive bail and "cruel or unusual punishment"; immunity from general search warrants; the right to a speedy trial; and immunity from *ex post facto* laws. Personal liberties of the individual guaranteed freedom of the press, freedom of conscience and religion, and the "right to bear arms for the defence of the State." The existence of standing armies in time of peace was declared "dangerous to Liberty."

The preamble to the constitution, based on the compact theory, gave reason for revolt against the mother country, saying that George III had "declared the inhabitants of these States out of the protection of the British Crown"; that the Continental Congress "had declared the colonies independent"; and that "in order to prevent Anarchy and Confusion," it had become necessary to establish a government "derived from the People only." The constitution, like other state constitutions of this period, was short, simple, and obscure. It was merely a general outline of governmental machinery. Unfortunately it contained no provision for amendment, and this very serious omission was destined to cause controversy for half a century. The most salient feature of the constitution of 1776 was the emphasis on legislative supremacy; this was a marked shift away from the executive supremacy that had characterized colonial days.

The governor and the whole executive department—consisting of the seven-member Council of State, secretary, treasurer, and attorney general—were now definitely to fall under legislative control. They were to be subject to election, removal, short term of office, and very limited powers. The governor's powers, especially, were now very much in check. Unlike his colonial predecessors, the governor had no control over elections or over the time and place of legislative sessions; he had no power to "summon, prorogue, or dissolve" a legislature; and he had no veto power. William Hooper observed that the only power the governor had was "to sign a receipt for his own salary." But this was not entirely true. The governor did have the power to initiate policies and recommend legislation; he had the powers of pardon and reprieve; he was commander-in-chief of the military and naval forces of the state; and he had general authority to "exercise all other executive powers of government" subject to the constitution and laws of the legislature. There was also the prestige of the office, and there were opportunities for great service by a strong executive through personal leadership. The governor now had influence rather than constitutional power. The qualifications for the office were that the man be at least thirty years of age, have five years of residence in the state, and own a freehold "in lands and tenements above the value of one Thousand Pounds." The governor was to be chosen annually by a joint ballot of the two houses of the legislature for a one-year term. He was to be eligible for reelection three years in any six successive years. He and other officials were to be paid "adequate salaries."

The legislative authority was vested in a General Assembly, consisting of a Senate and House of Commons, both of which were to be dependent on the people. Members of each house were to be chosen annually by ballot, one senator and two commoners for each county, plus one commoner for each of the six borough towns. Senators were required to have "a freehold of not less than 300 acres"; commoners, 100 acres. To vote for a state senator, a person must own at least 50 acres; but to vote for a commoner, payment of "public taxes" was sufficient. Each house was to elect its own speaker and other officers, pass on the qualifications of its own members, and pass bills into law. The two houses, sitting jointly each year, were to elect the governor, Council of State, and other executive officials, as well as judges and high-ranking military officers. A quorum in each house was to be a majority of *all* the members.

The state's judiciary was to consist of "Judges of the Supreme Courts of Law and Equity, Judges of Admiralty, and Attorney General"—all appointed by the General Assembly and commissioned by the governor to hold office during good behavior. Justices of the peace, on recommendation by "county representatives in the General Assembly," were to be appointed and commissioned by the governor to hold office "during good behavior."

The structure of local government remained largely as it had been. The constitution provided for creation by legislative enactment of the offices of sheriff, coroners, and constables in each county. Election, tenure, and duties were to be prescribed by law.

The constitution contained many provisions that clearly reflected the fact that North Carolinians had learned a great deal from their colonial experience. There was, for example, to be no established church or compulsory support of any religious organization, and it was guaranteed that "all persons shall be at liberty to exercise their own mode of worship." No clergyman, "while he continues in the exercise of the pastoral Function," could be a member of the General Assembly. No person "who shall deny the being of God, or the Truth of the Protestant Religion, or the Divine Authority of the Old or New Testament, or who shall hold Religious Principles incompatible with the Freedom and Safety of the State," was eligible for any public office. Multiple officeholding, surely one of the most deplorable features of colonial government, was effectively eliminated by a provision that "No person in this State shall hold more than one lucrative office at any one time." The importance of education was now given official recognition. Section 41 provided "that a School or Schools shall be established by the Legislature for the convenient Instruction of Youth, with such Salaries to the Masters paid by the Public, as may enable them to instruct at low Prices, and all useful Learning shall be duly encouraged and promoted in one or more Universities."

The last official action of the Halifax Congress was the adoption on December 18, 1776 of "an Ordinance for appointing a Governor, Council of State, and Secretary until the next General Assembly." It appointed Richard Caswell as governor and James Glasgow as secretary. The Council of State that the congress selected consisted of Cornelius Harnett, Thomas Eaton,

William Dry, William Haywood, Edward Starkey, and Joseph Leach; Harnett was appointed president. The new state government began operation in January 1777, when Caswell and the other officials took the oath of office. The first General Assembly of the independent state convened at New Bern on April 7. Samuel Ashe of New Hanover was elected speaker of the Senate and Abner Nash of Craven, speaker of the House of Commons. The General Assembly approved all of the officials who had been appointed by the congress the previous December. James Glasgow and members of the Council of State were formally elected by joint ballot of the two houses, and on April 18 Caswell was elected governor.

Having entered on the path of revolution with a great deal of reluctance, North Carolina faced the inevitable and set about solving her own problems. Loyalty to King George faded rapidly in most areas when it became known that he had ordered royal troops to fight against the colonists. The men who had taken the responsibility of acting and speaking for the whole body of people when it had become apparent that peaceful negotiations would not prevail, also stepped in to call assemblies, to appoint committees, and to lay the foundations of a new government. Through their own efforts these men created a favorable climate of public opinion that made it possible for their action to be accepted with little effective opposition. They dispensed "democracy" through a constitution that they not only wrote themselves, but which they also declared to be in force without ever offering the people an opportunity to debate its provisions or even to vote on its adoption. The new state government was launched on what turned out to be a stormy career.

EPILOGUE

The colony of North Carolina was an enigma to the Lords Proprietors as well as to the Crown and to many of the governors they appointed. None fully understood the numerous factors that divided the colony into opposing camps at many levels. The divisive influences of geography, religion, and social status shaped the history of the whole colony as well as of its counties and towns. In fact, the inhabitants regarded North Carolina as a "country" and even named a small stream flowing across the Virginia boundary, Country Line Creek. North Carolina was different from the other colonies, even from its foster mother to the north and her sister to the south. Although there were families of local influence, there were none such as the Lees of Virginia or the Laurenses of South Carolina who made their marks both at home and abroad. The colony had no notable centers of commerce and culture such as existed in other colonies between Boston and Charleston, but it did have its own little self-sufficient societies, such as they were, in Edenton, New Bern, Wilmington, Halifax, Hillsborough, Salem, and Salisbury.

People in this isolated colony, with its disparate communities, became insular. With few exceptions, throughout the seventeenth and eighteenth centuries little concern was shown for events transpiring elsewhere on the continent. Local government, with no interference from a higher authority, was the goal of most county leaders. At the provincial level, home-grown leaders insisted that their own interpretations of the people's rights in the

British scheme of government were correct. These leaders had little contact with their counterparts elsewhere, and until late in the colonial period they seldom showed signs of even the least awareness of events in other colonies.

Observers from elsewhere could not read the pulse of North Carolina. New Englanders and others who settled in the colony in 1664 gave up and returned home after a few years. Observers in New York, Boston, and Philadelphia tried without success to fathom the meaning of the events on the North Carolina frontier between 1759 and 1771. Because of the numerous Loyalists in this unusual place—who wanted more than anything else simply to be left alone—spokesmen for the "common cause" in other colonies on the eve of the Revolution wondered what reception their radical philosophy might receive in North Carolina.

North Carolina fitted into the British mercantile system perhaps better than most of the other colonies, due largely to the production of such articles as naval stores (tar, pitch, rosin, and turpentine) so eagerly sought by British leaders. It led the world in the production of these from 1720 until well into the next century. The colony developed a fairly large trade with the mother country and with the island colonies of the West Indies but never became a commercial colony comparable to her neighbors, Virginia and South Carolina, or to Massachusetts Bay, New York, and Pennsylvania. In fact, the experience of North Carolinians at the hands of Virginia and South Carolina merchants, who refused to accept their paper money and who often refused to pay full value for their produce, created in them a spirit of distrust of the merchant class and even of mercantile colonies. They turned inward, relying upon themselves for both markets and trade whenever they could, and often spoke disparagingly of the New England merchants whose ships docked at Edenton, New Bern, or Wilmington.

On the other hand, North Carolina had much in common with other colonies. There had been a serious Indian problem, climaxed by one of the deadliest wars in early American history, as well as prolonged and sometimes bitter controversies between the governor and the lower house of the legislature. As elsewhere, the legislature in North Carolina gradually gained power, especially in relation to "control of the purse." Again like some of the other colonies, a controversy between the older counties and the newer ones over representation in the assembly persisted throughout the colonial era. In no other province, however, was the east-west sectional struggle so bitter, culminating as it did in open warfare.

As in other colonies, particularly those in the South, an overwhelming majority of the people made their living from farming and related industries. The colony was predominantly one of small towns and small landholders, although individuals owned extensive tracts, some of more than ten thousand acres. A few North Carolina planters owned more than a hundred slaves each, but the colony never developed a plantation aristocracy such as that in Virginia and South Carolina. Nor did North Carolina ever have as many indentured servants, in sum or percentage, as did her two neighbors.

North Carolina was similar to several of the other colonies in that thousands of Scotch-Irish and Germans settled in the backcountry, yet it did not have as large a number or as high a percentage of these non-English settlers as did Pennsylvania. It did have the largest number of Highland Scots in any English colony.

Here, as in all of the continental colonies, the colony's leaders opposed England's "New Colonial Policy" after 1763. A strict enforcement of the Royal Proclamation of 1763 would have kept the colony from settling its lands between the crest of the mountains and the Mississippi River. North Carolina's opposition, however, was mild compared to that of Virginia in this instance. Little attention greeted the Sugar Act of 1764, the Currency Act of 1765, or the Quartering Act, but there was violent opposition to the Stamp Act, the first and only "direct tax" levied on the colonies by Parliament. The people of the colony, urged on by the Sons of Liberty, maintained that England had no right to levy such a tax, and they successfully resisted its enforcement. At Wilmington there were demonstrations, and at Brunswick an armed uprising, with the result that officials designated to receive the stamped paper were forced to resign. Not a single piece of such paper was sold in North Carolina. North Carolina's reaction to the Townshend taxes of 1767 was similar to that in other colonies—the organization of nonimportation associations, followed by a great drop in trade with the mother country.

Soon after the shooting war began at Lexington and Concord, Massachusetts, on April 19, 1775, Governor Josiah Martin fled, royal rule in North Carolina broke down, and a provisional government was set up. A provincial council replaced the governor, a provincial congress became the law-making body, and safety committees took charge of government in the counties. In Mecklenburg County on May 31 a strong set of resolves was drawn up, declaring that "all commissions civil and military heretofore granted by the Crown to be exercised in these colonies are null and void and the constitution of each particular colony wholly suspended."

Many people were loath to go to war with Great Britain. These Tories or Loyalists included many of the official class, merchants, some large planters and producers of naval stores (which were subsidized by Parliament), some Anglican clergymen, many Scottish Highlanders, and some naturally conservative people who simply dreaded a break with the empire. Yet a very skillful group of men succeeded in turning much of this indifference and outright opposition into support of the Revolutionary movement. Trained in English law, they were persuasive speakers, skilled politicians, and masters of propaganda. At public meetings, marches through towns, and evening sessions around huge bonfires, they swayed the thinking of their neighbors and secured the election to office of men who supported the American cause. Economic and social ostracism diligently applied in many communities brought new support to the cause and held opposition in check.

Many of these very leaders would have been content to see

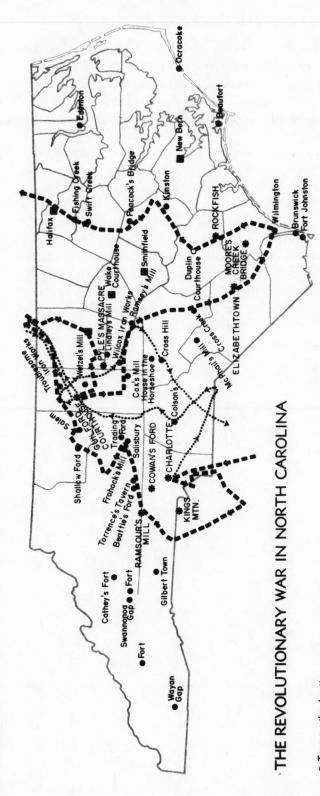

THE REVOLUTIONARY WAR IN NORTH CAROLINA

● Town or other location

□ Meeting place of state legislature

✳ Site of battle (name in capital letters)

■■■▶ March of Cornwallis, 1780-81

••••••▶ March of Greene, 1780-81

The Revolutionary War in North Carolina. Reprinted from the Atlas of North Carolina (Chapel Hill, 1967) with permission of University of North Carolina Press.

North Carolina make its own way in the world, remaining totally independent of both Great Britain and all of the other colonies, but neutrality proved impossible. Unhappy experiences under governors sent from England, New York, or even South Carolina, with merchants from Glasgow or Boston, and with Anglican clergymen from London, Coventry, or Liverpool convinced many men that they could do better for themselves without outside aid. They demonstrated this during the course of the Revolutionary War when officers from other states were denied command of North Carolina troops. The state also refused to ratify the United States constitution and remained outside the new union for well over a year. Some years afterwards, even in the face of desperate need for his services by the state, an outside engineer, employed by a state agency to plan internal improvements, was harrassed and finally driven away. More than half a century after the Revolution, North Carolina finally began to break out of the cocoon in which she had wrapped herself during her colonial experience.

BIBLIOGRAPHY

PRIMARY SOURCES

Anyone interested in the history of colonial North Carolina will find ample unpublished resources in the Public Record Office in London and in the State Department of Archives and History in Raleigh, while large masses of both official and private sources have been printed. The ten volumes of *Colonial Records of North Carolina*, (Raleigh, 1886–1890), edited by W. L. Saunders, have formed the main source from which the narrative history of the colony has been drawn. To date three volumes in a new collection of records, under the editorship of Mattie Erma Parker, have also appeared: *North Carolina Charters and Constitutions, 1578–1698* (Raleigh, 1963) provides the text of the various documents under which North Carolina was discovered, explored, settled, and first governed; *North Carolina Higher-Court Records, 1670–1696* (Raleigh, 1968) and *North Carolina Higher-Court Records, 1697–1701* (Raleigh, 1971) contain a wealth of social and political history. These sources are supplemented by documents that appeared in the *North Carolina Historical and Genealogical Register*, which was published in three volumes under the editorship of J. R. B. Hathaway of Edenton between 1900 and 1903. David B. Quinn's magnificent *Roanoke Voyages, 1584–1590* (London, 1955), published in two volumes by the Hakluyt Society, contains all of the known records associated with that very interesting phase of the colony's history. William S. Powell, ed., *Yᵉ Countie of Albemarle in Carolina* (Raleigh, 1958) is a collection of documents from the period 1664–1675 bearing on the earliest permanent settlement. Hugh T. Lefler, ed., *North Carolina History Told by Contemporaries* (Chapel Hill, 1965) is a well-rounded collection of edited documents that have been selected and arranged in chronological order for the general reader.

There are many special kinds of sources that historians and general readers alike have found helpful in understanding North Carolina's past. John Lawson, *A New Voyage to Carolina* was first published in London in 1709, but is most readily available in an edition recently edited by Hugh T. Lefler (Chapel Hill,

1967). Lawson's detailed comments on the Indians, his sympathy for them, and his skill in writing about them make his book a very important source in this area. Lawson has recorded a vast amount of information dealing not only with natural history and geography, but also with the early settlements of which he was a part. The knowledge he gained about the colony while serving as its surveyor-general is obvious throughout the book. Dr. John Brickell, a physician, plagiarized much of Lawson in *Natural History of North Carolina* (Dublin, 1737), but he also tells us a great deal about the daily life, particularly the illnesses, of North Carolinians in the early years of the eighteenth century. Adelaide L. Fries *et al.*, eds., *Records of the Moravians*, 11 vols. (Raleigh, 1922–1969) consist of diaries, letters, and other records kept by Moravians who were living in the vicinity of what is now Winston-Salem from 1752 until the middle years of the nineteenth century. These people were in frequent communication with areas other than their own and they often were hosts to visitors; their records are filled with useful and fascinating information on social, economic, political, and, in spite of their peace-loving nature, military history. Janet Schaw was a Scottish visitor to North Carolina on the eve of the Revolution who faithfully recorded her observations in a diary. Edited by Charles M. and Evangeline W. Andrews, *The Journal of a Lady of Quality* (New Haven, 1921), gives us much unique information on the daily life of the people at that time. The penetrating and often unkind comments of William Byrd about North Carolinians were recorded in his journal and are to be found in Louis B. Wright, ed., *The Prose Works of William Byrd of Westover* (Cambridge, Mass., 1966). Other pertinent writings of Byrd are also included in this volume, which is a classic of eighteenth-century American literature that has forever fixed North Carolinians in history as several notches below Virginians in all categories. Alexander S. Salley, Jr., ed., *Narratives of Early Carolina, 1650–1708* (New York, 1911) and William K. Boyd, ed., *Some Eighteenth Century Tracts Concering North Carolina* (Raleigh, 1927) contain the text of many tracts that throw much light on events occurring during the century and a quarter prior to statehood. The splendid index by Lester Cappon and Stella Duff to the *Virginia Gazette* is the key to a gold mine of information about eighteenth-century North Carolina that is yet to be worked by historians. During the many years of this century when North Carolina had no newspaper (and even when there was one) the *Virginia Gazette* circulated widely in the colony; news and advertisements from the southern colony appeared in almost every issue.

Among the standard reference works of value to the student of colonial history are David L. Corbitt, *The Formation of North Carolina Counties, 1663–1943*, rev. ed. (Raleigh, 1969); William S. Powell, *The North Carolina Gazetteer* (Chapel Hill, 1968); R. D. W. Connor, comp. and ed., *A Manual of North Carolina* (Raleigh, 1913), which lists officials of the government from 1663 onward; and Richard E. Lonsdale, ed., *Atlas of North Carolina* (Chapel Hill, 1967).

There are also adequate bibliographical guides available to the searcher for North Caroliniana. Hugh T. Lefler, *A Guide to the Study and Reading of North Carolina History*, 3rd ed. (Chapel Hill, 1969) is a classified listing of books and articles for the entire period of the state's history. Also dealing with the whole period are two compilations by Mary L. Thornton, *Official Publications of the Colony and State of North Carolina, 1749-1939* (Chapel Hill, 1954) and *A Bibliography of North Carolina, 1589-1956* (Chapel Hill, 1958). Both of these volumes are arranged by author but have adequate subject indexes. William S. Powell, "Carolina in the Seventeenth Century: An Annotated Bibliography of Contemporary Publications," *North Carolina Historical Review*, XLI (January 1964), 74–104, is an appraisal of thirty-seven tracts and broadsides. Douglas C. McMurtrie, *Eighteenth Century North Carolina Imprints, 1749-1800* (Chapel Hill, 1938) supplemented by William S. Powell, "Eighteenth Century North Carolina Imprints: A Revision and Supplement to McMurtrie," *North Carolina Historical Review*, XXXV (January 1958), 50–73, provides a guide to all known publications of the colony and early state. One of the best general guides to material on the colonial period is Lawrence H. Gipson, *A Bibliographical Guide to the History of the British Empire, 1748-1776.* (New York, 1969).

SECONDARY SOURCES

GENERAL WORKS

There has been no detailed study of the history of colonial North Carolina comparable to M. Eugene Sirman's work on South Carolina or Richard L. Morton's study of Virginia, but the authors of general histories published since the appearance of the *Colonial Records of North Carolina* have treated the period adequately. The first general history to appear after this compilation of primary documents became available was Samuel A. Ashe, *History of North Carolina*, 2 vols. (Raleigh, 1908; Greensboro, 1925). With numerous citations to contemporary sources, Ashe's work covered new ground and revealed for the first time much of the state's colonial history. Most of his interpretations have stood the test of time. R. D. W. Connor was the first trained historian to undertake a history of the state, yet his *History of North Carolina: The Colonial and Revolutionary Periods* (Chicago, 1919) added only slightly more to what Ashe had already said, but it did correct a few factual errors. Connor's *North Carolina: Rebuilding an Ancient Commonwealth* (Chicago, 1929) was largely a rewriting of his first work. Hugh T. Lefler and A. R. Newsome, *North Carolina: The History of a Southern State*, rev. ed. (Chapel Hill, 1963) varies little from Connor in its account of the colonial period. Lefler's *History of North Carolina*, 2 vols. (New York, 1956) also follows Connor in its treatment of the colonial and Revolutionary periods. Most general histories of the American colonies touch upon the subject of North

Carolina, but several go considerably beyond, presenting excellent factual and interpretative chapters. The third volume of Charles M. Andrews, *The Colonial Period of American History*, 4 vols. (New Haven, 1934-1938), for example, has two outstanding chapters on the Carolinas in which extensive new material appeared. The first volume of J. A. Doyle, *English Colonies in America*, 3 vols. (New York, 1889), contains a chapter on the two Carolinas and another on the social and economic life of the Southern colonies. There is a twenty-five-page chapter on North Carolina in Lawrence H. Gipson, *The British Isles and the American Colonies: The Southern Plantations, 1748-1754* (New York, 1967); Herbert L. Osgood, *The American Colonies in the Seventeenth Century* (New York, 1904-1907), and his *American Colonies in the Eighteenth Century*, 2 vols. (New York, 1924) also deal at length with the subject.

BIOGRAPHY

While considerable interest has been shown in certain actions of numerous North Carolinians of the colonial period, few well-rounded biographies have been written. None of the proprietary governors and only two of the royal governors have been the subject of book-length studies. Desmond Clarke, *Arthur Dobbs, Esquire, 1689-1765: Surveyor General of Ireland, Prospector and Governor of North Carolina* (Chapel Hill, 1957) and Marshall DeLancey Haywood, *Governor William Tryon and His Administration in the Province of North Carolina, 1765-1771* (Raleigh, 1903) are well researched and readable biographies of two of the most active royal governors. Alonzo T. Dill, *Governor Tryon and His Palace* (Chapel Hill, 1955) discusses at length an important aspect of Tryon's career, but more accurately might be classified as a history of New Bern rather than a biography of Tryon. There are concise sketches of each of the colony's royal governors in Blackwell P. Robinson, *The Five Royal Governors of North Carolina* (Raleigh, 1963).

In Samuel A. Ashe, ed., *Biographical History of North Carolina from Colonial Times to the Present*, 8 vols. (Greensboro, 1905-1917) will be found sketches of varying quality of numerous men of the pre-Revolutionary period, but many of these are more laudatory than objective. A few, however, were written by trained historians and are based on extensive research in contemporary sources.

Mary E. Lazenby, *Herman Husband, A Story of His Life* (Washington, 1940) stands almost alone in this category in that it deals with an eighteenth-century figure who held no important public office and who did not participate in the American Revolution; yet as a leader of the Regulators, Husband played an important role in the colony in the 1760s and 1770s. Griffith J. McRee, ed., *The Life and Correspondence of James Iredell*, 2 vols. (New York, 1857-1858) has long been acclaimed, but McRee's attempts to delete from the correspondence anything that might reflect unfavorably on his subject renders this work suspect. A completely new edition of Iredell's letters, now being prepared, will supplant much of McRee's pioneer work. R. D. W. Connor, *Cornelius Harnett: An Essay in*

North Carolina History (Raleigh, 1909) deals with another early Revolutionary leader.

Carefully documented articles published in various journals provide selected information of a biographical nature on many other participants in colonial and early Revolutionary War events in North Carolina. Randolph G. Adams, "An Effort to Identify John White," *American Historical Review*, XLI (October 1935), 87–91, questions the identification of John White, artist, with John White, governor of the Roanoke colony of 1587, while William P. Cumming, "The Identity of John White Governor of Roanoke and John White the Artist," *North Carolina Historical Review*, XV (July 1938), 197–203, provides the answer which has since been widely accepted.

Percy G. Adams, "John Lawson's Alter Ego—Dr. John Brickell," *North Carolina Historical Review*, XXXIV (July 1957), 312–326, examines the debt Brickell owed to Lawson for information that the doctor employed in his *Natural History of North Carolina*. The activities of two clergymen are examined in Fleming H. James, "Richard Marsden, Wayward Clergyman," *William and Mary Quarterly*, XI (October 1954), 578–591, and in Durward T. Stokes, "Henry Pattillo in North Carolina," *North Carolina Historical Review*, XLIV (October 1967), 373–391. A noted teacher is studied by Aubrey L. Brooks, "David Caldwell and His 'Log College,'" *North Carolina Historical Review*, XXVIII (October 1951), 399–407, while Robert W. Ramsey, "James Carter, Founder of Salisbury," *North Carolina Historical Review*, XXXIX (April 1962), 131–139, examines the career of a colonist from Maryland who played an important role in the development of a frontier county in North Carolina.

John Cannon, "Henry McCulloch and Henry McCulloh," *William and Mary Quarterly*, XV (January 1958), 71–73, clears up the confusion that once existed stemming from the similarity of these men's names. Participants in the Revolutionary movement have been the subject of several articles: Talbot M. Allen, "Samuel Johnston in Revolutionary Times," *Trinity College Historical Society Papers*, V (1905), 39–49; David L. Corbitt, "Thomas MacKnight," *North Carolina Historical Review*, XX (October 1925), 520–525; John G. Coyle, "Cornelius Harnett," *Journal of the American Irish Historical Society*, XXIX (1941), 148–156; Allen J. McCurry, "Joseph Hewes and Independence : A Suggestion," *North Carolina Historical Review*, XL (October 1963), 455–464; and Blackwell P. Robinson, "Willie Jones of Halifax County," *North Carolina Historical Review*, XVIII (January, April 1941), 1–26, 133–170.

ERA OF EXPLORATION AND DISCOVERY

Discussion of the natural resources and geography are presented in Kenneth B. Pomeroy and James G. Yoho, *North Carolina Lands* (Washington, D.C., 1964), see especially pp. 1–72, which include interesting comments on the ownership of the land; Cordelia Camp, *The Influence of Geography upon Early North Carolina*

(Raleigh, 1963); Gary S. Dunbar, *Historical Geography of the North Carolina Outer Banks* (Baton Rouge, 1958); H. Roy Merrens, *Colonial North Carolina in the Eighteenth Century* (Chapel Hill, 1964); Edmund Ruffin, *Sketches of Lower North Carolina* (Raleigh, 1861); Ben Franklin Lemert, "Geographic Influences in the History of North Carolina," *North Carolina Historical Review*, XIII (October 1935), 297–319; and Jasper L. Stuckey, *North Carolina: Its Geology and Mineral Resources* (Raleigh, 1965).

The American Indian in North Carolina is known to us today in a number of ways: first, through accounts of explorers and settlers who observed the natives; second, through the drawings of artists such as John White; and third, from archaeological discoveries. Information from these varied sources will be found in John Lawson, *A Voyage to Carolina*, ed. Hugh T. Lefler (Chapel Hill, 1967); David B. Quinn, *Roanoke Voyages, 1584–1590* (London, 1955); Paul Hutton and David B. Quinn, *The American Drawings of John White* (London and Chapel Hill, 1964); Joffre L. Coe, "The Formative Culture of the Piedmont," *Transactions of the American Philosophical Society*, LIV, pt. 5 (1954); William G. Haag, *The Archeology of Coastal North Carolina* (Baton Rouge, 1958); John R. Swanton, *Indians of the Southeastern United States* (Washington, D. C., 1946); Douglas L. Rights, *The American Indian in North Carolina* (Winston-Salem, 1957); Frank G. Speck, "The Catawba Nation and its Neighbors," *North Carolina Historical Review*, XVI (October 1939), 404–417; G. Melvin Herndon, "Indian Agriculture in the Southern Colonies," *North Carolina Historical Review*, XLIV (July 1967), 283–297; Stanley A. South, *Indians in North Carolina* (Raleigh, 1959); and Chapman J. Milling, *Red Carolinians* (Chapel Hill, 1940). Sanford Winston, "Indian Slavery in the Carolina Region," *Journal of Negro History*, XIX (October 1934), 431–440, discusses an interesting facet of Indian history.

The French and Spanish explorations of North Carolina are touched upon both in numerous secondary works and occasionally in collections of documents. David B. Quinn and Raleigh A. Skelton, *The Principall Voiages and Discoveries of the English Nation*, 2 vols. (Cambridge, Eng., 1965) is a handsome fascimile of the classic Hakluyt's "Voyages" with the addition of scholarly notes and an index. General Spanish interest in the region is discussed in Woodbury Lowery, *The Spanish Settlements within the Present Limits of the United States, 1513–1561* (New York, 1959) and in Paul Quattlebaum, *The Land Called Chicora* (Gainesville, Fla., 1956). Specific expeditions are recorded in the *Final Report of the United States De Soto Commission* (Washington, D.C., 1939); Stanley J. Folmsbee *et al.*, "Journals of the Juan Pardo Expeditions, 1560–1567," *East Tennessee Historical Society Publications*, XXXVII (1965), 106–121; Clifford M. Lewis and Albert J. Loomie, *The Spanish Jesuit Mission in Virginia, 1570–1572* (Chapel Hill, 1953); and L. A. Vigneras, "A Spanish Discovery of North Carolina in 1566," *North Carolina Historical Review*, XLVI (October 1969), 398–407; and James L. Wright, "Spanish Reaction to Carolina," *North Carolina*

Historical Review, XLI (Autumn 1964), 464–476. Verner W. Crane, *The Southern Frontier, 1670–1732* (Durham, 1928) discusses the Spanish problem in detail.

Although David B. Quinn, *Roanoke Voyages, 1584–1590* (London, 1955) is the ultimate source for information on the English interest in North Carolina during the sixteenth century, the introductory notes to Paul Hulton and David B. Quinn, *The American Drawings of John White* (London and Chapel Hill, 1964) provide a polished narrative. Further information will be found in Alexander Brown, *The Genesis of the United States*, 2 vols. (Boston, 1890); William S. Powell, "Roanoke Colonists and Explorers: An Attempt at Identification," *North Carolina Historical Review*, XXXIV (April 1957), 202–226; David B. Quinn, *Raleigh and the British Empire* (New York, 1949); Jean Carl Harrington, *Search for the Cittie of Ralegh* (Washington, D.C., 1962); and William S. Powell, *Paradise Preserved* (Chapel Hill, 1965).

THE PROPRIETARY PERIOD

North Carolina in the seventeenth century and the early eighteenth century is touched upon briefly in a few secondary accounts, in several monographs, and in a handful of articles, but the definitive work remains to be done. Wesley F. Craven, a native of North Carolina, deals with the colony in his *Colonies in Transition, 1660–1713* (New York, 1968) and in his *The Southern Colonies in the Seventeenth Century, 1607–1689* (Baton Rouge, 1949). There is a twenty-page survey of this period in William S. Powell, *Yᵉ Countie of Albemarle in Carolina* (Raleigh, 1958); further information may be found in Powell's *The Proprietors of Carolina* (Raleigh, 1963) and in his *The Carolina Charter of 1663* (Raleigh, 1954); and in Lindley S. Butler, "The Early Settlement of Carolina: Virginia's Southern Frontier," *Virginia Magazine of History and Biography*, LXXIX (January 1971) 20–28. E. Lawrence Lee, *Indian Wars in North Carolina, 1663–1763* (Raleigh, 1963) is a careful examination of a special subject. Culpeper's Rebellion has been adequately covered by several investigators: Hugh F. Rankin, *Upheaval in Albemarle, The Story of Culpeper's Rebellion, 1675–1689* (Raleigh, 1962); Mattie Erma Parker, "Legal Aspects of Culpeper's Rebellion," *North Carolina Historical Review*, XLV (April 1968), 111–127; and Charles M. Andrews, ed., *Narratives of the Insurrections, 1675–1690* (New York, 1915). Lindley S. Butler, "The Governors of Albemarle County, 1663–1689," *North Carolina Historical Review*, XLVI (July 1969), 281–299, takes a fresh look at the old accounts of the chief executives of the colony and, based on research in newly discovered sources, the author draws up a new list of governors. William P. Cumming, "The Earliest Permanent Settlement in Carolina, Nathaniel Batts and the Comberford Map," *American Historical Review*, XLV (October 1939), 82–89, and Elizabeth G. McPherson, "Nathaniel Batts, Landholder on Pasquotank River, 1660," *North Carolina Historical Review*, XLIII (January 1966), 66–81, examine the evidence which suggests that Batts was the first permanent settler in North Carolina. The origins of the very important colonial town of New Bern are discussed by Alonzo T. Dill, Jr., in two articles entitled "Eighteenth Century New Bern," *North Carolina Historical Review*, XXII (January 1945), 1–21, and XXII (July 1945), 292–319. Herbert R. Paschal, Jr., *History of Colonial Bath* (Raleigh, 1955) contains a carefully researched account of the colony's first town. The war involving the Tuscarora Indians and related topics are covered in Vincent H. Todd, ed., *Christoph von Graffenried's Account of the Founding of New Bern* (Raleigh, 1920) and "Journal of John Barnwell," *Virginia Magazine of History and Biography*, V (April 1898), 391–402, and VI (July 1898), 42–55. The final act of the Proprietary period is discussed in C. C. Crittenden, "The Surrender of the Charter of Carolina," *North Carolina Historical Review*, I (October 1924), 383–402.

EXPANSION AND IMMIGRATION

Many writers have been attracted by the fascinating aspects of the growth of North Carolina from the seed bed of the Albemarle into the Cape Fear area and the further expansion of the colony by the arrival of many groups of people in the Piedmont. However, no one has written about the earlier shift to the Pamlico River as the first of these great events. On the subject of Cape Fear we have E. Lawrence Lee, *The Lower Cape Fear in Colonial Days* (Chapel Hill, 1965); Duane Meyer, *The Highland Scots of North Carolina, 1732–1776* (Chapel Hill, 1961); James Sprunt, *Chronicles of the Cape Fear River, 1660–1916* (Raleigh, 1916); and Nina Moore Tiffany, ed., *Letters of James Murray, Loyalist* (Boston, 1901). James G. Leyburn, *The Scotch-Irish, A Social History* (Chapel Hill, 1962) deals with a people who settled in both the Cape Fear and in the Piedmont as does the even more inclusive volume by R. D. W. Connor, *Race Elements in the White Population of North Carolina* (Raleigh, 1920). A discussion of the Scottish settlers in general will be found in Ian C. C. Graham, *Colonists from Scotland: Emigration to North America, 1707–1783* (Ithaca, N. Y., 1956). The role played by a small but important group of people who settled within a compact area is recounted by Linville L. Hendren, "De Graffenreid and the Swiss and Palatine Settlement of New Berne, N. C.," *Trinity College Historical Society Papers*, IV (1900), 64–71.

Various aspects of the settlement of the Piedmont will be found in William P. Cumming, ed., *The Discoveries of John Lederer* (Charlottesville, 1958); Robert W. Ramsey, *Carolina Cradle, Settlement of the Northwest Carolina Frontier, 1747–1762* (Chapel Hill, 1964); Carl Hammer, Jr., *Rhinelanders on the Yadkin* (Salisbury, 1965) and Robert W. Ramsey, "Captain Samuel Cobrin's Company of Militia: The First Settlers of Gaston and Lincoln Counties," *Journal of North Carolina Genealogy*, XII (Winter 1966), 1773–1779, and XIII (Fall 1967), 1926–1933; William H. Gehrke, "The Transition from the German to the English Language in North Carolina," *North Carolina Historical Review*, XII (January

1935), 1–19; Francis C. Anscombe, *I Have Called You Friends, The Story of Quakerism in North Carolina* (Boston, 1959); and Adelaide L. Fries *et al.*, eds., *Records of the Moravians*, 11 vols. (Raleigh, 1922–1969). E. Merton Coulter, "The Granville District," *James Sprunt Historical Publications*, XIII, no. 1 (1913), 35–56, deals with the unique problem of the existence of a proprietary grant within the royal colony of North Carolina during the eighteenth century.

GOVERNMENT AND POLITICS

Politics and affairs of government are the primary concern of Charles Lee Raper, *North Carolina, A Study in English Colonial Government* (New York, 1904); Lawrence F. London, "The Representation Controversy in Colonial North Carolina," *North Carolina Historical Review*, XI (October, 1934), 255–270; Jack P. Greene, *The Quest for Power: The Lower Houses of Assembly in the Southern Royal Colonies, 1689–1776* (Chapel Hill, 1963); and Charles G. Sellers, Jr., "Private Profits and British Colonial Policy: The Speculations of Henry McCulloh," *William and Mary Quarterly*, VIII (October 1951), 535–557. Another aspect of McCulloh's political activity is investigated by James High, "Henry McCulloh, Progenitor of the Stamp Act," *North Carolina Historical Review*, XXIX (January 1952), 24–38. An interesting study of the service and wealth of the individual councillors will be found in William S. Price, Jr., " 'Men of Good Estates': Wealth Among North Carolina's Royal Councillors," *North Carolina Historical Review*, XLIX (January 1972), 72–82. Other aspects of offices and officeholders are discussed by Julian P. Boyd, "The Sheriff in Colonial North Carolina," *North Carolina Historical Review*, V (April 1928), 151–181; William C. Guess, "County Government in Colonial North Carolina," *James Sprunt Historical Publications*, XI, no. 1 (1911); Carl W. Ubbelohde, Jr., "The Vice-Admiralty Court of Royal North Carolina, 1729–1759," *North Carolina Historical Review*, XXXI (October 1954), 517–528; and by Jack P. Greene, "The North Carolina Lower House and the Power to Appoint Public Treasurers, 1711–1775," *North Carolina Historical Review*, XL (January 1963), 37–53. Enoch W. Sikes, "North Carolina, A Royal Province, 1729–1776," in the first volume of the thirteen-volume *The South in the Building of the Nation* (Richmond, 1909–1913) 441–462, concisely summarizes the whole period.

Two specialized studies of a single event in the colony clearly reveal the temperament of North Carolinians on the eve of the Revolution: C. Robert Haywood, "The Mind of the North Carolina Opponents of the Stamp Act," *North Carolina Historical Review*, XXIX (July 1952), 317–343; and E. Lawrence Lee, Jr., "Days of Defiance: Resistance to the Stamp Act in the Lower Cape Fear," *North Carolina Historical Review*, XLIII (April 1966), 186–202.

The role played by North Carolina in the British Empire has been generally ignored by recent scholars, but at least two mid-eighteenth-century authors in England were aware of it. In *An American Traveller: or, Observations on the Present*

State, Culture and Commerce of the British Colonies in America (London, 1767) attributed to Alexander Cluny, and *The Present State of Great Britain and North America* (London, 1767) believed to have been compiled by John Mitchell, the commercial value of North Carolina is set forth. Two specialized studies on a related theme are C. Robert Haywood, "The Mind of North Carolina Advocates of Mercantilism," *North Carolina Historical Review*, XXXIII (April 1956), 139-165, and Justin Williams, "English Mercantilism and Carolina Naval Stores, 1705-1776," *Journal of Southern History*, I (May 1935), 168-185. Certain aspects of a problem that plagued the colony for a great many years are explored by Marvin L. Michael Kay in "Provincial Taxes in North Carolina During the Administrations of Dobbs and Tryon," *North Carolina Historical Review*, XLII (October 1965), 440-453. Another question that developed during this period but which was not finally settled until many years afterward is dealt with in Louis DeVorsey, Jr., *The Indian Boundary in the Southern Colonies* (Chapel Hill, 1966). Alfred Moore Waddell, *A Colonial Officer and His Times* (Raleigh, 1890) relates the career of his relative, General Hugh Waddell, who was one of the most brilliant young men in North Carolina during the colonial period.

ECONOMIC AND SOCIAL HISTORY

There are two good works dealing with many aspects of the economy of North Carolina during the eighteenth century. C. C. Crittenden, *Commerce of North Carolina, 1763-1789* (New Haven, 1937) views all of the facets of commerce—regulations, markets, exports, imports, merchants, and transportation. H. Roy Merrens, *Colonial North Carolina in the Eighteenth Century* (Chapel Hill, 1964) deals with the same general subject but the material is approached from the point of view of the historical geographer rather than that of the historian. Merrens studies the role of the people in the economy—the use they made of the forests and their crops, plantations, and livestock. The part played by North Carolina's towns, small though they were, is also explained. Two old studies on a single theme, yet still interesting, are John S. Bassett, "Landholding in Colonial North Carolina," *Trinity College Historical Society Papers*, II (1898), 44-61, and Lawrence N. Morgan, "Land Tenure in Proprietary North Carolina," *James Sprunt Historical Society Publications*, XII, no. 1 (1912), 41-63. An unusual study in which a great deal of very interesting information was culled from the advertisements that appeared in colonial North Carolina newspapers is Wesley H. Wallace, "Property and Trade: Main Themes of Early North Carolina Newspaper Advertisements," *North Carolina Historical Review*, XXXII (October 1955), 451-482. Robert E. Moody, "Massachusetts Trade with Carolina, 1686-1709," *North Carolina Historical Review*, XX (January 1943), 43-53, is a detailed look at the intracolonial trade that often violated the navigation acts but which was one of the most important commercial ventures in which North Carolinians engaged. F. W. Clonts, "Travel and Transportation in Colonial North Carolina," *North Carolina Historical Review*, III (January

1926), 16–35, touches on a subject that was of deep concern in the colony throughout the eighteenth century. Another aspect of the same problem is explored by Alan D. Watson, "Ordinaries in Colonial Eastern North Carolina," *North Carolina Historical Review*, XLV (January 1969), 67–83. Closely related to commerce in North Carolina history has been the story of the many pirates who infested the coastal waters. Hugh F. Rankin collected data on more than a hundred such men and women in his *The Pirates of Colonial North Carolina* (Raleigh, 1960), and he presents his findings with a pleasant combination of scholarship and readability in *The Golden Age of Piracy* (Williamsburg, 1969). The old standard work on this subject, however, is still useful—Shirley C. Hughson, *The Carolina Pirates and Colonial Commerce* (Baltimore, 1894).

Social history has not often caught the attention of North Carolina historians. In many instances, however, very useful studies in this area have been made by architects, ministers, and other interested and qualified amateurs. Those who would seek to know more about the homes of early North Carolinians must turn to photographer Frances Benjamin Johnston and architect Thomas T. Waterman, *The Early Architecture of North Carolina* (Chapel Hill, 1941). Artist and art professor John V. Allcott has also prepared a very useful volume in this area: *Colonial Homes in North Carolina* (Raleigh, 1963). For arts and crafts there is no better source than *The Arts and Crafts in North Carolina, 1699–1840* (Winston-Salem, 1965) by former historic site specialist and later antique dealer James H. Craig. A former secretary of state, J. Bryan Grimes, edited two volumes from which extensive information may be gleaned on the life style of North Carolinians: *Abstract of North Carolina Wills* (Raleigh, 1910) and *North Carolina Wills and Inventories* (Raleigh, 1912). Guion G. Johnson, *Ante-Bellum North Carolina, A Social History* (Chapel Hill, 1937) bears in part on the colonial period and suggests how useful a similar work on an earlier period would be. Abbot E. Smith, *Colonists in Bondage* (Chapel Hill, 1947) deals with the many people who came to the colonies as servants as a means of gaining their freedom.

The subjects of religion and education have attracted a few writers with special interests but none willing to make a broad study of either subject. Approaching this need, however, are two works by Stephen B. Weeks: *Religious Development in the Province of North Carolina* (Baltimore, 1892), and *Church and State in North Carolina* (Baltimore, 1893). Spencer Ervin, "The Anglican Church in North Carolina, 1663–1823," *Historical Magazine of the Protestant Episcopal Church*, XXV (June 1956), 102–161, and Sarah M. Lemmon, "The Genesis of the Protestant Episcopal Diocese of North Carolina, 1701–1823," *North Carolina Historical Review*, XXVIII (October 1951), 426–462, examine the establishment of the Anglican Church in the colony, while Lindley S. Butler, "The Seventeenth Century Origins of North Carolina Friends," *The Louisburg College Journal of Arts and Sciences*, II (June 1968), 1–11, discusses the first body of Christians in Albemarle County. William S. Powell's introduction to the facsimile reprint of Clement Hall's *A Collection of Many Christian Experiences* (Raleigh, 1961) is a sympathetic appraisal of the work (first printed in New Bern in 1753) of one of the most devout Anglican missionaries in any of the American colonies. Charles Woodmason, *The Carolina Backcountry on the Eve of the Revolution*, ed. Richard J. Hooker (Chapel Hill, 1953) is a frank report of the religion, the morals, and sometimes the politics of the people on the frontier of both Carolinas. David T. Morgan, Jr., "The Great Awakening in North Carolina, 1740–1775," *North Carolina Historical Review*, XLV (July 1968), 264–283, and Haskell Monroe, "Religious Toleration and Politics in Early North Carolina," *North Carolina Historical Review*, XXXIX (July 1962), 267–283, discuss two interesting aspects of religion as it was practiced in the colony. There also are histories of many of the denominations, but they are of uneven quality and generally touch only lightly on the colonial period. Two of the most useful are George W. Paschal, *History of North Carolina Baptists*, 2 vols. (Raleigh, 1930) and Jacob L. Morgan *et al.*, eds., *History of the Lutheran Church in North Carolina* (Salisbury, 1953). Two books by Frederick L. Weis offer, respectively, lists of colonial clergy and concise biographical information: *The Colonial Churches and the Colonial Clergy of the Middle and Southern Colonies, 1607–1776* (Lancaster, Mass., 1938) and *The Colonial Clergy of Virginia, North Carolina and South Carolina* (Boston, 1955).

Herbert R. Paschal, Jr., "Charles Griffin: Schoolmaster to the Southern Frontier," *East Carolina College Publications in History*, II (1965), 1–16, reexamines the career of the earliest known schoolmaster in the colony and, based on new research, reappraises Griffin's pioneering work in the Albermarle section. Aubrey L. Brooks, "David Caldwell and His Log College," *North Carolina Historical Review*, XXVIII (October 1951), 399–407, summarizes all that can be discovered from the surviving records of the most important and the longest lived school in the colony. Edgar W. Knight, ed., *Documentary History of Education in the South before 1860*, 5 vols. (Chapel Hill, 1949–1953), and his *Education in the South* (Chapel Hill, 1924), supplemented by R. D. W. Connor, "The Genesis of Higher Education in North Carolina," *North Carolina Historical Review*, XXVIII (January 1951), 1–14, and William S. Powell, *Higher Education in North Carolina* (Raleigh, 1970) adequately cover the subject of education at all levels.

Books, printing, and journalism have received the passing attention of a number of writers and the subject is one to which further attention should be given. Stephen B. Weeks was a pioneer in this area and his *The Press of North Carolina in the Eighteenth Century* (New York, 1891) and "Libraries and Literature in North Carolina in the Eighteenth Century," *American Historical Association Annual Report for 1895* (Washington, 1896), 169–267, have not been entirely superseded. Mary L. Thornton, "Public Printing in North Carolina, 1749–1815," *North Carolina Historical Review*, XXI (July 1944), 181–202, and Robert N. Elliott, Jr., "James Davis and the Beginning of the Newspaper in North Carolina," *North Carolina Historical Review*, XLII (January 1965), 1–20, trace the origins of printing and journalism in the colony. C. C. Crittenden, "North Carolina Newspapers Before 1790," *James Sprunt Historical Publications,* XX, no. 1 (1928) is a useful study and guide. William S. Powell, "Patrons of the Press: Subscription Book Purchases in North Carolina, 1733–1850," *North Carolina Historical Review,* XXXIX (October 1962), 423–499, deals with a wide spectrum of books and readers, while Helen R. Watson, "The Books They Left: Some 'Liberies' in Edgecombe County, 1733–1783," *North Carolina Historical Review,* XLVIII (July 1971), 245–257, is much more specific.

Slavery in the nineteenth century is a subject adequately covered in numerous studies, a few of which made a modest attempt to review the eighteenth century. John S. Bassett, *Slavery and Servitude in the Colony of North Carolina* (Baltiore, 1896) is still useful despite its age. James A. Padgett, "The Status of Slaves in Colonial North Carolina," *Journal of Negro History,* XIV (July 1929), 300–327, and Ernest J. Clark, "Aspects of the North Carolina Slave Code, 1715–1860," *North Carolina Historical Review,* XXXIX (April 1962), 148–164, supplement Bassett.

THE BACKCOUNTRY

John S. Bassett, "The Regulators of North Carolina, 1765–1771," *American Historical Association Annual Report for 1894* (Washington, 1895), 141–212, was the first scholarly investigation of this subject and is still valid. All of the known documents pertaining to this lengthy east-west struggle appear in William S. Powell *et al.,* eds., *The Regulators in North Carolina, A Documentary History, 1759–1776* (Raleigh, 1971). A concise statement of the theory behind the unrest of this period may be found in Helen H. Miller, *The Case for Liberty,* chap. 9 (Chapel Hill, 1965). An even fuller account of the events leading up to the Battle of Alamance in 1771 is contained in Alonzo T. Dill, *Governor Tryon and His Palace* (Chapel Hill, 1955) and in Carl Bridenbaugh, *Myths and Realities: Societies of the Colonial South* (Baton Rouge, 1952). Robert O. DeMond, *The Loyalists in North Carolina* (Durham, 1940), a work badly in need of revision in light of newly available sources, touches upon the subject in a study that traces internal dissension in North Carolina through the period of the American Revolution.

REVOLUTION AND INDEPENDENCE

Events in North Carolina on the eve of the Revolution were dramatic and moving and their telling has drawn the best efforts of numerous scholars. Two studies by E. Lawrence Lee, *The Lower Cape Fear in Colonial Days* (Chapel Hill, 1965) and "Days of Defiance: Resistance to the Stamp Act in the Lower Cape Fear," *North Carolina Historical Review,* XLIII (April 1966), 186–202, tell of the bold, successful, and bloodless efforts of the dauntless Cape Fear patriots during some very troubled times. The sweep of events during these years is reviewed by Charles G. Sellers, Jr., "Making a Revolution: The North Carolina Whigs, 1765–1775," in J. C. Sitterson, ed., *Studies in Southern History* (Chapel Hill, 1957)

23–46. C. Robert Haywood, "The Mind of the North Carolina Opponents of the Stamp Act," *North Carolina Historical Review*, XXIX (July 1952), 317–343, is an interesting examination of the reasoning of those who played leading roles in these events. Louise Dunbar, "The Royal Governors in the Middle and Southern Colonies on the Eve of the Revolution," in Richard B. Morris, ed., *The Era of the American Revolution* (New York, 1939), 214–268, and Ella Lonn, *The Colonial Agents of the Southern Colonies* (Chapel Hill, 1945) explain many of the events of this period.

Two broader studies which should be consulted in conjunction with the more specialized works are John Alden, *The South in the Revolution, 1763–1789* (Baton Rouge, 1967), and Elisha P. Douglass, *Rebels and Democrats: The Struggle for Equal Political Rights and Majority Rule During the American Revolution* (Chapel Hill, 1955).

The clash of arms in North Carolina, which represented the opening of the Revolutionary War, is related in Hugh F. Rankin, "The Moore's Creek Bridge Campaign, 1776," *North Carolina Historical Review*, XXX (January 1953), 23–60, and Laura P. Frech, "The Wilmington Committee of Public Safety and the Loyalist Rising of February, 1776," *North Carolina Historical Review*, XLI (January 1964), 21–35. R. D. W. Connor, *Revolutionary Leaders of North Carolina* (Greensboro, 1916) is an excellent source for concise biographical sketches of a number of men prominent in the movement for independence. Connor's *Cornelius Harnett: An Essay in North Carolina History* (Raleigh, 1909) is biographical insofar as Harnett is concerned and narrative of the stirring events of his time. E. W. Sikes, *The Transiton of North Carolina from Colony to Commonwealth* (Baltimore, 1898) is a clear explanation of the complicated steps through which the leaders of North Carolina carried their constituents from being subjects of the Crown to becoming subjects of the state without their approval. An interesting study of the various sources drawn upon by the leaders of North Carolina in preparing the first constitution will be found in Earle H. Ketcham, "The Sources of the North Carolina Constitution of 1776," *North Carolina Historical Review*, VI (July 1929), 215–236.

INDEX

Abercromby, James, 123, 124
Adams, Rev. James, 207
Adams, Samuel, of Mass., 251–52
Agents, 123; sent to England, 48; to acquire supplies for war, 267
Agriculture, 47, 106, 151, 153–54, 155–59
Alabama River, explored, 86
Alamance, Battle of, 237–38, 275
Alamance County, 100, 202
Albany Congress, 138
Albemarle County, 38, 43–55, 192, 193
Albemarle section, 121–24, 155, 193–97, 224
Albemarle Sound, 2, 30, 32, 48
Alderson, Simon, Sr., 57
Alexander, Rev. James, 213
Allen, Eleazer, 87
Amadas, Philip, 6, 7, 10
Amherst, Maj. Gen. Jeffery, 145
Anabaptists, 61
Anderson, John, 202
Anglican Church, 6, 31, 33, 46, 64, 191–92, 194, 195, 197, 198, 199, 203, 206–208, 213, 217, 265
Anne, Queen, 60, 196
Annual Register, 214, 278
Anson County, 92, 108, 200, 218, 219, 228, 234
Antiproprietary party, 47, 48, 51
Arbuthnot, Capt. Thomas, 140
Archdale, John, 81, 193–94, 195
Archdale Precinct, 57
Artisans, 42, 64, 104, 177, 180, 220, 274
Arundell, Capt. John, 10
Ashe, Col. James, 277
Ashe, John, 244, 258, 270

Ashe, John Baptista, 210
Ashe, Samuel, 288
Assembly, 51, 114, 116, 118–22, 125; first state, 225; last royal, dissolved, 264
"Attachment clause," 256
Attmore, William, 225
Augusta Conference (1763), 148–49
Ayllón, Lucas Vásquez de, 3

Backcountry, 89, 99, 110, 166, 169, 277. *See also* Regulators
Bacon's Rebellion, 50, 55
Baptists, 61, 199–200, 217
Barbados, 36, 39, 40, 42, 43, 84, 181
Barbados Adventurers, Corporation of, 40
Barker, Mrs. Penelope, 259
Barker, Thomas, 123
Barlowe, Arthur, 6, 7, 9
Barnwell, John, fights Indians, 72–80
Barré, Col. Isaac, 242
Bath (town), 57, 74, 76, 174, 214, 218, 224
Bath County, 56, 57, 72
Batts, Nathaniel, 32
Bay River Indians, 72
Bean, William, 111
Bear Inlet, 136
Bear River Indians, 68
Beaufort, 135, 211
Beaufort County, 57
Bell, Thomas, 210
Bennett, John, 211
Berkeley, Sir William, 31, 32, 36, 37
Berkeley, John, Lord, 36
Bertie County, 152
Bethabara, 104, 145

309